Palgrave Insights into Apocalypse Economics

Series Editor
Richard Westra
Centre for Macau Studies
University of Macau
Macau, China

This series is set to become the lodestone for critical Marxist and related Left scholarship on the raft of apocalyptic tendencies enveloping the global economy and society. Its working premise is that neoliberal policies from the 1980s not only failed to rejuvenate capitalist prosperity lost with the demise of the post-Second World War 'golden age' economy but in fact have generated a widening spectrum of pathologies that threaten humanity itself. At the most fundamental level the series cultivates state of the art critical political economic analysis of the crises, recessionary, deflationary and austerity conditions that have beset the world economy since the global meltdown of 2008–2009. However, though centered on work that critically explores global propensities for devastating financial convulsions, ever-widening inequalities and economic marginalisation due to information technologies, robotised production and low wage outsourcing, it seeks to draw on exacerbating factors such as climate change and global environmental despoliation, corrupted food systems and land-grabbing, rampant militarism, cyber crime and terrorism, all together which defy mainstream economics and conventional political policy solutions.

For critical Marxist and related Left scholars the series offers a non-sectarian outlet for academic work that is hard-hitting, inter/trans-disciplinary and multiperspectival. Its readership draws in academics, researchers, students, progressive governmental and non-governmental actors and the academically-informed public.

More information about this series at
http://www.palgrave.com/gp/series/15867

Richard Westra

Periodizing Capitalism and Capitalist Extinction

palgrave
macmillan

Richard Westra
Centre for Macau Studies
University of Macau
Macau, China

ISSN 2523-8108 ISSN 2523-8116 (electronic)
Palgrave Insights into Apocalypse Economics
ISBN 978-3-030-14389-3 ISBN 978-3-030-14390-9 (eBook)
https://doi.org/10.1007/978-3-030-14390-9

This Palgrave Macmillan imprint is published by the registered company Springer Nature Switzerland AG.
The registered company address is: Gewerbestrasse 11, 6330 Cham, Switzerland

Praise for *Periodizing Capitalism and Capitalist Extinction*

"In his new book, Richard Westra takes up two long-standing and crucial questions in the study of capitalism. How do we conceptualize and periodize the different historical phases of capitalist development in general and this long period of neoliberal globalization in particular? What are the signs of a fundamental impasse in capitalism's dynamics of accumulation, it's terminal crisis, and the emergent political conditions pointing toward a social transformation? There are few texts that take these issues up, and Westra provides a timely and important map to these debates. In a conjuncture in world politics where social forces on the right are taking an authoritarian turn and new movements on the left are beginning to surface, this book is written with the right temper of careful assessment and necessary sense of political urgency."

—Greg Albo, *York University, Canada*

"After systematically critiquing alternative accounts presented over the last 150 years, Westra develops his own explanation of the discontinuities in continuity of capitalism. His book will appeal to all those with a theoretical, historical, and practical interest in the nature, trajectory, and crisis-tendencies of capitalism up the current stage of consumerism."

—Bob Jessop, *Lancaster University, UK*

"Many analysts have sought to identify and analyze distinct periods in capitalist history, from Marx, Hilferding, and Lenin, through recent examinations of neoliberalism, globalization, and financialization. Richard Westra fills a gap in this literature by offering a comprehensive account, along with a critique, of those efforts. He offers a gloomy conclusion, that the current stage is not a stage of capitalism at all but a period of disintegration of its foundations."

—David M. Kotz, *University of Massachusetts Amherst, USA*

"Determining the historical periods of capitalist development is one of the most complex problems faced by Marxist political economy. Richard Westra reviews the relevant literature with great skill, and discusses novel approaches that draw on Uno School Marxism. His book is a powerful contribution that will serve as reference point."

—Costas Lapavitsas, *SOAS University of London, UK*

Contents

List of Figures

List of Tables

1

Introduction to Periodizing Capitalism

Through the waning years of the twentieth century and into the twenty-first, a cottage industry of sorts has erupted around how best to characterize the extreme and in many ways frightening transformations of capitalist economies. Designations offered for the current era certainly tell a tale: "gore capitalism" (Valencia 2018); "carceral capitalism" (Wang 2018); "authoritarian capitalism" (Bloom 2016); "totalitarian capitalism" (Liodakis 2010); "crack capitalism" (Holloway 2010); capitalism that has reached its "cancer stage" (McMurtry 1999); and so forth. These, along with ubiquitous references to "globalized", "neoliberal", and "financialized" capitalism, are all intended to emphasize some striking feature of capitalist economies to differentiate capitalism as it supposedly "really exists" today from the capitalisms of the past.

What is particularly revealing about this spate of writings is that, with a few notable exceptions, its elaboration upon those aspects of economic goings-on deemed most idiosyncratic of current seismic transformations proceeds with little account taken of an earlier growth industry on theorizing capitalist change in the post–World War II (WWII) period. As will be shown in this book, the genre of work on post-WWII capitalism is extremely fecund. A diverse group of authors from around the world set

R. Westra, *Periodizing Capitalism and Capitalist Extinction*, Palgrave Insights into Apocalypse Economics, https://doi.org/10.1007/978-3-030-14390-9_1

out to conceptualize the modus operandi of an era of capitalism widely referred to as a "golden age" of prosperity among advanced economies. This writing, of course, was hardly triumphalist. Its critical bent spurred theorists to not only explore economic and institutional contours of the era, along with processes that purportedly launched these, but extrapolate from existing tendencies future prospects for capitalism.

That such extrapolative ventures in virtually no case captured the global economic shifts that shape today's world is hardly surprising. It is not only a question here of social science itself being an explanatory science rather than predictive, which is de rigueur in natural science (we will attempt to navigate this thorny epistemological and ontological thicket in later chapters). Rather, the problem rests with the conceptual frameworks and analytical procedures that have been applied to understanding momentous capitalist change. And, indeed, it is precisely to answer such big theoretical questions of capitalist transformation that calls forth the research agenda of periodizing capitalism, which is the concern of this book.

After all, the view that such a creature known as a capitalist economy really exists is largely accepted axiomatically. Where things begin to get messy is over questions of the "kinds" of capitalist economies that have populated modern history. Then we enter the realm of an even greater problematic when attempts are made to delineate broad "types" of capitalism in the context of sweeping world historic transformations of capitalism as captured in the aforementioned notion of capitalism reaching a "cancer stage", for example. If humanity finds itself today in such a "stage" of capitalism, there, of course, needs to be theorizing of what the key elements of this era of capitalist history are that differentiate it from previous periods. But theory must also account for the way these elements mark different kinds of capitalist economies such that notwithstanding their empirical differences (e.g. between the United States [US] or Japan's economy), it is still possible to classify them as representatives of this "cancer" species of capitalism. Finally, the crux of the matter, which is often occluded in the analysis of capitalist change, is the ultimate conceptual touchstone for determining whether an era of economic history or a particular type of economy, "cancerous" or not, is *capitalist* in the first place.

While this issue will be revisited at points over the following pages, it may be safely asserted here that mainstream economics, from its "classical" birth through its neoclassical progeny, offers little foundation for thinking systematically about capitalism and capitalist change. After all, its basic orientation is that "the *Invisible Hand of Providence*...coordinated and reconciled all disparate and conflicting interests of blind human beings (like 'monads') into a world of the (Leibnizian) Pre-established Harmony" (Sekine 2013: 245). Thus, the fundamental approach of mainstream economics to really existing capitalism revolves around the question of how human economic life is best compelled to obey the dictates of "the market" as captured today by neoclassical models and the "virtual economy" these depict, to adopt the apt expression of Blaug (2003: 147–8). And, though there is a case to be made that classical political economy at least grappled with how social wealth is produced through "real" market workings (which potentially leads to problematizing capitalist change), neoclassical economics shifts the very course of mainstream economic thinking away from such interests toward the narrow concern over distribution of "given" means (Dasgupta 1987: 77).

It is largely (though not solely, as we shall see) in the hands of Marxian economics and political economy that the research program of periodizing capitalism unfolds. Two overarching research frameworks may be preliminarily delineated. Though, to be sure, they are not necessarily mutually exclusive. First, building on Marx's words spiking his various writings to the effect that capitalism is driven by an "inner" logic or "laws...winning their way through and working themselves out with an iron necessity" (Marx 1977: 91), Marxist approaches have endeavored to create an explanatory "chain link" between the "laws" as they understand these and historical transmutations of capitalism (Laibman 2005: 293). The merit of these approaches is that they seek to ground their analysis of capitalist change on some "essence" or constant of capitalism which it is then claimed shapes capitalist development notwithstanding the dramatic historical recasting it undergoes across its major historical stages or phases. Where these miscarry, on the one hand, stems from the chosen constant that is conceptualized as the prime mover of capitalism and, on the other hand, due to the inclinations of such theorizations to box in historical difference, contingency, and agency.

A second broad research approach to periodizing capitalism largely anchors its analysis in the systemization of empirical history to produce what are dubbed "stylized facts" or "ideal types" of institutional or economic trends in capitalist economies (Hollingsworth and Boyer 1998). In its dedicated Marxian political economy version, this broad approach to periodizing capitalism carries over elements of the first in setting out a matrix of core economic "forms" which orient the systemizing of empirical history in a capitalist period. Marxist approaches of this cast also eschew determinate explanations of capitalist transmutation bound to purported trans-capitalist economic "laws". Most importantly, Marxist approaches here offer refined explanations of how, notwithstanding crises tendencies inhering in capitalism, a pattern of relatively stable accumulation over decades is nevertheless managed.

A significant contingent of non-Marxist perspectives falls into this broad category of periodizing capitalism according to systemizations of empirical history. Interestingly, these approaches sprouted during the post-WWII era. And, while such analyses of the post-WWII period of capitalism self-identified as non-Marxist, that they were either inspired by questions Marxism asked (as opposed to neoclassical economics silence) or tacitly imbibed in their work Marxian foci on technological change, forms of business organization, and the like is instructive.

Yet, where Marxian and non-Marxian variants of periodizing capitalism through systemizing empirical history miscarry is over what gave the first genre its confidence. That is, the attempt to set out a constant or invariable substance of capitalism that defines *it* or its operations in their most fundamental incarnation. Initially, the move of theory away from its tethering to a constant of capitalism was heralded as a positive, liberating step, opening up a vista for greater historical play and accounting for difference and contingency which "orthodox" Marxism supposedly frustrated (Hirst and Zeitlin 1991). However, in the end, it left periodizing capitalism at the mercy of ad hoc constructions of stylized facts based upon this or that salient feature of the age. And, as adverted to above, in their reveling in historical idiosyncrasies of an era, the life span of such theories was inevitably short as momentous, unforeseen economic change overwhelmed them.

Eliding elaboration of a constant or invariable substance of capitalism leads to a bigger problem for the periodization of capitalism research program. Capitalist economies have existed in human history for a few hundred years, possibly longer depending on the theoretical approach to this question. Economic historians of both Marxist and non-Marxist persuasions engaged in extensive, long-running international debate over the genetic markers of the capitalist era, the process by which capitalism emerged from the womb of precapitalist society and on what initially differentiated capitalist economic modalities from those engaged in within "feudal" economies (see, for example, Aston and Philpin 1987; Anderson 1996). Why this debate raged for so long, in fact, it arguably continues today in some academic circles, is precisely because no benchmark for what capitalism *is* in its most fundamental incarnation was accepted by all parties to the dispute. Travails of this theoretical gap are only compounded by the "gray" historical conditions that prevail during times of epochal social change, as was the existential condition of the period of transition away from feudalism in Western Europe.

As will be argued in later chapters, it is the case particularly with regard to periodizing post-WWII capitalism and conceptualizing the economic changes occurring at the close of the twentieth century that dearth of theoretical reflection on how to apprehend capitalism in its most fundamental incarnation hamstrings thought in ways not unrelated to difficulties faced in treating the transition from feudal economies to capitalism. This follows from the fact that an array of economic practices adopted in so-called golden age social democratic, welfare state capitalism "governed" capitalist market operations with a degree of programming and coordination in many ways more akin to socialism than capitalism (Kapp 1939). What is important to grasp here is that it is not simply a question of the existence of a "mixed" economy that confronts theory and empirical analysis. Rather the core problem is that of historical determinacy of the economic "forms" composing the "mix". In the case of feudal economies in their process of disintegration, it will be shown that the sprouting within them of what are perceived as ostensibly capitalist practices does not necessarily beget capitalism per se. Much the same may be said of germinating socialist economic forms within capitalist economies. These do not necessarily lead to the rise of socialism itself.

Two Foundations for Periodizing Capitalism in Marx's Writing

Given the central role Marxian economics and political economy, both directly and tacitly, plays in periodizing capitalism as a research program, it is necessary to acknowledge upfront that ambiguities in Marx's own writings impel thinking along two broad paths. First, in the famous "Preface" to *A Contribution to the Critique of Political Economy*, Marx states (1904: 11–2):

> In the social production which men carry on they enter into definite relations that are indispensable and independent of their will; these relations of production correspond to a definite stage of development of their material powers of production. The sum total of these relations of production constitutes the economic structure of society...At a certain stage of development, the material productive forces of production in society come into conflict with the existing relations of production...From forms of development of the forces of production these relations turn into their fetters. Then comes the period of social revolution...

Approaching the development and transformation of capitalism through this lens crystallized what in many ways became the received view within Marxist theory of a capitalist teleology with socialism as its historical outcome. In Marx's magisterial economic work, *Capital*, the first volume of which was published in his lifetime, Marx lends further credence to this position with the short quote offered earlier, that capitalism manifests "laws...working themselves out with an iron necessity". And, in the closing pages of Volume I of *Capital*, Marx reinforces that. He puts it thus (Marx 1977: 928–9):

> ...as soon as workers have been turned into proletarians, and their means of labour into capital, as soon as the capitalist mode of production stands on its own feet, the further socialization of labour...and other means of production...takes on a new form...The monopoly of capital becomes a fetter upon the mode of production which has flourished alongside and

> under it. The centralization of the means of production and socialization of labour reach a point at which they become incompatible with their capitalist integument. This integument is bust asunder…The expropriators are expropriated.

It is precisely this view of capitalism taking on "a new form" en route to fulfilling its historical telos that binds the periodization research program to the notion that Marx's constant of capitalism are its "laws" driving it toward breakdown from which socialism, supposedly already gestating within capitalism, springs. Socializing of the means of production in the sense of competition yielding ever-enlarging units of capital that tend to monopolize sectors and increasingly "organize" production constitutes morphing features of capitalism which struck Marx in his final decades of life. As will be explored in the next chapter, it is these tendencies Marx discusses preliminarily that are seized upon following his passing by the initial efforts at periodizing capitalism of the earlytwentieth century.

What is imperative to grasp in the Introduction to this book are the ramifications of this approach to capitalist change attributed to Marx for not only periodizing capitalism but determining the ultimate limits to capitalism as a historical mode of economy. Commencing with the theorizing of capitalist change at the close of the nineteenth century following Marx's passing and continuing with attempts to capture further economic shifts of the post-WWII era, a peculiar theme comes to characterize this genre of Marxist literature. That is, on the one hand, theorizations of capitalist change explain the extension of trends toward monopolization and "organizing" of capitalism treated by Marx and ways these "fetter" human material reproduction notwithstanding the productive power of increasingly advanced socialized forces of production. On the other hand, theorizing the "new form" of capitalism calls forth explanation of why, despite material conditions for socialism purportedly ripening within socialized, "organized" production, the working class proves incapable of assuming its historic revolutionary role in "expropriating the expropriators".

Where this apprehension of Marx's writings become most problematic, however, resides in the fashion by which it forces theory to account for all economic change in terms of capitalism. That is, if the constant of capitalism is accepted as its "law" advancing and socializing the forces of production until a point is reached where this ultimately conflicts with capitalist social relations of production, rendering them unsustainable and ushering in an "a period of social revolution", as Marx expressed it in the famous "Preface", then all "new forms" of economy that arise along this historical course must be considered capitalist. Viewed from another angle, capitalism is thereby endowed with historical staying power almost akin to that imparted to it by mainstream economics. It is forever until dismounted by proletarian action through revolution or ascendance of socialist political parties in democratic electoral processes.

Paradoxically, the longer capitalism persists or even argumentation to that effect made by the Left for its transfiguring in yet another form as per the above schema, the more pronounced becomes its ideological fallout fomenting disincentives for socialist change. Marx, of course, in the heady days of the early workers' movement believed the end of capitalism to be nigh. Marx himself had been convinced that the looming horror of capital subsuming human economic life would impel workers as an increasingly organized social class to violently destroy it. With his passing, Marx's prominent followers including Friedrich Engels increasingly looked toward elections as the vehicle for ushering in socialism. However, the story of electoral socialism is one of initial optimism as industrial workers rapidly grew proportionally among adult populations in major economies. Ultimately it led to mounting disappointments when the share of the proletariat dropped and socialist party platforms gravitated toward social democratic reforms of capitalism rather than calls for socialist change, diluting their programs to "catch" non-industrial working class and even "middle class" voters (Przeworski 1985; Przeworski and Sprague 1986).

Further, capitalist development in advanced economies, notwithstanding capitalist ills elaborated by Marx, underpinned a welter of benefits for working people of all stripes into the second half of the twentieth century, including greater life expectancies, modern health and sanitation infrastructure, public education, wide access among populations to consumer durable material goods and private homes, rising real wages and working conditions a far cry from Engels' "satanic mills"—not to mention accoutrement of the welfare state such as pensions which invest people in the perseverance of capitalism. Put differently, capitalism has been associated with delivering the goods, so to speak, particularly when it dons its social democratic, welfare state garb. For working people of various stripes to now forsake capitalism with its potential socio-material betterments for socialism, even in the latter's idyllic representations, will entail stepping into the unknown. It is for this reason that even though, today, there is a resurrected Zeitgeist for socialism reflected in the growing support for avowedly socialist political candidates or programs—Bernie Sanders in the US, Jeremy Corbyn in Britain, DiEM25 in the European Union (EU), for example—the platforms they outline shrewdly hark of social democratic reforms of capitalism, as the qualifier "democratic" is strongly emphasized whenever their "socialism" is publicly called to account (Westra 2018: 9–10). The point to be made is that the perceived existence of capitalism offers some solace even to those desirous of socialism. This is the case because if the latter is not attained, capitalist economic workings, as odious and crises ridden as these may be, are counted on to ensure human material reproduction on some basic level.

Yet, Marx's writings offer another theoretical undergirding for periodizing capitalism and thinking about the delimitations of capitalism as a historical society. In the closing section of *A Contribution to the Critique of Political Economy*, Marx observes (1904: 300):

> The bourgeois society is the most highly developed and most highly differentiated historical organization of production. The categories which serve as the expression of its conditions and the comprehension of its own organization enable it at the same time to gain insight into the organization and the conditions of production which had prevailed under all past forms of society…The anatomy of the human being is the key to the anatomy of the ape.

Marx's alternative narrative here may be taken as essentially foregrounding his earlier statement in the famous "Preface". That is to say, in the "Preface", he approaches capitalism within a conceptual framework delineating a process of change playing out across the sweep of human history that capitalism allegedly follows. In this latter quote, Marx admits that the very conceptual infrastructure and categories of analysis of his pithy theory of human economic history in the "Preface" are dependent on an in-depth study of capitalism.

This position is further corroborated by Marx's own characterization of his theorizing of the capitalist economy. Marx clearly affirms that his crowning economic treatise, *Capital*, is intended as the founding work of a "new science". His object of study in *Capital* is the "capitalist mode of production" in its "pure state" (Marx 1977: 89–90). Thus, though Marx conducts his scientific investigations on the economy of Britain, which constitute the initial, "*locus classicus*" of capitalist development, the empirics of *Capital* Marx asseverates are simply "used as the main illustration of the theoretical developments I make" (Marx 1977: 90). Instead, *Capital*, as the foundation of the "new science", is grasped as developing a "purely theoretical position" (Marx 1977: 99). That is to say, *Capital* offers what is variously designated a "pure" (Uno 1980), "general" (Levine 1978), or "basic" (Itoh 1988), theorizing of capitalism that sets out to systematically capture capital in its most fundamental economic incarnation and, thus, to "define" what capitalism as a mode of production *is*.[1]

Unfortunately, this theoretical approach to periodizing capitalism is almost universally overlooked within the literature. Yet, its very raison d'etre is precisely to provide the necessary conceptual touchstone for differentiating capitalism from other forms of economy and to inform our determinations on whether an era of economic history or kind of economy is *capitalist* in the first place. As intimated above, in the heady days accompanying early stirrings of working-class radicalism, even Marx himself did not belabor in correspondences and public speeches what he had set out as the scientific kernel of his research program. Rather, Marx chose to emphasize trends exposed by his studies of capitalism that he believed augur socialist change. However, into the twentieth century, no evidence exists of tendencies fixated upon by Marx bringing about the desired socialist historical outcome. Yet advanced economies continue to experience such seismic transmutations as to render them essentially unrecognizable from capitalism as grasped by Marx in his day. These conditions suggest a pressing need for placing Marx's "pure" or "general" theorizing of capitalism at the center of the periodization research program.

There is, to be sure, one particular theoretical approach within the broad literature to periodizing capitalism that closely follows Marx on his position that as the foundation of a new science it is in fact his economic studies in *Capital* that undergird the pithy approach to human economic history in toto sketched in the "Preface", and constitute the touchstone for periodizing capitalism and explorations of economic history to answer questions of the coming into being and passing of capitalism. A discussion of this approach will take place in Chap. 6 of the book. Its treatment at that juncture does not reflect its development in chronological terms in relation to other theories. Nor is it a measure of its importance to the literature. What will be revealed is that even though two hugely influential Marxian schools of thought on periodizing capitalism that crystallized in the waning years of the post-WWII golden age blaze a theoretical trail approximating in some ways the approach in question, they end up plagued by their inability to fully harness the power of Marx's *Capital* in their historical determinations over current economic change. These, along with other theories, the present volume demonstrates, hit an explanatory wall in the "gray", often befuddling, empirical milieu confronting us in the twenty-first century.

When Marx's theorizing of what capitalism *is* in its most fundamental incarnation is correctly marshaled as the constant of capitalism, informing our historical judgment on the existence and potential transmutability of capitalism, the recent spate of frightening, even apocalyptic, appellations applied to current economies take on a new light. That is, it is argued, adjectives "gore", "carceral", "totalitarian", "crack", "cancer", and so forth, along with the conditions they delineate, point away from what can reasonably be explained as a stage or phase of capitalism. Rather the political economic goings captured in these and other theories with rubrics such as financialization and globalization conjure up the specter of capitalist disintegration and extinction: Such a scenario unfolding in a fashion reminiscent of the Dark Ages which followed the collapse of the Roman Empire. However, the current looming dark age holds out scant "promise" of any new, progressive economic forms germinating as has been claimed marked its historical precursor (Stavrianos 1976).

Put differently, the inescapable conclusion the theoretical and empirical explorations this book points to is that the time is upon us to tear away the security blanket working people of all stripes take refuge under. This is the false comfort provided by the belief that if there is no socialism, then there must still be capitalism, in some guise, as the devil we know, able to manage the economic reproduction of human societies into the foreseeable future. To fully grasp what is in store for humanity, however, demands a journey through over a century of writing on capitalist transformation. It is a journey proceeding through the prism of works of original and influential thinkers of capitalist change and the most powerful schools of thought on periodizing capitalism that this book takes readers on.

The focus of the book is multifaceted. Debates swirling around how to grasp the seismic economic changes over the past 150 years since Marx wrote *Capital* are covered. Answers to the question of why, despite anarchic and crises tendencies of capitalism captured in radical analysis, capitalism manages to congeal in relatively stable periods of accumulation and prosperity are explored. The volume carefully evaluates arguments on the economic forces bringing phases of capitalist stability to an end. And it exposes current tendencies that place capitalism on the endangered species list. Such tendencies euphemized in sweet-sounding terminology like globalization demand painstaking theoretically informed investigation. Thus, this volume is largely a theoretical treatise. In this sense, it contravenes current trends in critical writings on the current economy that leave readers bobbing in whirlpools of facts, many informative to be sure, but with little conceptual moorings beyond the assertion of keywords that, themselves, require extensive interrogation. Nevertheless, in the latter chapters, theory is turned back upon the empirical world with a much sharper eye. In the end, no analytical stone is left unturned in this book on the research field of periodizing capitalism.

Outline of the Book

Chapter 2 picks up on indicators Marx left in his work for the periodization research agenda. It tracks how Marx's early followers such as Karl Kautsky treated questions raised by Marx of "formal" and "real" subsumption of the labor and production process and that of the enlarged footprint of merchant "capital". From the ensuing debates, it is argued, emerged the theorizing of *imperialism* as a new stage of capitalism. However, with the smell of revolution in the air prior to World War I (WWI), there was scant interest among prominent theorists of imperialism including Rudolf Hilferding, Nikolai Bukharin, and V. I. Lenin in refining Marx's pure or general theory of capitalism. Marxist sights instead were riveted upon the historical trends within major capitalist economies presaging socialism along with questions surrounding animation of the working class to perform its historic role. Theories of imperialism promulgated by these Marxist theoreticians produced a wealth of empirical data on the genuine institutional changes marking early twentieth-century capitalism. But they also become forerunners of a theme in Marxist writing that treats eras of capitalist change in the context of the question of why, despite material conditions for socialism as initially specified by Marx appearing ripe, revolutionary classes fail to grab the moment.

Chapter 3 delves into questions of the momentous transmutation of capitalism in the post-WWII era. It tracks the effort of Marxist theorizations seeking to extend the fundamental insights of theorists of imperialism on the "organized" or "socializing" tendencies of capitalism as manifested in the monopoly industrial structure of imperialist economies. Prominent Marxists Paul Baran and Paul Sweezy investigate the impacts of expanding monopolization and oligopoly on accumulation. Their ultimate interest is in highlighting the way exigencies of "monopoly capital" accumulation "fetter" potentialities for economic development inhering in the productive power of labor, pointing, thus, to the necessity for socialism. Instructively, the influential non-Marxist writing of John Kenneth Galbraith blazes a similar empirical trail as Baran and Sweezy in drawing out the implications for capitalism of changes in business structure and attenuation of competition under the new corporate forms. Taking account of his work as a contribution to periodizing capitalism literature in this chapter is important for the contrary conclusion he arrives at. Rather than a historical telos of socialism, Galbraith suggests the requisites of technological and organizational change compel a systemic convergence of capitalism and socialism. Finally, the chapter explores the economic analysis of Belgian Marxist Ernest Mandel.

Mandel, in my view, produces the most sophisticated approach to periodizing capitalism among Marxian theoreticians of this early post-WWII era. His conceptual framework crucially offers a Marxian political economic explanation of why the scenarios offered by Baran and Sweezy as well as Galbraith never come to pass.

Chapter 4 begins with a switch of course by introducing three perspectives on periodizing capitalism that employ the epistemological approach of systemizing empirical history in stylized facts or ideal types. However, while demonstrating an epistemological affinity, the three theories operate from markedly divergent ideological positions. The writing of Daniel Bell is avowedly anti-Marxist, that of Scott Lash and John Urry if not neo-Marxist, at least Marxist friendly, while the work of Michael Piore and Charles Sabel may be classified as non-Marxist though, with interest in Marxist concerns. What ultimately brings these perspectives on periodizing capitalism together for the purpose of this chapter is their orientation both in, and to, time.

The work discussed in Chap. 3 captures the economic and institutional tendencies capital exhibits in the period of roughly 1950–1970. In the case of the Marxist writers, in particular, it is maintained that notwithstanding the qualitative differentiation of post-WWII capitalism from early twentieth-century imperialism, the roots of the post-WWII economy can be traced back to tendencies identified by theorists of imperialism. Bell, Lash and Urry, and Piore and Sabel all write from the vista of the 1970s and 1980s. For them, whatever case had been made for a constant of capitalism around which its transformation into the post-WWII era revolved, the 1970s constitutes a watershed. That is, if capitalism from its inception has evinced tendencies toward industrial agglomeration and gigantism that, in turn, brought on the need for increased "organization" at both the level of business and that of the state (early Marxist theorizations of periodizing capitalism, to recapitulate, have always interpreted this in terms of the "ripening" of economies for socialist transition), such tendencies are now reversed. Advanced economies from the crisis of the 1970s and unraveling of the golden age, so the argument goes, are becoming "disorganized" and manifest trends toward "post-industrialism" as exemplified by burgeoning service and financial sectors. To Piore and Sabel, organizing of capitalism, which reached its apogee in integrated mass-production systems, has succumbed to crisis egression, which depends upon humanity imbibing a new technological orientation.

Finally, the chapter is brought to a close with an examination of two approaches to periodizing capitalism that contextualize the foregoing transformations in terms of a broader historical process of change which by no means is brought to a close in "post-industrial" society and the like. The self-identified Marxist approach to periodizing capitalism of Giovanni Arrighi, for example, offers a sweeping theory of "systemic cycles" of capital accumulation. Where Arrighi constitutes a potential corrective to the aforementioned three perspectives in this chapter derives on the one hand from his focus on capitalism as a "world system" as opposed to the empirical concentration of the above three theories largely upon comparative national data. On the other hand, and more importantly, is what Arrighi has to say about trends toward "disorganization" claimed as the new telos of capitalist economies supplanting earlier tendencies toward "organization". That is, for Arrighi, rather than an end state for capitalism, such conditions are part of a recurring historical pattern where interregnums of financial expansion endowing capital with greater "flexibility" punctuate intervening periods of "systemic cycles" of capitalist accumulation. Carlota Perez innovatively develops "long wave" theory to explain the succession of capitalist stages in terms of the emergence of new "techno-economic paradigms". Perez's view of the 1980s and 1990s as gestating a new "microelectronics paradigm" of economy points to the fact that the period following the demise of the golden age does not bring about a "post-industrial", society but a new structuring of capitalist industry and institutional support system. If this chapter offers one major lesson for the study of capitalist change, it is that theories too strictly wedded to ad hoc systemizing of empirical history are sure to have a short shelf life.

Chapter 5 critically explores key writings of two major, and highly original, emergent Marxist schools of thought on periodizing capitalism. The work of these schools is noteworthy, first, because of their essentially simultaneous promulgation on both sides of the Atlantic—the *Regulation School* (RS) in France and the Social Structures of Accumulation (SSA) school in the US. For RS, there is a single progenitor, Michel Aglietta (though the work of Robert Boyer follows on the heels of Aglietta's and is seen as instrumental to the development of RS). SSA, on the other hand, originated with the writing of a triumvirate, David Gordon, Richard Edwards, and Michael Reich. Its cardinal follow-up writings also tend to be products of collectivities drawing in these authors and later generations of important contributors. Second, RS and SSA periodizing of capitalism is noteworthy from a strictly Marxist stance in its eschewal of conceptualizing a prime mover or constant of capitalism that connects stages of capitalism as a telos. Its position here yielded a seminal theoretical innovation that combined epistemological strategies of stylized facts with elaboration of core capitalist political economic "forms" or "structures". The result is the periodizing of capitalism at an "intermediate" or "mid-range" *level* of theory. Third, this device of mid-range theory, which enables elaboration upon institutional constituents of long-term accumulation as well as limiting factors in a historically non-determinist fashion, renders RS and SSA relatively adaptable in the face of seismic capitalist change. RS and SSA emerged in the late 1970s and early 1980s. Both theorize what they apprehend as the initial phases of capitalism from its inception. Each, however, focuses much of its attention on the post-WWII stage of capitalism, the crisis of that period, and the structural changes of the late 1970s and 1980s leading to twenty-first-century transmutations euphemized variously as neoliberalism, globalization, and financialization. These latter extensions of RS and SSA are followed up on, however, in Chaps. 7 and 8.

Chapter 6 introduces a lesser-known yet comprehensive approach to periodizing capitalism initially developed following WWI but refined in basic form by its progenitor, Japanese Marxist economist Kozo Uno, by the 1950s. As I alluded to above, it is Uno's perspective on periodizing capitalism that closely follows Marx in anchoring Marxian political economy in Marx's theorizing of capitalism in *Capital* as a pure or basic theory of capital. Uno, formatively in Japanese language, and later Uno's student Thomas Sekine in English, reconstructed and completed the material of Marx's unfinished *Capital. Capital* in this endeavor is intended as a "definition" of what capitalism as a mode of production *is* in its most fundamental economic incarnation. The raison d'etre for Uno's procedure here is to establish a conceptual touchstone to inform our determinations over whether an era of economic history or kind of economy is *capitalist.*

It is argued that notwithstanding the family resemblance among the Uno approach, RS, and SSA, the absence in the latter two perspectives of a clear reference to what constitutes the conceptual touchstone for differentiating capitalism from other modes of economy significantly limits their analysis of twenty-first-century economic change. Instructively, Uno had arrived at the conclusion by the 1950s that Marxian political economic study of capitalism necessitated three "levels of analysis" with a "stage theory" that periodized capitalism "mediating" between the pure theorizing of capital in its fundamental incarnation and analysis of capitalist history. But with language barriers and relative insulation of Japanese academia at the time, there was no cross-fertilization of ideas between Uno's work and that of RS or SSA. Today, unfortunately, while a second and third generation of Marxist scholars both based in Japan and around the world working in the Uno School tradition, all writing in the English language medium, have carefully studied and integrated insights of RS and SSA where pertinent, there has been little reciprocal interchange. With a few exceptions, to be sure, RS and SSA proponents proceed as if the Japanese approach did not exist even though it pioneered by decades the basic notion of mid-range theory RS and SSA are founded on.

On periodizing capitalism, as covered in the chapter, the Uno approach maintains capital accumulation has congealed into four world historic stages, with the post-WWII stage constituting its final stage. While there is debate among scholars working in this tradition over the extent to which even the post-WWII golden age can be classified as capitalist given the way market operations are governed with a degree of programming and coordination in many ways more akin to socialism than capitalism, there is agreement on the course of the twenty-first century. That is, economic goings-on euphemized variously as neoliberalism, globalization, and financialization entail little measure of cohesive substance of capitalism. Rather as picked up in descriptions of current political economic pathologies cited in the opening paragraph of this book, an analysis of the Uno School claims that if the world finds itself in any kind of phase, it is one of capitalist disintegration with human barbarism a-la-Dark Ages looming on the horizon (see Table 1.1).

Chapter 7 collects the conceptual and empirical strands of the periodizations of capitalism to track the actual economic changes that fol-

Table 1.1 Brief history of periodizing capitalism

Theorist/school	Periodization	Key features
Karl Marx	Formal subsumption of labor process, pre-1800s	Merchant "putting out" system
	Real subsumption, 1800s	Industrial revolution and factory system
Karl Kautsky	Petty commodity society	Small independent traders
	Capitalism proper	Large-scale manufacturing
R. Hilferding, N. Bukharin	Imperialism 1895–1917	Monopoly combines, finance capital
V. I. Lenin		Acquisition of imperialist territories
P. Baran, P. Sweezy	Monopoly capitalism 1950–1970	Organized capitalism, rising "surplus"
		Underconsumption despite sales effort
J. K. Galbraith	New industrial state 1950–1970	"Technostructure" management
E. Mandel	Late capitalism 1950–1975	Technological dynamism in drive for surplus profit
D. Bell	Post-industrial society 1972–	Expansion of service sector
Lash and Urry	Disorganized capitalism 1980s	Crisis of organized capitalism
		Domestic and international factors
Piore and Sabel	Flexible specialization 1980s	Crisis of mass production, re-emergent craft production networks
G. Arrighi	US systemic cycle of accumulation 1950–1990s	US hegemony and financial dominance
C. Perez	Microelectronic technological paradigm 1971–2000s	Technological revolution brings to bear institutional and cultural change
Marxist Regulation School	*Fordism* 1950–1975/ post-*fordism* 1975—"regimes of accumulation"	Mass production and mass consumption "norm"
	1980s—globalization, financial deregulation	Flexibility over production rigidity
Social Structures of Accumulation Theory	Postwar SSA 1950–1970s	Class accord and welfare state
	Neoliberal SSA 1980s–	Deregulation, asset bubbles, rising inequality, speculation economy

(*continued*)

Table 1.1 (continued)

Theorist/school	Periodization	Key features
Uno School	Sekine post-WWI capitalist disintegration	Law of value no longer regulates economy, role of state hypertrophies
	Albritton 1950–1970s stage of consumerism	Interpenetration of economic, political and ideological practices, mass production and consumption of consumer durables
	Albritton/Westra 1980s– capitalist disintegration	Financialization and disarticulation of production-centered economies, Indirect costs and intangible assets subvert market operations

Source: Author

lowed the breakdown of the post-WWII golden age economy. It looks at the way important expositors of RS (though with a few outliers) essentially gravitated away from Marxism to join a cohort of "heterodox" economists in a research agenda on "models" or "varieties" of capitalism. In some way, the unceremonious collapse of the Soviet Union and the bite of China's post-Mao, "market reforms" drove RS exponents and other critical scholars to blithely accept that capitalism was the only game in town. And to play required a seat at the policy table to propose, at best, progressive reforms amid hegemonic neoliberal fixation upon competitiveness and economic growth. What this section of the chapter confirms is the poverty of the epistemological procedure of stylized facts animating the models of capitalism debate in the face of deep-rooted, complex, and disconcerting seismic economic change.

Taking off from the theorizing of capital and periodizing of capitalism in the Japanese Uno School tradition, the chapter undertakes a step-by-step historical analysis of the most significant economic transmutations shaking advanced capitalist economies during the final decades of the twentieth century and into the twenty-first century. It examines the impacts of the disintegration of full-scale industrial production-centered economies, captured in discourses on globalization, on both the mass commodified labor forces capital maintained in the post-WWII period in its heartlands and the activities of erstwhile production-centered corporations themselves, which morph into "brands" that no longer make anything. Also specified is precisely what is entailed by financialization and the perverse fashion by which financialization and globalization interpenetrate to the detriment of humanity. Chapter 7 then concludes by tracing the patterns through which the transformations of capitalist finance produce a financial and historical regression to antediluvian practices most associated with ancient usury that expropriate wealth rather than intermediate in its generation and augmentation.

Chapter 8 begins with a theoretical retrospective on Marx's important expose in Volume III of *Capital* on the way capital subsumes land and establishes a modus vivendi with its owner as landed property in order to incorporate it into the capitalist production-centered economy directed toward profit making. Carrying crucial ramifications for understanding current economic shifts is the specific principle of this modus vivendi, its application to financialization, and its role in maintaining rent and interest on lending as subsidiary to the capitalist chrematistic of production-centered profit making. What is preliminarily argued is that the impact of transformations in production and finance toward an economy of wealth expropriation are exacerbated by technological change. The latter not only brings to bear an increasing proportion of indirect costs on vestiges of capitalist production, which further discombobulate it, but also hypertrophies the economic force of "intangible assets" to which varying modalities of rent accrue. This trajectory that operates alongside predatory expropriations of financialization is tantamount to the "landlordization" of capitalism.

In this light, the chapter assesses reloaded views of SSA and monopoly capitalism which maintain that the period following the demise of the post-WWII golden age economy led to the reconstitution of capitalism in but another stage. And that the global financial meltdown of 2007–2008 reflects the discontents of that. Rather it is argued based on the full spectrum of theoretical insights on periodizing capitalism gained in this volume that there is very little remaining of what can reasonably be referred to as production-centered capitalist "market" substance of major economies. Even the form taken by recent crises has morphed from crises patterns marking over a century and a half of capitalism's existence. Capitalist rationality of advanced economies has largely been leeched out through the shape shifting of giant transnational corporations into financial arbitragers that outsource work to non-commodified labor forces in third-world locales. Even global financial, banking, securities, bond markets, and so on, have now been commandeered and manipulated by machinations of governments.

In the short conclusion of Chap. 9, the book reflects back on writings adverted to at the outset of this introduction, which provided apocalyptic appellations for the current economic state—gore, carceral, authoritarian, cancer, and so forth—to show that the pathologies that these works point not to a form of capitalism but to the extinction of the capitalist species. It suggests that the technocratic management by neoliberal states of capitalist decay means that in lieu of a concatenation of unforeseen events, there will be no final great meltdown to bring the masses onto the streets demanding change akin to Marx's envisioned heroic class struggles. Rather the extinction of capitalism will unfold as a slow and agonizing death as dystopian scenarios of starvation, disease, and urban violence break down the last fabrics of social control, sending the über wealthy with their private contracted security forces scurrying for "safe zones" either on earth or on other planets.

Note

1. As will be discussed in Chap. 6, capitalist change had largely been theorized within the field of Marxist studies as following the general course of history where, as cited in the famous "Preface", at a certain point, the development of the forces of production in society "come into conflict with the existing relations of production" to commence an area of revolution and change. This animated early followers of Marx to scour his writings on capitalism for references on how that process comes about. As the next chapter shows, Marx's followers fixated upon Marx's statements about the "organizing" of capitalism as the antechamber for socialism and believed the earliest trends toward enlargement of businesses were precursors of Marx's vision. While Marx's general theory of the course of history known as historical materialism is not "wrong", and captures some

enduring truths about epochal historical change, it does not explore, nor make reference to, the specificities or dynamics of any one historical economy. Of all the historical economies, it is capitalism that Marx studied exhaustively. And there are vital epistemological and ontological warrants for Marx's lifelong lucubration upon *capital* and capitalism. What will be revealed as discussion as this book proceeds is that, as per Marx's own emphasis and theorizations of capitalism, there is a more fundamental and specific "contradiction" that drives capitalism than the general historical contradiction Marx posits between the development of the forces of production and relations of production in the "Preface". This is the signal lesson from the second basis for thinking about periodization of capitalism in Marx's work that revolves around his theorizing of capitalism as a "pure" theory of capital.

References

Anderson, P. 1996. *Lineages of the Absolutist State*. London: Verso.

Aston, T.H., and C.H.E. Philpin. 1987. *The Brenner Debate: Agrarian Class Structure and Economic Development in Pre-industrial Europe*. Cambridge: Cambridge University Press.

Blaug, M. 2003. The Formalist Revolution of the 1950s. *Journal of the History of Economic Thought* 25 (2): 145–156.

Bloom, P. 2016. *Authoritarian Capitalism in the Age of Globalization*. Northampton: Edward Elgar.

Dasgupta, A.K. 1987. *Epochs of Economic Theory*. New York: Basil Blackwell.

Hirst, P., and J. Zeitlin. 1991. Flexible Specialization versus Post-Fordism: Theory, Evidence and Policy Implications. *Economy and Society* 20 (1): 1–56.

Hollingsworth, J.R., and R. Boyer. 1998. *Contemporary Capitalism: The Embeddedness of Institutions*. Cambridge: Cambridge University Press.

Holloway, J. 2010. *Crack Capitalism*. London: Pluto Press.

Itoh, M. 1988. *The Basic Theory of Capitalism: The Forms and Substance of the Capitalist Economy*. Basingstoke: Macmillan.

Kapp, K.W. 1939. Economic Regulation and Economic Planning. *The American Economic Review* 29 (4): 760–773.

Laibman, D. 2005. Theory and Necessity: The Stadial Foundations of the Present. *Science & Society* 69 (3): 285–315.

Levine, D.P. 1978. *Economic Theory Volume One: The Elementary Relations of Economic Life*. London: Routledge and Kegan Paul.
Liodakis, G. 2010. *Totalitarian Capitalism and Beyond*. London: Routledge.
Marx, K. 1904. *A Contribution to the Critique of Political Economy*. Chicago: Charles H. Kerr & Co.
———. 1977. *Capital Volume I*. New York: Vintage Books.
McMurtry, J. 1999. *The Cancer Stage of Capitalism*. London: Pluto Press.
Przeworski, A. 1985. *Capitalism and Social Democracy*. Cambridge: Cambridge University Press.
Przeworski, A., and J. Sprague. 1986. *Paper Stones: A History of Electoral Socialism*. Chicago: University of Chicago Press.
Sekine, T. 2013. Towards a Critique of Bourgeois Economics. In *Towards a Critique of Bourgeois Economics: Essays of Thomas Sekine*, ed. J. Bell. Berlin: Owl of Minerva Press.
Stavrianos, L.S. 1976. *The Promise of the Coming Dark Age*. San Francisco: W.H. Freeman.
Uno, K. 1980. *Principles of Political Economy*. Sussex: Harvester Press.
Valencia, S. 2018. *Gore Capitalism*. South Pasadena: Semiotext(e).
Wang, J. 2018. *Carceral Capitalism*. South Pasadena: Semiotext(e).
Westra, R. 2018. *Socialism in the Twenty-First Century*. Hauppauge, NY: Nova Science Publishers.

2

Capitalist Development and Theories of Imperialism

To provide a rather brief and selective historical contextualization to the discussion in this chapter, several factors related to precapitalist economic conditions contributed to capitalist development in Britain and Western Europe. Evidence indicates that with the demise of the slave-based Roman Empire and remaking of society under feudal relations of production following the Dark Ages, a significant cluster of labor-saving inventions in agriculture, construction, manufacture, and transportation proliferated. Particularly noteworthy was technological innovation in shipbuilding, navigation instruments, and naval armament. Western Europe found itself corralled by the breakdown of order in the Mongol Empire and expansion of the Ottoman. This impelled a search for maritime trade routes to the East and the material wherewithal of plying and defending these. Effects of that early endeavor were manifested in the advantage Western Europe would enjoy for centuries in controlling the oceans of the world.

European quests across the world's oceans operated economically, with a centripetal force siphoning wealth of the globe into the newly forming nation-state containers that emerged as centers of global capital accumulation. Gold and silver pillaged from the Americas, for example, provided

R. Westra, *Periodizing Capitalism and Capitalist Extinction*, Palgrave Insights into Apocalypse Economics, https://doi.org/10.1007/978-3-030-14390-9_2

a then-unrivaled economic stimulus. Britain and Europe also battened on the new transcontinental trading system the traversing of the world's oceans created. This was particularly the case as trade shifted from luxury goods such as spices and silk to new "bulk" consumer products extracted from exploitative plantation economies fashioned by British and European colonialism. Further, plantation economy importation of labor sparked a trans-Atlantic slave trade. Estimates vary over both the total numbers of human beings brutally transported from Africa across the more than three centuries the slave trade was plied by Europeans. They similarly vary on the extent to which commercial stimulus and capital accumulation from the historical holocaust of "triangular trade" of slaves and sugar with the West Indies and America fed development of Britain and Western Europe. What is certain is that Africa was devastated and significant investments drawing from the trade found their way into the industrial revolution in Britain or the United Kingdom (UK).

Debate over the genesis of capitalism, with greatest implications for its early periodization, swirls around the transformation of social relations in agriculture. In Britain, by the mid-seventeenth century, feudal systems of land tenure were significantly eroded. But this did not lead automatically to the formation of capitalism in agriculture. Rather, a diverse array of land-leasing arrangements subsequently formed. These often entailed subsistence guarantees and off-farm "service" employment opportunities for peasant farming families. Further, the enclosing of commons and pastures proceeded slowly until the eighteenth century when it gathered pace, suggesting that direct links radical historiography posits between the revolutionary tumults of mid-seventeenth-century Britain and the rise of capitalist agriculture are tenuous (Overton 1996: 205). Arguably, the revolutionary tumults, along with the spread of new ideas that generated them, can themselves be traced to the unique way sovereignty in British feudal society was "parcelized", leaving significant "space" outside of staid socioeconomic relations for new transformatory classes and forces to germinate (Anderson 1996).

Monetizing of socioeconomic relations in agriculture accelerated under the impetus of mercantile trading activities, which expanded their scope from the mid-seventeenth century. Potential export earnings from corn sold in European markets led to rationalizing of land use on the part of landlords to increase crop yields. This process was exacerbated by the lure of monies for conversion of farmland into pasture to graze sheep. In this way, the wool industry and its orientation toward export through the seventeenth and into the eighteenth century played a big part in uprooting what remained of peasant tenancy. Nevertheless, a considerable social and political armature remained firmly in place in Britain to support the maintenance of staid socioeconomic relations. The Poor Laws and the Speenhamland order, the latter promulgated as late as 1795, all sought to ensure that even as subsistence guarantees and employment opportunities in local off-farm work were eliminated, the disenfranchised masses were to be supported by parishes with charity or make work programs and their mobility restricted (Polanyi 1957).

Marx's Periodization of Capitalism as Formal and Real Subsumption of Production

Marx has always been crisply clear that economic "forms" associated with capitalism existed in most modes of precapitalist society. However, their role was always external to the substantive economic principles through which material reproduction of those societies was guaranteed. Put differently, Marx observed: "In all forms of society there is one specific kind of production which predominates over the rest, whose relations thus assign rank and influence to the others" (Marx 1973: 106–7). Hence, while things like markets, wages, profits, money, and so forth exist in precapitalist economies, there are other "principles" such as slave production in antiquity, or peasant subsistence farming and community reciprocity carried out under conditions of politico-religious hierarchy in feudal society, that predominate.[1]

Nevertheless, it is precisely in the maelstrom of epochal historical transformation where precision of thought is called upon to discern the approximate point where the substantive economic principles governing material reproduction in one mode of economy decompose and/or are supplanted by others in an era of socioeconomic transition. It thus falls to a manuscript fragment—"Results of the Immediate Process of Production"—now appended to the first volume of *Capital* (Marx 1977), though not widely available prior to the 1930s, where Marx draws upon his then largely completed theorizing of what capitalism *is* in its basic incarnation to engage in a historical retrospective on its coming into being. Failure to grasp Marx's careful distinctions here, as we shall see, impinges on both the apprehending of *Capital* and the theorizing of imperialism.

Marx's copious historical research preparation for *Capital* alerted him to the growing "internalization" within feudal society of that gamut of economic forms characteristic of capitalism that had operated external to feudal modalities of material reproduction. In particular, Marx recognized how social dislocations and rationalization of agriculture "freed" an enlarging segment of the peasant populace from their conditions of livelihood in subsistence farming and access to common forests. Swooping in to take advantage of the subsequent precariousness was an increasingly assertive merchant class. What lured them to Britain's rural parishes were two conditions in particular. First, the centralized facilities of craft and luxury production of goods which re-emerged following the Dark Ages were located in urban areas and were strictly managed by closed guilds guided by strict codes of quality and ethical pricing. Second was the precapitalist intra-family division of labor peasants survived on. To furnish their own wool garments from sheep tended on common pastures, spinning was done by women and children, while men did the weaving during their off-farm time.

To Marx, what is dubbed "putting out" production commenced in a benign enough fashion within feudal society. Simultaneously circumventing guild restrictions while employing peasants who found their subsistence livelihood increasingly compromised, merchants intervened in rural economies by commissioning family members to work woolen garments for them and even provided raw materials in that endeavor. While one can read back into this the genesis of capitalism, Marx argues that because family workers still maintained their own means of production and controlled their own work rhythms, such activities did not substantially alter existing precapitalist social relations of production.

However, for Marx, when merchants in the wool industry began to invest in "proto-industrial" activities, gathering small groups of workers in production units under one roof to specialize in one or another facet of the wool production process with means of production merchants themselves supply, this constituted a nascent form of capitalism. Marx refers to it as the "formal" subsumption by capital of the labor and production process. It is "formal" because *merchant capital*, as an antediluvian form of capital, now directs the labor process. But it does not transform the means of production which it simply takes over from family cottage labor techniques. Further, Marx makes the important point that such formal subsumption by merchant capital occurs in various guises under diverse precapitalist conditions without necessarily inducing substantive transformation of the labor and production process toward capitalism. He offers three determinant criteria to confirm whether capitalism is in the making: First is the compulsion for work. Are peasant workers enmeshed in paternalistic, interpersonal hierarchical social relations simply being enticed to devote some of their off-farm free time to merchant "putting out", for example? Second is the question of "time" relating to the extent to which the income workers receive from merchant "putting out", as opposed to farming (or rural "services"), factors into reproducing their livelihoods, or is merely supplemental to it?[2] Third is the scale of the operation where work is carried out (Marx 1977: 1019–31).

Where intense debate swirls in Left historiography over the development of capitalism (commensurate with that over capitalism in agriculture) surrounds the period from the sixteenth century to the eighteenth century and the swelling economic footprint of merchant capital in Europe and the world. It is true that European mercantile activities spearheaded by merchant capital imbricate the world in a transcontinental trading system. But the notion that this trading system solely by virtue of linkages established between areas like Britain (which we now know ultimately did transition to capitalism) and far-flung corners of the world enmeshed in precapitalist modes of economy materializes a "capitalist world system" is wrongheaded on too many levels.

At that of history, there was nothing very "systemic" inhering in world trade during the era in question. Rather than reflecting market forces of supply and demand, pricing of traded goods was extremely haphazard. Part of the problem related to the fact that the bulk of traded commodities were agricultural goods produced under myriad working conditions and subject to large seasonal and climatic vagaries. As well, early colonial exploits were marked by rapidly shifting political conditions rendering trade a precarious endeavor. There was little assurance of profit making or even business survival as trade "bottlenecks" sprung up randomly and then unexpectedly disappeared. Even into the early nineteenth century, major global trade flows largely involved remittances of colonial military personnel and goods pillaged by colonial governments (Bayly 2004: 135).

On the level of theory, the view of capitalism as a "world system" germinating in sixteenth-century global mercantile linkages essentially "naturalizes" capitalism. It does this, as touched on above, because economic forms associated with capitalism such as "exchange" of goods and so on make appearances across the sweep of precapitalist history. Yet they do so in ways external to the predominating principle of material reproduction characteristic of those precapitalist societies. One concrete example of what this means is this: Portuguese, and later, Dutch merchants traded with feudal Japan. But their contact with Japan was confined to *Dejima* or "protruding island", constructed off the coast of Nagasaki, where merchants were interned and their goods off-loaded. Whatever the volume or frequency of such "exchanges", the manner by which the goods entered Japan was determined by feudal authorities according to custom and interpersonal hierarchical relations of the Tokugawa Shogunate, bearing little resemblance to capitalist market practices.

Thus, whether the question is one of mercantile connections between separate territories internationally or that of mercantile relations between historically separate communities within a given territory, Marx places emphasis for determinations of capitalist substance upon the emergence of human labor power as a commodity. In his example of "putting out", where recruitment by merchants of family labor is casual and does not involve merchant direct control of work time or merchant provision of production implements, Marx maintains even formal subsumption cannot be said to have taken place. Formal subsumption of the labor and production process only occurs when the direct producing class is increasingly "freed" from hierarchical interpersonal bonds that bind it to place and task and from access to its means of labor and material reproductive conditions. That is when workers find themselves "free", with only one commodity or "asset" left to trade—their power to labor.

Again, while the presence of merchant capital certainly is a factor in transitions away from precapitalist economy to capitalism, ultimately the consummating of capitalist relations of production derives from internal forces of precapitalist social class dissolution. Marx captured this under the rubric of "primitive accumulation" (Brewer 1990: 40–1). Where merchant capital may be claimed as a phase of capitalism is predicated upon its increasing control and management of the labor process in key production sectors of the period. In eighteenth-century Britain, this was wool production for export. Marx's arguments for formal subsumption of the labor and production process can thus be apprehended as his formative effort at periodizing capitalism in its initial stage of development.

"Real" subsumption of the labor and production process, for Marx, refers to the rise and consolidation of capitalism "proper" in its paradigmatic *industrial* form. Formal subsumption sees capital take control of production as it finds it. Real subsumption, as Marx explains, arises on the basis of formal subsumption to constitute an "otherwise *specific mode of production—capitalist production*—which transforms the nature *of the labour process and its actual conditions*...capitalist production now establishes itself as a mode of production *sui generis*" (Marx 1977: 1034–5). And, it is predicated upon the existence of capitalism as a mode of production in its own right that enables Marx to theorize its "abstract" economic workings in *Capital* (Brewer 1990: 36).

Karl Kautsky, Socialist Telos, and Capitalist Change

Discussion of the unique ontology of capitalism enabling Marx to capture its inner workings in an abstract "pure" or "basic" economic theory in *Capital* is reserved for Chap. 6 of this book. Here it is necessary to understand that, as we note in the introductory chapter, it was the version of Marxism as a theory of historical directionality that largely took hold among Marx's followers. This claim is not intended to lay "blame" for a wrong turn in the Marxist research program solely at the feet of those who carried the banner of Marxism into the twentieth century.

Marx himself, as quotes from him set out in Chap. 1 clearly show, helped lead his followers toward the conclusions they arrived at. As well, to reiterate, from the final decades of Marx's life to the turn of the twentieth century, the scent of revolution was in the air. Hence, there was little incentive among Marx's prominent followers to painstakingly complete and refine his theory of capital in the unfinished *Capital* as a timeless definition of what capitalism in its most fundamental incarnation *is*. Instead, following the lead of Marx's revolutionary incantations, spiking his works seemed more apropos.

There is, however, another crucial factor shaping the way Marx's writing in *Capital* was apprehended that carries weighty implications for the theorizing of imperialism. As Brewer reminds us (1990: 58), following his passing in 1883, a temporal gap existed in the further development of Marx's thought. When development of Marx's research program was revived, the field of science that Marx claimed his economic study of capitalism contributed to had been hijacked by an approach from natural science. This is the methodology of "positivism", a genre of empiricism that identifies causality with observation of event regularities. It was in the hands of Marx's most prominent disciple, confidant of Engels and leader of the Second International, Karl Kautsky, that Marx's thinking would be reconstructed in a positivist mold.

Kautsky's first step in this play was to codify the various intellectual regions of Marx's thought as a single overarching theory. He is thus responsible for coining the very term "Marxism" to denote this body of theory tracing its lineage to Marx (Haupt 1982: 276–82). For Kautsky, the newly minted Marxism constitutes a master theory of historical directionality scientifically confirming socialism as its telos. Marx's writings in *Capital* are, according to Kautsky, but a subtheory of this master theory of "historical materialism" sketched by Marx in the famous "Preface". *Capital*, then, as per the scientific formula of positivism, purportedly "proves" how history is driven by inexorable "laws" with socialism as their outcome (Westra 2009: 46–7).

Marx made clear that his theoretical discussion of the "commodity" in the opening chapter of *Capital* treated "*the commodity* as the universally necessary social form of the product [that] can only emerge as the *consequence of the capitalist mode of production*" (Marx 1977: 949). And a decade before he published the first volume of *Capital*, though was most certainly deeply submerged in preparing the sequential architecture of its argument, Marx declared (1904: 304):

> It would thus be impractical and wrong to arrange the economic categories in the order in which they were the determining factors in the course of history. Their order of sequence is rather determined by the relation which they bear to one another in modern bourgeois society, and which is the exact opposite of what seems to be their natural order or the order of their historical development. What we are interested in is not the place which economic relations occupy in the historical succession of different forms of society.

Kautsky, notwithstanding Marx's cues, and the fact there is evidence that Kautsky was familiar with Marx's manuscript fragment on formal and real subsumption (Marx 1977: 943–4), argues in his widely read popularization of *Capital* that Marx's work therein be read as a genetic theory of capitalist historical development. What Kautsky alleges is that from the fifteenth century in Western Europe, feudalism as a mode of production is supplanted by a vaguely defined entity dubbed a petty or "simple commodity production" society. Then laws of history transform this society into capitalism as its "small business" economy is "gradually destroyed and supplanted by large scale capitalist concerns" (Kautsky 1887/1903: Chapter 6). In the final chapter of *The Economic Doctrines of Karl Marx*, Kautsky picks up on Marx's words from *Capital* Volume I to the effect that "organized" or socialized production "which has only been half carried out by capital" is consummated by socialism "as a necessary consequence" of the "law" of history (Kautsky 1887/1903: Chapter 7).

Marx, of course, never theorized such a thing as a "simple commodity" society—and for good reason. A "simple commodity" society would never be viable as a historical mode of economy. When Marx in our earlier quotation states, in any mode of economy "one specific kind of production predominates over the rest", his point is not intended simply for descriptive purposes. Rather, its analytical import is to focus attention on the predominating principle of material reproduction in the society in question. In feudal societies, for example, "exchanges" of goods took place in local markets and wages (often in kind) were paid for services or labor rendered. But basic goods in the society produced by peasants beyond what their families withheld for survival were commandeered by landlords and "redistributed" to other claimants according to hierarchical politico-religious prescriptions and social obligations.

Marx's careful distinction between nascent "putting out" in which off-farm cottage work of peasants was bought by merchants for market sale *and* formal subsumption of peasant labor by merchant capital where peasant family members would forgo farm work for employment in early "sweat shops" was set against the backdrop of centuries of dissolution of precapitalist social relations. At no time during this period preceding real subsumption of the labor process and industrial revolution were peasant producers ever a "class", reproducing their livelihood as independent "simple commodity sellers". With industrial revolution looming, where formal subsumption transitions to real subsumption, it is the market principle of capitalism that emerges as the "social" mechanism ensuring supply of basic goods meets social demand. Prior to this, as the astute economic historian Karl Polanyi shows for the first transition to capitalism in Britain, paternalistic Poor Laws and Speenhamland persisted into the nineteenth century precisely to compensate for decayed feudal relations under conditions where the capitalist labor market had not yet come into its own (Polanyi 1957: 83).

Put differently, private labor is never directly social. In precapitalist class societies, it is rendered social through hierarchical interpersonal relations of domination and subordination within which direct producers are enmeshed. Private production in capitalist economies is rendered social ex post by price taking among atomistic participants in integrated systems of self-regulating markets. "Freed" from precapitalist social relations of extra-economic compulsion along with their means of production, the direct producers make their labor power available in these integrated systems of markets to be shifted by capitalists to production of *any* good according to the changing patterns of social demand and opportunities for profit making. It is only because the labor power of the direct producing class is *not* bound to the production of a single good or "simple commodity" (as in feudal craft production) that impersonal markets carry the potential for supply to efficiently meet demand across society.

Further, there is the overlooked question of incentive and motivation for work. Independent artisans, as the historical record reveals, worked to ensure their own needs and those of their families were met. After that, they simply went on vacation (Duplessis 1997: 262–4). A society solely dependent on such an arrangement would be saddled with an inelasticity of supply and permanent shortages. This is why Marx emphasized how formal subsumption of the labor process in "putting out" industries commences when merchant capital sheds its dependence on peasant cottage and artisanal work rhythms to separate workers from their means of production and concentrate their labor in shops under control and supervision of merchant capital itself.

Kautsky's argument over a so-called "small business" economy being "gradually destroyed and supplanted by large scale capitalist concerns" by the late nineteenth century, at the time of his books' publication, also has little historical foundation. Nor is it a "doctrine" Marx espouses as Kautsky alleges. The "highest stage" of capitalism Marx theorized is that of industrial capitalism typified by the cotton industry. And, even as *Capital* made its way into print, the changes wrought by industrial revolution which entailed the production of production machinery by machines as occurred for steam-powered cotton factories had not spread across the entire economic landscape in Britain (Brewer 1990: 46–7). Again, as can be taken from our quotations from Marx above, Marx did detect tendencies in capitalism of his day where competition eliminated weaker firms to concentrate and centralize capital in the stronger. But the degree to which monopoly was actually established in a production sector during Marx's lifetime tended to be exaggerated by his followers (Brewer 1990: 126).

More problematic are claims of an impending capitalist breakdown and the ensuing socialist revolution made by Kautsky on Marx's supposed authority. When he published *The Economic Doctrines of Karl Marx*, the second volume of *Capital* had just become available but Volume III had not. If Kautsky is correct about one thing in this work, it is that the economic crisis that struck Western Europe and the world in the closing decades of the nineteenth century differed in scale, scope, intensity, and duration from the decennial cyclical oscillations of capitalist business cycles marking the British economy from the midpoint of the century (Kautsky 1887/1903: Chapter 7). However, notwithstanding Marx's suggestive radical statements in the closing chapters of the first volume of *Capital*, Marx never argues that "laws" of capital manifested in its tendencies toward crises simultaneously impel capitalism to self-destruct as it animates the working class to revolution. In *Capital* Volume III, which Kautsky did not read, Marx explains how the logic of capital is not self-defeating. Regarding the decennial nineteenth-century business cycle oscillations theorized in *Capital*, Marx demonstrates how capital recuperates from these by raising its organic composition to incorporate labor-saving technologies. But Marx passed away in the midst of the great economic crisis of the late nineteenth century and had no opportunity to fully assess its implications for the future of capitalism.

Without Marx's reflections on the crisis, Marxists worldwide were left with the analysis of Kautsky whose position as leader of the Second International endowed him with great influence over Marxist thinking. Why this matters for the theorizing of imperialism and warrants the digression on Kautsky in this chapter is because of the way his ideas and apprehension of Marx's work shaped the foci of theorists of imperialism. Kautsky's averment that revolution was nigh and it, along with the severe economic tumult that enveloped Europe and the world, was proof of "laws" purportedly theorized by Marx, engendered a crisis for Marxism when capitalism entered the twentieth century reloaded and transformed (see Fig. 2.1).

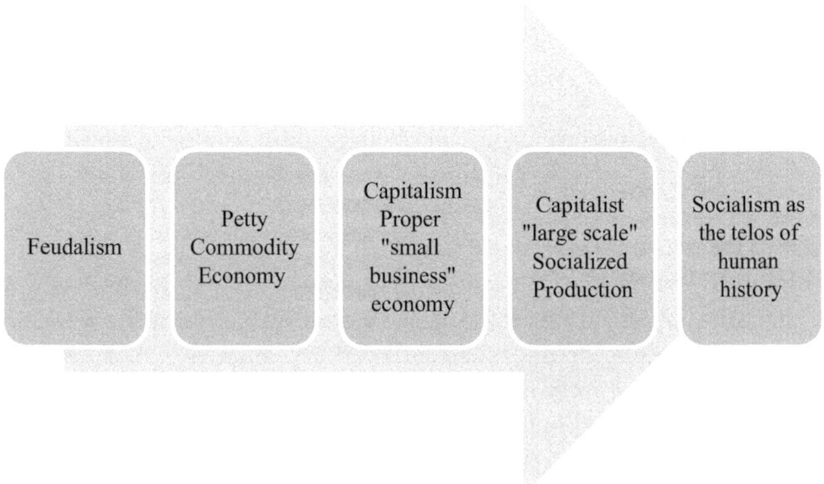

Fig. 2.1 Karl Kautsky and the historical trajectory of capitalism (Source: Author)

Imperialism as a Stage of Capitalism

That Marxism potentially faces a crisis of confidence here (see McDonough and Drago 1989), of course, hinges on the imbibing of Kautsky's reconstruction of Marx's thought and Kautsky's spurious arguments on the historical trajectory of capitalism. Textual examination of writings by major theorists of imperialism reveals the extent to which they did in fact follow Kautsky's lead (Gronow 1986). No major challenge arose among them to the view of *Capital* as a genetic theory of capitalist historical development. Also, Kautsky's contention that a "petty commodity" economy came to life with the decomposition of feudalism in Western Europe and furnished the ground from which capitalism sprung is accepted as factually correct. Capitalism "proper", driven by the "laws" Marx supposedly established in *Capital*, so it was further acknowledged, did progress inexorably toward its demise even as it gestated socialism within it, thus verifying Marx's prognosis as claimed by Kautsky. What the generation of theorists of imperialism were forced to confront, however, is the following.

Yes, the development of the forces of production "socialized" capitalism, rendering it ripe for socialism. But, in spite of a cataclysmic economic crisis wracking the European continent and the world economy, there was no socialist revolution. This problematic compelled the theorists of imperialism to explore the economic and political physiognomy of the period of capitalism following the economic crisis that closed the nineteenth century. In this endeavor, there was no question of Marx being "wrong". Rather, their efforts were advanced as "up-dating" Marx, particularly on the transmutation of the monopoly form of capitalist enterprise (Brewer 1990: 89). In addition to this empirical issue, there emerged an important theoretical concern. Capitalist change sweeping across early twentieth-century major economies could not be grasped in terms of a simple extrapolation of historical trends of capitalism from the mid-nineteenth century. Therefore, notwithstanding Marx's accepted prediction of expanding monopolization, or Kautsky's contention that capitalism manifested inexorable historical "laws", early twentieth-century capitalism is recognized as a new "kind" of capitalism. In this kind of capitalism, both the tendencies Marx predicted and purported capitalist inexorable "laws" a-la-Kautsky continue to operate yet take on new forms and express new "contradictions" that were not foreseen by Marx. Hence, the theorizing of early twentieth-century capitalism in terms of its transubstantiating into an imperialist "stage" of capitalism constitutes the first major widely recognized step in the world historic periodizing of capitalism.

Below we discuss the writings of the three major Marxist theorists of imperialism: Rudolf Hilferding, Nikolai Bukharin, and V. I. Lenin. It is true that the work of Rosa Luxemburg is often included in the group of Marxist writers on imperialism. The reason for this, as argued by Brewer (1990: 58ff), is what Luxemburg brings in to debate over the historical trajectory of capitalism and its purported inherent tendencies toward crises. That is treatment of the interrelation between that part of the world considered advanced capitalist at the time (Britain and Western Europe) and the large non- or precapitalist part of the world. Luxemburg, accordingly, is heralded as prefiguring post–World War II (WWII) theorizing of imperialism, not as a stage of capitalism per se, but as an explanatory concept for widening wealth asymmetries between advanced or developed capitalist economies and non- or "underdeveloped" economies within a "capitalist world system". However, important as Luxemburg's work is perceived to be in that regard, from the perspective of this chapter, its contribution is largely tangential.

Indeed, it may be argued that theories "defining" capitalism as a "world system", the essential contours of which are put in place from the sixteenth century (or earlier?) and persist to this day, obviate the very research agenda on periodizing capitalism that is the topic of this book. While Luxemburg sought to enrich Marx's analysis of the global expansion of capitalism "to some degree pushed into the background in *Capital* by the theoretical task of analysing a pure capitalist mode of production" (Brewer 1990: 67), periodizing capitalism is interested in the distinguishing variegated forms and dynamics the international dimension of capital manifests across capitalist stages. But this hinges on the central recognition that the political economic study of capitalism at a crucial level demands theoretical attention to the historical transmutability of capital. And that is the starting point for Marxists Hilferding, Bukharin, and Lenin.

Rudolf Hilferding and Finance Capital

Published initially in 1910, though largely written around 1905, Hilferding's tome *Finance Capital* "deserves credit" as the path-breaking work in theorizing imperialism, and influenced later work by Bukharin and Lenin in significant ways (Brewer 1990: 88). In the opening sentence of his preface, Hilferding places his work firmly within the research field of periodizing capitalism. The mission of *Finance Capital* he declares is "to arrive at a scientific understanding of the economic characteristics of the latest phase of capitalist development" (Hilferding 1981: 23).

As noted above, the key thread from Marx's writing, which is picked up by Hilferding, is the twin tendency within capitalism toward the concentration and centralization of capital. The former referred to the sheer magnitude of capital applied by an enterprise to production; the latter referred to the way competition leads to smaller, weaker firms being absorbed by the stronger and increasingly larger. It is precisely the confluence of concentration and centralization of capital from which major sectors of advanced capitalist economies become the preserve of monopoly or, more widespread, oligopoly businesses. What Hilferding brings to this discussion is thorough analysis of a capitalist nuance on which Marx left only a few scattered remarks in *Capital* Volume III. This is the generalized transformation of the form of enterprise through the legal device of limited liability joint-stock companies that would ultimately spawn the modern corporation. The spread of joint-stock companies leads to a qualitative transformation within capitalist economies in the relationship between property ownership and investment. Where Hilferding makes his most profound intervention into periodizing capitalism is on the question of changes in capitalist finance and credit system brought on by investment requirements of the new early twentieth-century commanding heights industries. As we shall see in later chapters, understanding of what today is dubbed "financialization" is indebted to Hilferding's work.

Under the entrepreneurial business structure of industrial capital theorized by Marx as the "pure" or paradigmatic form of capital, investment horizons are largely constrained by the capital individual business owners and, potentially, their families hold. Nevertheless, with the real subsumption of the labor and production process by capital, Marx explains how industrial capital simultaneously subsumes the activities of money lending and credit issuance to create modern banking (Marx 1991: 738).

The fundamental activity of capital, of course, is profit making. And the efficiency of capitalist profit making is secured to the extent the capitalist circuit of (money-commodities-money increased) M-C-M′—capital as money invested in means of production and labor power that produces commodities that are then sold at profit, to be reinvested—proceeds uninterrupted (see Fig. 2.2). Where modern banking enters the picture is to hold monies temporarily rendered "idle" in the course of the capitalist production-centered circuit. Capitalist businesses necessarily maintain depreciation and contingency funds as well as monies set aside for shorter periods according to investment schedules of this or that part of business operations. When such idle funds are withdrawn from the capitalist profit-making circuit and deposited in the banking system, they cease to be capital. That is, idle money in the hands of banks becomes a commodity or "asset" the "ownership" or custody of which entitles banks to the income stream of *interest.* Banks, institutions standing "outside" the circuit of capital, play a vital "social" role for capital. This is financial intermediation. Idle money

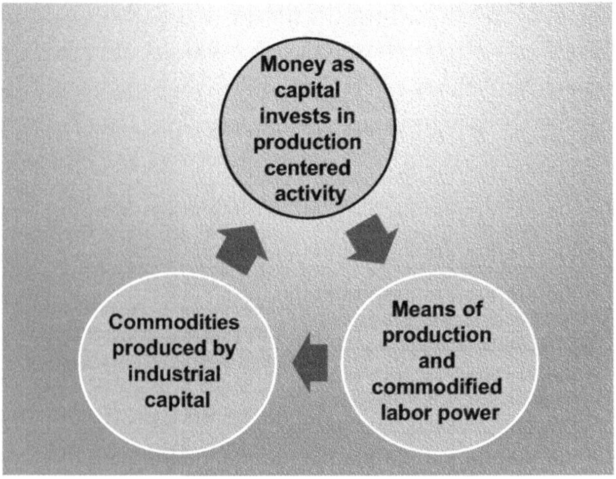

Fig. 2.2 Circuit of industrial capital (Source: Author)

generated at various points across the economy is lent by banks wherever it is needed, thus increasing the magnitude of available productive capital in the economy at large. Banks profit from the spread between interest paid to depositors and lenders' interest that is paid to banks by borrowers. Banking networks constitute the money market as interest rates themselves are determined by the supply and demand for funds (see Fig. 2.3).

As Hilferding makes clear, the very existence of idle money withdrawn from the profit-making circuit of capital entails a "contradiction" of sorts at the heart of the capitalist modus operandi (1981: 79). Thus, capital necessarily strives to ensure funds withdrawn from its circuit do not remain idle for long. Along with varied businesses notwithstanding their differing branches of commodity production that access the "socialized funds" in money markets, so "commercial capitalists" that perform tasks of both wholesale and retail buying and selling of commodities borrow from the money market. This only further accelerates the efficiency of profit making or value augmentation because the faster production-centered businesses sell their commodities the more rapidly profits may be reinvested. In this way, the credit system by design "activates" idle money in the capitalist economy. Finally, Hilferding draws attention to the essential "relationship" role banks play not only in evaluating the

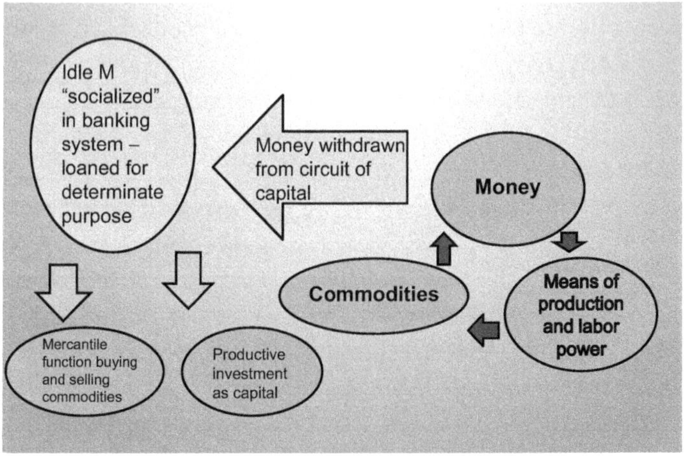

Fig. 2.3 Idle M in production-centered economy (Source: Author)

creditworthiness of business they deal with in the money market but in the way banks discount commercial bills among businesses as productive capitalists extend credit to each other (Hilferding 1981: 82ff).

Why Hilferding opens his book with a discussion of "relationship banking" in the commodity economy as it operates under the auspices of industrial capital is to set the stage for his elaboration upon the seismic transformation advanced economies undergo in the early twentieth century. Factoring into these changes is the rise of a new set of commanding heights industries, those of heavy steel production and industrial chemicals, in major economies; this is known as the "second industrial revolution" (Landes 1969). The sheer scale of operations in heavy steel and chemicals, along with tightly coupled backward and forward linkages within their production processes, required integration of previously separate industrial branches in a single concern. That this not only brought to bear enormous upfront costs of fixed capital but extended investment periods before plants ever entered production called for levels of financing vastly outstripping capital outlays marshaled by any one entrepreneur and their family.

Meeting the financing challenges of the new, gargantuan monopoly and oligopoly businesses populating the commanding heights of major advanced economies gives birth to capital or equity markets. The role of capital markets is further mobilizing of idle funds within society beyond that accessed by the money market. What the legal device of limited liability joint-stock companies enables is the raising of capital investment by businesses through the selling of stocks or shares in the business. This changes the relationship in capitalist economies between property ownership and investment because ownership is no longer the prerogative of entrepreneurs or business "founders" but becomes distributed across various hands throughout society. Varied specialized institutional arrangements for managing the new capitalist credit system materialize among advanced economies including the stock market itself and "investment banks". In Hilferding's empirical illustrative case of Germany, it was its giant, increasingly monopolistic multipurpose banks themselves that tend to superintend stock market activities. Power of big banks to further promote monopolization and extra-market economic collusion among major companies they increasingly intervened in the affairs of is further enhanced by the spread of the joint-stock form of enterprise and the banks own investment in these (Brewer 1990: 92). Growing dependence of industry on big banks to the extent that "bank capital… [as] money… is actually transformed…into industrial capital", Hilferding dubs "finance capital" (Hilferding 1981: 225). And it is this new form assumed by capital that Hilferding maintains constitutes the hallmark of the new phase of capitalism.

Hilferding further addresses the peculiar cognitive distortions arising with transformations in the credit system of the new phase of capitalism that carry implications for perceptions of the "kind" of economy capitalism is. First, shareholding appears to render businesses "publicly" owned. However, the joint-stock form of enterprise facilitates control in the hands of major capitalist stockholders of an exponentially greater magnitude of capital than they themselves paid in to a company as well as power over other shareholding "owners" (Hilferding 1981: 119). Second, while the funds paid in to an ongoing profit-making business function as capital, the share or stock held by an investor does not constitute a claim on the capital in operation within the enterprise. It is simply a title to income in the form of dividends. That shares or equities are traded in the capital market does not change the fact that the only capital that "really exists is the industrial capital and its profit" (Hilferding 1981: 111). And when stockholders withdraw from a business by selling their shares, this entails ownership titles changing hands but does not disrupt the production-centered circuit of capital. Hence, Hilferding refers to equities as "fictitious capital" (see Fig. 2.4). As we will see in later chapters, the notion of fictitious capital as a claim on a revenue stream priced in money emerges as an omnibus concept for activities associated with financialization.

With the changes in the basic structure of business and enabling financial infrastructure of capital markets managed by finance capital explained, Hilferding turns to the implications of this for those facets of the political economy of the new phase more widely associated with the concept of *imperialism*. Hilferding proceeds step by step from the way monopolization and oligopoly fostered by finance capital impact the capitalist business cycle and endogenous crises propensities of capitalism. However, because Hilferding's work largely underpins in most aspects

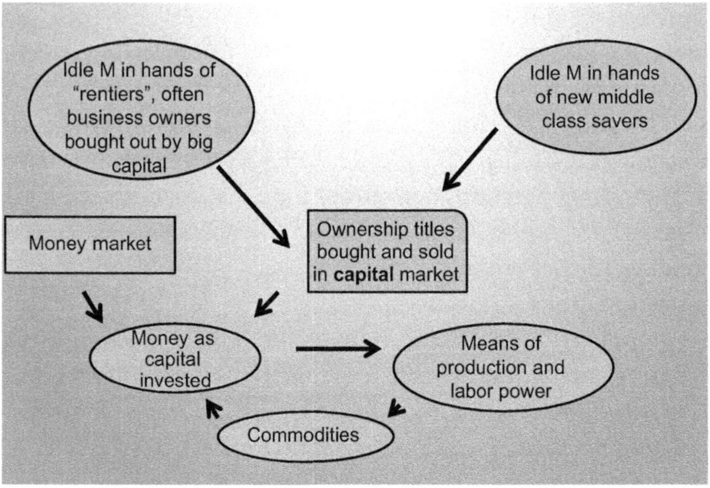

Fig. 2.4 Idle M and capital market (Source: Author)

the "popularization" of the theorizing of imperialism by Bukharin and Lenin, it is through the prism of their writings that we will gather the remaining strands of Hilferding's formative contribution.

Nikolai Bukharin and Imperialist State Policy

It is from the exigencies of suppressed competition by finance capital–run monopoly combines within major national economies that a radical shift in the role of the capitalist state is impelled according to Hilferding (1981: 301ff). If industrial capital in Britain battened on laissez-faire policy internationally and required only a "night watchman" state domestically, the imperialist era demands a state with a more active policy posture. Hilferding covers the rudiments of this. To protect its cartels in the domestic market, finance capital calls upon the state to erect tariff walls against foreign competition. But, as tariff barriers increasingly become the rule among major economies, to accommodate the enormously expanded productive power of second industrial revolution industries, the state is recruited by capital to covet "economic territory" across the globe and maintain these territories as "preserves" for "national" monopolies by encasing them with protective tariffs as well (Hilferding 1981: 326).

Where Bukharin's work takes off in its endeavor of periodizing capitalism is by emphasizing "that imperialist policies arise only on a certain level of historic development" (Bukharin 1973: 110). Part of this "historic development", as traced by Hilferding, involves the legal, organizational, and technological changes of the early twentieth century. Bukharin highlights the way large-scale, organized productions, under the mastery of great capitalist "magnates", "have taken possession of the entire economic life". State power, in turn, becomes "the domain of a financial oligarchy" that manages the productive and political apparatus of advanced capitalist societies. However, for Bukharin, this process, which proceeds "from below", is transposed into the international dimension of capital.

> Every one of the capitalistically advanced "national economies" has turned into some kind of a "national" trust. This process of the organisation of the economically advanced sections of the world economy…has been accompanied by an extraordinary sharpening of their mutual competition…the economic subjugation of entire regions by "national" banking combines… has thrown into the sharpest possible relief the clash of interests between "national" groups of capital…A mighty state military power is the last trump in the struggle of the powers. (Bukharin 1973: 108)

Indeed, as summarized by Brewer, Bukharin sees two forces at work within the world economy as a whole. The concentration and centralization of capital identified by Marx and further elaborated by Hilferding constitutes the force of "nationalization" of capital under the auspices of finance capital with the state it has commandeered. Then there is the force of "internationalization" of capital that engenders an increasing interdependence among regions of the world economy. These, however, are now divided into national imperialist "blocs". Hence the tension between these two opposing tendencies constitutes the central contradiction of capitalism in its imperialist phase, driving it toward economic breakdown and war (Brewer 1990: 111). For Bukharin, there is no escape for capitalism from this trajectory. There has been massive investment in its material accouterment by imperialist states. Not only were much of the world's modern railway and communications systems constructed during the early twentieth century but the technological infrastructure for resource extraction in mining and other essential raw materials, along with deep-water port and loading facilities for efficiently shipping goods around the globe, is similarly put in place during this historical period. For this reason, Bukharin maintains imperialism as a "policy of conquest". Though he follows up, "not every policy of conquest is imperialism". Imperialism implies "the existence of a developed world economy" in thrall to finance capital. And the policy of conquest is that of finance capital marking the imperialist period "as a definite historical entity" (Bukharin 1973: 114–5).

Notwithstanding his statement on the "definite historical" markers of the imperialist era, Bukharin returns later in his book *Imperialism and World Economy* to the question of a socialist historical telos and its working out in the imperialist "entity". We will treat this momentarily.

V. I. Lenin and the Export of Capital

To be fair to Bukharin, my remark above on his and Lenin's "popularizing" of the notion of imperialism is mostly directed at Lenin whose pamphlet essentially reproduces the work of Hilferding and Bukharin. Nevertheless, Lenin offers an important definitional nuance and somewhat divergent emphasis from them. At the outset, Lenin is unambiguous in slotting his work within the research mission of periodizing capitalism. "If it were necessary to give the briefest possible definition of imperialism we should have to say that imperialism is the monopoly stage of capitalism", he declares (Lenin 1975: 83). Following Marx and Hilferding, Lenin notes how concentration and centralization of capital feeds monopolization with such businesses then ascending to the commanding heights of advanced economies. In line with Hilferding and Bukharin, Lenin agrees that finance capital creates a "financial oligarchy" atop imperialist states. Lenin also follows Bukharin on the question of the international thrust of "monopoly associations which share the world among themselves". Where Lenin picks up on discussion by Hilferding, though lays a greater emphasis here, is upon the fact that in the imperialist stage of capitalism "the export of capital as distinguished from the export of commodities acquires exceptional importance" (Lenin 1975: 77).

We will return below to questions of why export of capital takes place during this period and what its impact is on both capital-exporting and capital-importing economies. There is no question, however, of the significance of capital export for the imperialist era. Of course, the export of capital being referred to in this phase of capitalism is that of international portfolio investment. Figures, here, speak for themselves. In the period 1870 to 1913, international portfolio investment averaged approximately 50 percent of global GDP. Through the years 1910–1913, Britain's net foreign investment equaled 53 percent of its domestic savings. And, in 1913–1914, 42 percent of foreign investment from Britain landed in Latin America, Asia, and Africa (Westra 2016: 126–7).

Though Hilferding and Lenin search for one, there is no answer to the question of what connects the export of capital to the structural economic changes associated with imperialism and what the impact of such exports are globally that can be traced to Marx's "basic" or "pure" theory in *Capital*. Certainly, as Hilferding notes, capital carries an innate tendency to move where potential for profit making is greatest. And this may entail migration of capital from where it is abundant to where it is scarce. But there is little evidence that falling profits in advanced imperialist economies spurred capital export to colonies. And even to the extent it can be shown that non-developed economic territories were fertile ground for profitable investment, particularly in resource extraction, this would not explain the significant export of capital to more developed areas such as Canada nor tell us whether extra profits were actually made through capital export to colonies (see Hilferding 1981: 313ff; Lenin 1975: 58–9; and the summary in Brewer 1990: 100–4).

However, there is an argument to be made from structural features of the stage of imperialism to explain why qualitative expansion of capital export takes place in the era. In Marx's theorizing of business cycles under the real subsumption of production by industrial capital, cyclical oscillations follow the advent of a "superabundance" of capital in relation to the size of the working population. That is, with the attainment by businesses of best practice technology across the economy, the capitalist competition and economic growth which proceed apace tend to absorb the industrial reserve army. It is this condition of overaccumulation of capital in relation to the size of the working population that drives capital into recession and crisis as wage pressure on profits precipitate business closures, fall in demand for goods, and contagion in credit markets. To extricate itself, capital raises its organic composition by incorporating newly available technologies at a time when crisis has destroyed weaker capitalists and devalued capital and commodities throughout the economy. On the basis of new labor-saving technologies, the industrial reserve army is reconstituted and wage pressures contained for capital to commence another cycle of accumulation.

But in the imperialist era as costs of fixed capital become increasingly exorbitant, the sorts of decennial cyclical oscillations from prosperity to recession and depression that devalue or destroy capital become anathema to it. As well, the formation of average rates of profit in industries across the division of labor, which is coupled in the era of industrial capital with relative price congruence in the economy at large, is thwarted by the market power of giant monopoly cartels managed by finance capital. Accumulating surplus profits thus earned by monopoly combines contributes to the massive expansion of their production capacity. Yet this no longer occurs in synchronization with the absorption of the industrial reserve army as the resultant superabundance of capital does not generate mounting unemployment. Rather, overaccumulation of capital leads not to crises but to bouts of overproduction of commodities (Uno 2016: 144–7).

Yet the same protectionist policies which are simultaneously adopted across advanced economies to shield monopoly surplus profit from competitors shut what safety valve the world economy in the period of laissez-faire potentially offered to capital. In this way, tariff protection in the age of imperialism differs from policies directed toward protecting nascent industry until it gained sufficient strength to compete on world markets as advocated by the Friedrich List. Instead, they foster the "dumping" at below-market prices of excess commodities on the world market in order to carve out large parts of it as exclusive preserve for a nation's finance capital. Export of capital thus supported this as it promoted industries like transportation and raw material extraction that create demand for export of commodities from the "national" economy, particularly of heavy steel–related products (Uno 2016: 207–10). Ironically, this all entailed little that was "rational" in any "basic" capitalist market sense. Much portfolio international investment was simply driven by "national governments which encouraged the commercial interests of their own citizens to preempt rival, mining, telegraph, railway or commodity companies" (Bayly 2004: 231).

Finally, while Hilferding and Lenin allude to the potential capital export held out for capitalist development within imperialist territories, this was not a central concern of their writing. Such was the case, as Brewer explains, because all Marxist theorists of imperialism believed the end of capitalism to be nigh (Brewer 1990: 103–4, 120–2). It is arguably a great tragedy of the era, and in fact of world history, that legacies of the specific orientation of imperialist material infrastructure toward extractivism, along with the way "economic territories" were carved up or created ex nihilo, with scant regard for inhabitants of those lands, persists to this day. In sparsely populated areas like British "white settler colonies", where indigenous inhabitants could be herded off the land to "reservations" of various sorts, imperialist capital export and European emigration manifested itself in development and prosperity. Across much of what became the "third world" in the post-WWII era, nothing of the kind occurred. Emigrant settler colonialists conspired with imperialist administrators to gain economic advantage and excluded native populations from resource and trade access through formal and informal apartheid practices. Precapitalist ruling classes were often recruited as allies in suppressing broad-based capitalist change and benefitted from the maintenance of property rights and social practices rooted in the past (Frieden 2006: 68ff).

Imperialism as the "Highest Stage" of Capitalism

Hilferding, Bukharin, and Lenin all expected "organized" capitalism as fashioned in the imperialist stage to constitute the antechamber of socialism. Given that he wrote his book early in the imperialist period,

Hilferding follows Marx's exhortations most closely in arguing that the socializing role played by finance capital finds its parallel in collectivist struggles of the labor movement. He expected these to transcend the false social dilemmas of laissez-faire versus protectionism to call for abolition of capitalism. However, in the closing pages of his book, Hilferding flirts with the possibility of electoral socialism as working-class political parties gain momentum from their day-to-day struggles against imperialist ills (Hilferding 1981: 365–8). History, though, has been extremely unkind to electoral socialist pretentions, as Hilferding himself would discover later in his life.

Bukharin and Lenin, writing under the dark clouds of war, harbored no illusions over supposed benefits bourgeois democracy holds out for a peaceful transition to socialism. And while both accepted Marx's essential premise of historical materialism, that epochal change in history is propelled by the contradiction between the productive forces developing within society which outgrow their relations of production to then usher in an era of social revolution, each argued that imperialism brought new contradictions to bear upon socialist change. Again, the issue of capitalism in the imperialist era being "overripe" for change is a theme found throughout their writing on imperialism. But, for Bukharin, as we have seen, the tendencies within the national state toward monopolization and the formation of "state capitalist trusts" call forth tendencies to monopolize territories internationally. From this dynamic, Bukharin laments, we perpetually find "capitalist society…whirling in the mad hurricane of world wars" (Bukharin 1973: 158). Lenin summarizes things along similar lines. The primary contradiction of the imperialist state, he declares, is "the disparity between the development of the productive forces and accumulation of capital on the one side, and the division of colonies and spheres of influence for finance capital on the other". Monopoly capital will not seek only to divide the world but "re-divide" it through war (Lenin 1975: 78–9, 92).

Because the socialist historical outcome was expected to be consummated in the aftermath of WWI, both Bukharin and Lenin turned their ire on Kautsky, who claimed that the same forces that manifested themselves in national economic spaces toward monopolization will potentially play out internationally. Thus, whereas Bukharin and Lenin saw the contradiction of imperialism in tendencies of imperialist powers to divide and re-divide the globe in an endless bloody struggle, Kautsky envisioned the rise of a super- or "ultra-imperialism" in which capital arrives at a "peaceful" global monopoly or "trust". And it is on that basis that Kautsky suggests the proletariat can reinforce the "peaceful" course of capitalism to bring an end to imperialism. With this, the possibility of countering the global capitalist trust with organized global proletarian action is created (Brewer 1990: 128–33).

Whether Kautsky made a valid projection, that capitalist or imperialist powers might unite in a hegemonic endeavor to share the spoils of global exploitation (US-led "coalitions of the willing" today?), or as Bukharin and Lenin argue were destined to battle it out until capitalism and imperialism are vanquished by proletarian revolution, is beside the point. Energies devoted in Marxist circles to debates swirling around imperialism and its telos as the final or "highest stage" of capitalism (as per the title of Lenin's book), and what the correct political strategy might be to consummate the socialist historical outcome, diverted attention from a critical question (see Fig. 2.5).

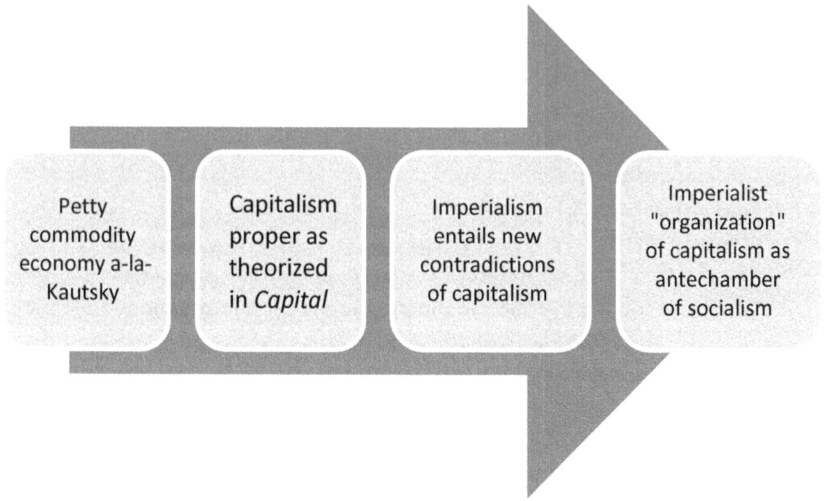

Fig. 2.5 Theorists of imperialism and the historical trajectory of capitalism (Source: Author)

That is, with an aura of déjà vu, as occurred following Marx's passing, when Marxist debate turned on why socialist revolution did not occur at that juncture of capitalism's then most severe crisis, there was little pause for thought on the "kind" of theory early periodization of capitalism produced. So, embroiled in political debate and seeking to directly extrapolate political positions from theories of imperialism, Marxists lost sight of what was actually accomplished theoretically by theorists like Hilferding, Bukharin, and even Lenin. And as we shall see, the enslaving of theory by the view that its role was to validate socialism as the telos of human history would persist as, much to the chagrin of socialists, did capitalism.

Notes

1. The notion of economic principles as it is used in this book combines insights of Marx and Karl Polanyi (1957). In Marx's reference above, as to how in "all forms of society there is one specific kind of production which predominates over the rest", what Marx alludes to is the central means for differentiating among historical modes of production. Marx was always clear that while markets existed in antiquity, for example, they are not the "specific kind of production", which was idiosyncratic of that epoch of human existence. Where Polanyi contributes to understanding the question that concerned Marx is in elaboration upon those other "kinds of production", besides that of the capitalist market, which predominate in other modes of production. Polanyi sets out two further "kinds" or principles of economy other than the market. The first is what Polanyi refers to as "reciprocity". It predominates in the very earliest societies, though it persists in various forms across history into the present. It entails modalities of cooperative human relations including communal "sharing", "gift" giving, customary and communal practices of "give and take", and so on. Second, for Polanyi is "redistribution". This operates as the central principle in more advanced geospatially larger-scale social units and involves the movement of goods, tribute, tithes, taxes, and so forth from scattered producers to the center. These are then reallocated or redistributed from the center according to hierarchical status of social claimants. Marx, for his part, understood what Polanyi dubs reciprocity as "primitive communism" and redistribution in terms of interpersonal economic relations of domination and subordination as characteristic of slave and feudal modes

of production. For our purposes, it is possible to think about redistribution in Polanyi's sense as the "kind of production" predominant in Soviet style socialist societies and as a principle operating in the shadow of the capitalist market in the welfare states of the post-WWII era.

2. Marx importantly argues that in all human societies the direct producers whether slaves, serfs, or proletarians must receive the product of their "necessary labor" for the work they perform within existing social class structures. What Marx means is that in every society there is some basic level of livelihood and sustenance that the direct producing class requires to guarantee that they will be able to continue to labor, day after day, and to reproduce as a social class. Even slaves must be well fed, Marx argued, otherwise they will perish leaving the masters to do their own work or relentlessly hunt for new slaves which is ultimately a dead end. Where the notion of workers receiving the product of their necessary labor assumes significance in the context discussed here is over the relative contribution to the reproduction of the direct producing class of wages paid in merchant putting out operations and traditional sources of peasant sustenance in household farming and services for the landlord class. We cannot talk about the commodification of labor power until workers are separated from their means of production and access the product of their necessary labor only via wages. Under formal subsumption of the labor process the extent to which the direct producers are supported by their farming activities as subsistence peasantries, or through wages, is ambiguous, particularly during periods of epochal change as societies in Britain and Europe experienced from the seventeenth to the nineteenth century. We will return to this question in later chapters as the persistence of subsistence peasantries in the global economy that make family labor available for foreign capital in sweat shops, and the like, demands renewed analysis.

References

Anderson, P. 1996. *Lineages of the Absolutist State*. London: Verso.

Bayly, C.A. 2004. *The Birth of the Modern World 1780–1914*. Malden, MA: Blackwell.

Brewer, A. 1990. *Marxist Theories of Imperialism*. London: Routledge.

Bukharin, N. 1973. *Imperialism and World Economy*. New York: Monthly Review Press.

Duplessis, R. 1997. *Transitions to Capitalism in Early Modern Europe*. Cambridge: Cambridge University Press.
Frieden, J. 2006. *Global Capitalism: Its Fall and Rise in the Twentieth Century*. New York: W.W. Norton.
Gronow, J. 1986. *On the Formation of Marxism*. Helsinki: The Finnish Society of Sciences and Letters.
Haupt, G. 1982. Marx and Marxism. In *The History of Marxism*, ed. E. Hobsbawm, vol. 1. Bloomington: Indiana University Press.
Hilferding, R. 1981. *Finance Capital*. London: Routledge & Kegan Paul.
Kautsky, K. 1887/1903. *The Economic Doctrines of Karl Marx*. https://www.marxists.org/archive/kautsky/1903/economic/index.htm. Accessed 2 Aug 2018.
Landes, D.S. 1969. *The Unbound Prometheus*. Cambridge: Cambridge University Press.
Lenin, V.I. 1975. *Imperialism: The Highest Stage of Capitalism*. Moscow: Progress.
Marx, K. 1904. *A Contribution to the Critique of Political Economy*. Chicago: Charles H. Kerr & Co.
———. 1973. *Grundrisse*. Middlesex: Penguin Books.
———. 1977. *Capital Volume I*. New York: Vintage Books.
———. 1991. *Capital Volume III*. London: Penguin Classics.
McDonough, T., and R. Drago. 1989. Crises of Capitalism and the First Crisis of Marxism. *Review of Radical Political Economics* 21 (3): 27–32.
Overton, M. 1996. *Agricultural Revolution in England: The Transformation of the Agrarian Economy 1500–1850*. Cambridge: Cambridge University Press.
Polanyi, K. 1957. *The Great Transformation*. Boston: Beacon Press.
Uno, K. 2016. *The Types of Economic Policies under Capitalism*. Leiden: Brill.
Westra, R. 2009. *Political Economy and Globalization*. London: Routledge.
———. 2016. *Unleashing Usury: How Finance Opened the Door to Capitalism Then Swallowed It Whole*. Atlanta, GA: Clarity Press.

3

From Monopoly to "Late" Capitalism

Marxist innovative political economic thinking essentially languished in a dead zone during the interwar period: Though some threads of discussion from theories of imperialism were picked up, specifically on issues related to forces making for the expected capitalist "breakdown" which would see societies in remaining advanced capitalism follow the Soviet Union's transition to socialism (Howard and King 1992: 3ff). And, while it might have been expected that in the wake of the world's first socialist revolution, culminating in creation of the Soviet Union, socialist debate and theorizations would flourish, the opposite was the case. Following the passing of Lenin and rise of Stalin, a chill set in crushing socialist critical thought not only in the Soviet Union but also among communist parties around the world beholden to Soviet international leadership. Stalin, as de facto head of the Third International or "Comintern", reduced a living Marxism to a few tired maxims and ruthlessly expunged deviations from these along with those proffering them. Nevertheless, as World War II (WWII) played out, progressive Marxist political economic shoots began to sprout in the UK, the US, and elsewhere.

It is instructive that one of the bright lights of Marxian political economic revival who took up the challenge of making sense of how

R. Westra, *Periodizing Capitalism and Capitalist Extinction*, Palgrave Insights into Apocalypse Economics, https://doi.org/10.1007/978-3-030-14390-9_3

the "moribund" capitalism of Lenin managed to reload from the middle of the twentieth century had emigrated from the Soviet Union in 1928. From his position at Stanford University, Paul Baran initially intervened in debate over points Hilferding and Lenin treated only in passing. This was the impact of capitalism upon the development prospects of the world beyond the advanced capitalist economies. This aspect of Baran's writing will be treated only in passing in the present chapter and will figure indirectly in later chapters of this book dealing with current capitalist disintegration. However, what concern us here are Baran's theoretical innovations in understanding the changed modus operandi of capital accumulation in advanced countries following WWII. In this endeavor Baran is joined by Paul Sweezy. Sweezy had already published his work during the interwar era in the US on questions raised by Keynes over "effective demand" management as a new engine of growth. Sweezy's interest was in the way economic tendencies toward monopoly and oligopoly impacted that (Screpanti and Zamagni 2005: 446–7).

Where the discussion below takes off is on the collaboration between Baran and Sweezy. With each bringing to the theoretical table answers to questions from two discrete lines of inquiry, the *monopoly capital* perspective of Marxism was birthed. It produced the first major Marxian attempt at periodizing capitalism anew after the theorizing of imperialism. From there the chapter turns to the non-Marxist work of John Kenneth Galbraith. Galbraith, as we shall see, sketches a somewhat similar empirical picture of the post-WWII capitalist economy in the US as do Baran and Sweezy. Yet, Galbraith's conclusions on the future economic prospects for capitalism radically diverge from Baran and Sweezy's Marxist position. Finally, the chapter turns to the important work of Ernest Mandel. If Baran and Sweezy along with Galbraith focus on the grasping the dynamics of the post-WWII phase of capitalism, Mandel produces a sweeping approach to periodizing capitalism which locates the WWII stage in the context of changes in the modalities of capital accumulation through two previous stages.

Monopoly Capital

Baran and Sweezy maintain that what they theorize as monopoly capitalism constitutes the "last phase" of capitalist development. Proceeding along lines initially sketched by Marx and later by theorists of imperialism, they invoke the "ripeness" argument to the effect that, notwithstanding the ills of monopoly capitalism, it "has produced the objective potentialities for the emergence of [socialism]" (quoted in Foster 2014: xxxix). At a fundamental level, Baran and Sweezy develop the concentration and centralization position that the ascendance of giant monopolistic and oligopolistic firms to commanding heights of major economies imbues capital with a modicum of "rationality", absent in its small, entrepreneurial business phase. Yet, in his formative work, Paul Baran throws down the gauntlet:

> The dream of "organized capitalism," of a "Ford-versus-Marx" solution of all economic and social ills and of "economic democracy" assuring justice and welfare to all became the shortest-lived utopia on the historical record. (Baran 1957: 7)

In terms of raw empirics there is nothing necessarily objectionable in Baran and Sweezy's work. In fact, they produce an important critical introduction to the momentous changes capitalism undergoes in its post-WWII monopoly phase or stage. Similar observations are made by later writers in the Marxist tradition. Let us review their main points.

First, Baran and Sweezy change the language used by theorists of imperialism to denote the business system realized by capitalist concentration and centralization from concerns, cartels, monopolies, and so on, to the "giant corporation". They discern a decisive transformation of commanding heights businesses toward a "recognizable pattern" which includes most prominently (1) a shift in control of major corporations to a managerial layer. That includes chief executive officers (CEOs) and boards of directors; (2) the emergence of the layer as a "self-perpetuating group" effectively severed from any responsibility to stockholders; and (3) the attainment of financial independence of the corporation through its ability to generate funds internally from its own earnings. This liberates corporate action from subjection to banks, though the corporation may still borrow funds in financial markets. And it frees management action as internally generated funds are wholly at their disposal (Baran and Sweezy 1966: 16–7).

Second, the new structure of the post-WWII commanding heights form of business leads to a widening of goals of the corporation as it augments the ability of the corporation to attain these. This change in the abilities of business constitutes a major factor for Baran and Sweezy in what they perceive as a pressing necessity to revamp the Marxian political economic conceptual infrastructure. At the center of this change, according to Baran and Sweezy, is the fact that the modern corporation is better equipped as a vehicle of profit maximization compared to the capitalist entrepreneur. Why this is the case rests on the running of companies not by the erstwhile entrepreneur but by the organization or "company men" of the management stratum. The rise of this cohort according to Baran and Sweezy is a reflection of a transformation of the class structure in capitalist societies where members of the middle and upper-middle classes enter the propertied class through positions in the corporation. As upper level management, they acquire significant stock holdings and this then aligns their interests with major capitalist stockholders in driving the success of their firms. Baran and Sweezy put it thus: "The replacement of the individual capitalist by the corporate capitalist constitutes the institutionalization of the capitalist function" (Baran and Sweezy 1966: 44).

Third, following from the foregoing Baran and Sweezy argue two signal differences from entrepreneurial firms mark the corporation. One is the corporation manifests a longer time horizon. The other is that it is a more rational calculator. These lead to discrete changes in behavior of corporations. The behavioral attributes are "a systematic avoidance of risk-taking" and "an attitude of live-and-let-live toward other [corporations]" (Baran and Sweezy 1966: 47–8). Baran and Sweezy's "live-and-let-live" argument overturns what had been the received view of Marxist theorists of imperialism. They had expected monopoly and oligopoly firms to duel it out in national markets initially until the most dominant businesses gained the edge. Then dominant national accumulators were expected to turn to world markets to do battle with imperialist competitors. On the basis of the three major empirical nuances, Baran and Sweezy turn to what is the most controversial aspect of their writing.

Economic Surplus and Underconsumption

Nothing detracts from the potential periodizing post-WWII capitalism as monopoly capital holds out for Marxian political economy than Baran and Sweezy's reliance on the notion of "economic surplus". The idea of an economic surplus is initially put forth by important forerunners of "classical" political economy, the *physiocrats* typified by writings of Francois Quesnay. Quite simply, the economic surplus constitutes the net product, a physical quantity, which remains after inputs used to produce it are replaced. Quesnay developed the concept in relation to the predominating agricultural economy of his time. His interest was in explaining how economic reproduction of society unfolded on the basis of one "productive" class capable of producing a surplus, the farmers working the land, and the existence of "unproductive" classes of landlords and rudimentary manufacturers. Quesnay considered the latter to be "unproductive" because their output, he believed, simply replaced the value of inputs. Only the land could yield the "gift" of surplus to support other "consuming" classes (Screpanti and Zamagni 2005: 55–7).

Baran and Sweezy reproduce the *physiocrat* definition verbatim: "The economic surplus, in the briefest definition, is the difference between what society produces and the costs of producing it" (Baran and Sweezy 1966: 9). For Baran and Sweezy, the economic surplus in aggregate is an indicator of the productivity and wealth of a society. Its composition, on the other hand, indicates how the surplus is utilized by a society: for example, consuming it, wasting it, investing it, and so on. Baran, in an earlier work, elaborated upon the concept of economic surplus by breaking its definition down into three categories. "Actual" economic surplus is the "difference between society's *actual* current output and its *actual* current consumption". Baran claims actual economic surplus has existed in virtually all historical societies. Potential economic surplus is "the difference between the output that could be produced…and what might be regarded as essential consumption". Echoing the *physiocrats*, Baran suggests the realization of potential economic surplus is possibly thwarted by excess consumption on the part of certain classes, "lost" through capture by "unproductive" classes, wasted or foregone by structural unemployment of potential "productive" workers with their potential "effective demand" (Baran 1957: 22–4). Finally, a "planned economic surplus" purportedly characterizes a socialist planned economy in which productive resource utilization and consumption gravitate to an "optimum" level (Baran 1957: 41).

Several reasons are given by Baran and Sweezy and adherents to the monopoly capital school for what, as we will see momentarily, is a surprising and impoverishing retreat in ostensibly Marxist work from Marx's scientific advancements in political economy. Baran offered the first in his early publication. In dealing with non- or underdeveloped economies where capitalist social relations of production have not taken root, Marx's conceptualization of "surplus value" does not apply it is claimed. Thus, the notion of an economic surplus is brought in to gauge the extent of wealth and resources available to underdeveloped economies for investment in development. This idea became the foundation for analysis of various shades of so-called world system theories which viewed underdevelopment as a result of the economic surplus of non-developed economies being siphoned off by developed economies through colonial, imperialist, and neocolonial policies. Baran, and later Baran and Sweezy maintain as the second reason the need for a comparative metric for distinct modes of economy, especially capitalism and socialism, such that it can be demonstrated how the latter provides a potential "optimum" utilization of resources of society as opposed to non-optimum deployment under capitalism. In their terminology, the "potential economic surplus" marking capitalism will find its most rational allocation in a planned socialist economy.

Finally, the concept of economic surplus is central to the fundamental argument of their book *Monopoly Capital*. This is the case because in it Baran and Sweezy argue that Marx's theory of the falling rate of profit in *Capital* needs to be supplanted as an explanatory tool for dynamics of the post-WWII monopoly capitalist stage. Its replacement is what Baran and Sweezy refer to as the "tendency of the surplus to rise". For them, "the tendency of the surplus to rise" purportedly follows from the structural and behavioral changes capital experiences in its commanding heights form of the giant corporation. Its "live-and-let-live" inclination and risk aversion mitigates potentially destructive price competition. Yet even as prices rise the corporation cuts costs with gales of technological innovation as a method of capturing market share from competitors. All the while profit margins widen in the face of working-class wages held close to a subsistence level notwithstanding their mass consumption, hence the rising surplus (Baran and Sweezy 1966: 53ff). This, then, is the point of passage to their arguments for "underconsumption" and pathologies of monopoly capital it leads to. We will return to that below.

Brewer is spot on in his critique of the notion of economic surplus as shifting away from Marx's explicit concern with social class relations of production and understanding of human labor as the wellspring of social wealth (Brewer 1990: 142). Indeed, for Marx, the metabolic interchange between human beings and nature through which the labor and production process furnishes the use values required for human sustenance constitutes the foundation of all human existence. Across the sweep of human history, societies are differentiated according to Marx by their social class relations. Class divided societies, which have populated much of human history, differ according to the way surplus *labor* is extracted from the direct producing class. Surplus labor is that work performed by the direct producers over and above their necessary labor which is devoted to ensuring the material reproduction of direct producers as a class. Even slaves, Marx notes, must receive the product of their necessary labor or as a class they would perish, leaving the masters to work for themselves or quickly hunt for new slaves. In capitalist society, whatever the expression of the wage in monetary terms or fluctuations in relative prices, wages must be able to purchase on the market goods equal to the product of the worker's necessary labor or work to ensure the material reproduction of society would fall to the capitalists.

Believing they help clarify with their categories of economic surplus why capitalism is a historically delimited, ill-ridden society and socialism a society best suited to human flourishing, Baran and Sweezy confound a question Marx answers so elegantly. Marx offers two approaches to socialism drawing upon his conceptualizing of necessary and surplus labor. In the first, Marx takes the example of Robinson Crusoe alone on his island.

Whatever kind of work Robinson performs, it is *his* work. Work for Robinson is a necessity (necessary labor). And in that endeavor he must "divide his time with precision between his different functions". Robinson catalogues during his stay on the island what useful objects he amassed, the sorts of labor required to furnish them, and the labor time on average specific quantities of the objects cost him. "All the relations between Robinson and these objects that form his self-created wealth are here so simple and transparent". Marx continues:

> Let us…imagine, for a change, an association of free men, working with the means of production held in common, and expending their many different forms of labour-power in full self-awareness as one single social labour force. All the characteristics of Robinson's labour are repeated here, but with the difference that they are social instead of individual…The total product of our imagined association is a social product. One part of this serves as fresh means of production and remains social. But another portion is consumed by the members of the association as means of subsistence. This part must therefore be divided amongst them. The way this division is made will vary with the particular kind of social organisation of production and corresponding level of social development attained by the producers. (Marx 1977: 169–72)

In short, for Marx, building on concepts of necessary labor and surplus labor, in an imagined classless, socialist society where exploitation and appropriation of surplus labor of the direct producers are extirpated, all social wealth in every form and dimension may be considered "necessary". This includes productive work performed by members of society beyond what is required to support themselves to ensure the "unproductive" aged, infirm, children, artists, singers, cooks, students, professors, and so on share in the division of the social product. Whether Robinson or the imagined socialist association decide to devote extra work time amassing goods for a rainy day or seek to raise the general level of productivity for the future makes no difference to the basic distinction.

Marx approaches the same question from a different angle in Volume III of *Capital* (Marx 1991: 958–9). There he declares:

> Surplus labour in some form must always remain, as labour beyond the extent of given needs. It is just that in the capitalist, as in the slave system, etc., it has an antagonistic form and its obverse side is pure idleness on the part of one section of society. A certain quantum of surplus labour is required as insurance against accidents and for the progressive extension of the reproduction process that is needed to keep pace with the development of needs and the progress of population. ...The real wealth of society and the possibility of a constant expansion of its reproduction process does not depend on the length of surplus labour but rather on its productivity...The realm of freedom really begins only where labour determined by necessity...ends...Just as the savage must wrestle with nature to satisfy his needs, to maintain and reproduce his life, so must civilized man, and he must do so in all forms of society and under all possible modes of production... Freedom, in this sphere, can consist only in this, that...the associated producers, govern the human metabolism with nature in a rational way... accomplishing it with the least expenditure of energy...The reduction of the working day is the basic prerequisite...

Though Marx here continues to distinguish between necessary and surplus labor for socialism, his interest is in highlighting the need to transform the relationship between them from that existing in class societies. In this way, the performance of surplus labor is still considered a part of necessary labor devoted to the socialist goal of human flourishing. As well, Marx's emphasis on the reduction of the working day as central to the leap from human necessity to socialist freedom only reinforces his economic insight that the only new cost society incurs at any given point in its reproduction process is its allocation of available labor power. That is to say, at the beginning of the production process the cost of all material inputs has already been met. Marx refers to this as "dead labor". If work in a capitalist economy halts at that point during the working day where labor produces the equivalent in value of its necessary labor the capitalist would break even and there would be no accumulation. Baran and Sweezy's regression to the *physiocrats* concept of economic surplus opens the door to accepting that "factors of production" other than human labor constitute the wellspring of social wealth. This is indubitably not the case for any "kind" of human society in history including monopoly capitalism. And focus upon some "optimal" utilization of an economic surplus by Baran and Sweezy paints a rather benign picture of what is wrong with capitalism as it reduces socialism to resolution of a technical problem.

From what has just been discussed it is easy to dismiss the idea that the conception of economic surplus helps shed light on the plight of underdeveloped economies. In those economies as drawn attention to in the foregoing quote from Marx, particularly to the extent the direct producers remain enmeshed in precapitalist social relations of production and subsistence economies, labor remains trapped in the realm of necessity and low productivity. While an increase in performance of surplus labor may be enforced upon the direct producers the degree to which much of the working day continues to be devoted to simply reproducing their livelihood to yield a limited surplus product, the possibility for increasing social wealth is limited. In many underdeveloped economies so much of future potentialities for development hinges upon control over extraction of natural resources which is what forged patterns of economic relations between advanced capitalism and the rest of the world from the stage of imperialism. And, as touched on in the previous chapter, when comprador ruling classes and settler colonialists interject their partial interests into these economies to shape their international export or trade relations, all the ingredients are thus emplaced for persisting poverty and underdevelopment. When social relations of production across the division of labor in society are transformed by capital as occurred in once impoverished, colonized South Korea and Taiwan, capitalist development will proceed as it did among initial advanced capitalist economies.

Finally, let us return as promised to the specific issue of the "tendency of the surplus to rise" and its corollary for Baran and Sweezy, "underconsumption". As touched on, Baran and Sweezy argue that "Marxian analysis of capitalism still rests…on the assumption of a competitive economy" (Baran and Sweezy 1966: 4). Monopoly capital, as they explain, shifts the modus operandi of capitalism away from ruinous price wars toward a "live-and-let-live" orientation among commanding heights corporations. Not only do corporate monopolists batten on maintenance of high prices but also their aforementioned technological innovation to covet market share entails a major change in investment patterns according to Baran and Sweezy. That is, rather than being compelled by competitive pressure technological innovations are driven by "careful calculations" of corporations to expand firm profitability as a whole. This new pattern of innovation under monopoly capital, Baran and Sweezy maintain, removes the constraint existing in a competitive economy for businesses to assess depreciation periods and costs, thus monies ostensibly accumulating for that purpose only add to the "surplus" in corporate hands (Baran and Sweezy 1966: 93, 99). In sum, because monopoly capital generates an ever-expanding surplus "yet fails to provide the consumption and investment outlets required [to absorb it] the normal state of the...economy is stagnation" (Baran and Sweezy 1966: 108).

In their empirical elaboration upon why potential surplus absorbers within the monopoly capitalist economy come up short, the insights Baran and Sweezy produce into pathologies of capitalism in the post-WWII period constitute the more interesting parts of their book. Discussion of the "sales effort" reveals frenzied efforts of capitalist business to sell marginally "differentiated" products through increasingly sophisticated manipulations of advertisers. Also traced is the growing role played by government spending in attempting to engender "effective demand". Baran and Sweezy further explore the ratcheting up of US military spending leading to ongoing imperialistic adventurism abroad. Finally, their original exploration of "quality of life" issues under monopoly capitalism anticipates later writings in critical sociology and political science on urban decay and alienation in US consumer society.

Critical literature on Baran and Sweezy's revisions of Marx and defense of an underconsumption theory of capitalist crises which, importantly, other Marxists have also argued for abound. Perhaps the most widespread critique is that underconsumption theories neglect the fact that demand in capitalist economies is hardly limited to personal consumption of the worker or even the individual capitalist. Instead, significant demand flows from other capitalist businesses for producer goods which cascades among such producers across the economy (Brewer 1990: 138; Howard and King 1992: 120–1). As well, Baran and Sweezy offer no convincing argument for limits on state and military spending. Indeed, Baran and Sweezy's writings on monopoly capital appeared just as state and military spending was ratcheting skyward. As we shall see in Chap. 5, later approaches to periodizing capitalism furnish a far more sophisticated analysis of the role of the capitalist state in the post-WWII era. Further, Baran and Sweezy have been taken to task over their view of monopoly suppressing competition (Howard and King 1992: 122–3). Particularly international competition among giant corporations becomes increasingly frenetic within a decade of Baran and Sweezy's writing. In fact, if, as Baran and Sweezy intimate, underconsumption is an intrinsic condition of capitalism it is unclear why accumulation should be struck by cyclical crises which have marked capitalism from its inception.

But, from the perspective of the literature on periodizing capitalism surveyed in this book, there exists a far deeper problem with their work. Baran and Sweezy uncritically recapitulate the view of Kautsky and theorists of imperialism that Marx's economic writings constitute a genetic theory of capitalist development with socialism as its telos. In this way, capitalism develops in a "petty commodity" economy which then morphs into capitalism. Capitalism turns into imperialism. Finally, imperialism is supplanted by monopoly capital. Given its purported analysis of a short-lived formation wedged between its "petty commodity" precursor and imperialism, which now according to Baran and Sweezy has transitioned to monopoly capitalism, Marx's economics in *Capital* is largely consigned to the dustbin except as a repository of radical quotations. Baran and Sweezy also hold fast to Kautsky's position on a prime mover or constant of capitalism driving it toward breakdown (see Fig. 3.1). From *Capital* through theories of imperialism, this constant is supposedly the tendency for the profit rate to fall. Under monopoly capital, so the argument goes, it is "the tendency for the surplus to rise".

However, as maintained in Chap. 2, Kautsky's reconstructing of Marx's theories makes nonsense of Marx's work. Indeed, from the perspective of the alternative grasp of Marxist theory adverted to in our introductory chapter Marx's economic studies in *Capital* constitute a pure or general theory of capital not a genetic theory of capitalist development. Marx's discussion of the falling profit rate in Volume III of *Capital* factors into the discussion of the capitalist business cycle. What Marx emphasizes is that under pure market conditions capital accumulation proceeds apace with businesses competing at a given level of development of the productive forces until the industrial reserve army is absorbed. This foments a condition of overaccumulation of capital in relation to the size of the working population which drives capital into recession and crisis. To

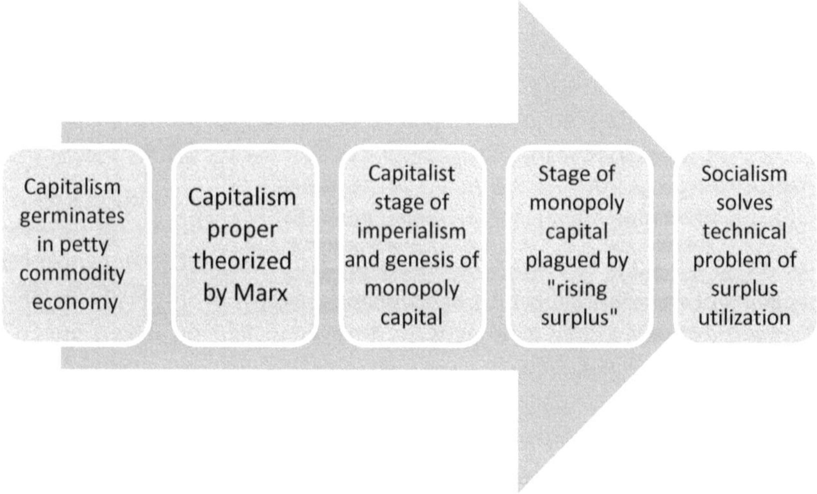

Fig. 3.1 Baran and Sweezy and the historical telos of socialism (Source: Author)

maintain capitalist relations of production and labor power as a commodity, capital is forced to revolutionize the forces of production. Because the new technologies are labor saving, the industrial reserve army is thereby reconstituted as capital begins another business cycle.

Hilferding, as we recounted in Chap. 2, had already pointed to the way monopoly pricing strategies impacted the business cycle. And that monopoly combines were able to renovate their technologies at selected points during the business cycle in ways no longer synchronizing with absorption of the industrial reserve army. Instead of overaccumulation generating unemployment it leads to bouts of overproduction of commodities. This was the rationale for the export of portfolio investment and "dumping" of commodities in foreign markets. It was in these markets where imperialist monopolies competed. Though we will return to this in later chapters, for post-WWII period commanding heights corporations producing expensive consumer durables, there is no question of "dumping" these in foreign markets. But, because of an even greater anathema to cutthroat price competition and devaluation of capital given their mammoth investment requirements, corporations necessarily evolve an alternate mechanism to confront tendencies toward overaccumulation. These were business cycle oscillations around expansions to full capacity utilization followed by maintenance of overcapacity while keeping price fluctuation to a minimum (Westra 2016: 141).

Below, in taking up the periodizing of capitalism by Ernest Mandel, we will revisit the falling rate of profit issue. For now, let us close this extended section on monopoly capital theory with a few words about "economic surplus". The fact is the hallmark of capitalism is its reproduction of human material life as a byproduct of value augmentation or profit making. Value is augmented through the production of surplus value. Surplus value is but the materialization in mercantile wealth of surplus labor performed by commodified labor power. How big private businesses are and how they compete do not change this fundamental aspect of capitalist economies. What we will discover in later chapters is that without the concept of surplus value and its division into profit, rent, interest, and dividends it is impossible to grasp the true impacts of economic transformations associated with "globalization", "financialization", increasing economic weight of so-called intangible assets, and so on. The notion of an "economic surplus" may appear at first glance to simplify. Unfortunately that which simplifies often misleads and obfuscates and regressing to a concept promulgated by *physiocrats* is a textbook example of that adage.

The Capitalist-Socialist New Industrial State

While the periodization of capitalism is largely a Marxist endeavor, the non-Marxist work of John Kenneth Galbraith is an indispensable contribution to exploring the dynamics of early post-WWII capitalism. It emerged at the approximate temporal point as writings of Baran and Sweezy and covers similar empirical terrain. Yet Galbraith paints a quite different picture of the US economy in itself and in relation to the socialist Soviet Union. Of particular significance is the bridge, of sorts, Galbraith's intervention establishes to later Marxist writings which take issue with Baran and Sweezy's position on post-WWII economic stagnation. As we will see, looking back from the vantage point of the 1980s, the post-WWII era is identified as a "golden age" of capitalist prosperity in comparison to the preceding period of war and depression, and to the neoliberal decades that follow. Galbraith is clearly a cheerleader of this view. "No society has ever before provided such a high standard of living as ours, hence none is as good", he proclaims (Galbraith 1972: 164).

What are the ingredients of this? Like Baran and Sweezy, Galbraith takes up the question of the transformed business structure of the giant corporation. First, there are exigencies of the new technologies; their high investment costs, set up requirements, and extended time horizons for profitability. This demands both the planned generating and mobilization by individuals, businesses, and governments of significant savings to supply the necessary capital. Galbraith, as other commentators on post-WWII capitalism, acknowledges the important contribution of internal funding for the modern corporation. Second, with capital relatively abundant, its owners' power is diminished. Galbraith, here referring to stockholders, remarks on the "quaintness that attaches to the suggestion that the United States is run from Wall Street" (Galbraith 1972: 57). Third, however, the coalescing of readily available capital with imperatives of technology, organization, and planning in the corporation feeds a power shift in advanced economies, according to Galbraith, redolent of that from land to capital centuries ago. That shift being to the new resource of specialized management—a cohort Galbraith famously dubs the "technostructure".

There is a notable similarity between Galbraith's conceptualizing of the technostructure and the "self-perpetuating" managerial cohort of "company men" in Baran and Sweezy's analysis. In social class terms, Baran and Sweezy recognize that this cohort emerges from the middle and upper-middle classes. However, for Baran and Sweezy, the "capitalist function" is simply "institutionalized" in the monopoly capitalist corporation with the company man (sic) ideologically predisposed to act in the capitalist interest. For Galbraith, on the other hand, there is a virtual power shift from capital to the technostructure such that the new goals of the economy are set by the technostructure, not capital. Growth of the firm, stable revenue stream, technological innovation, strategies of price-making, demand management, wage policies, and social expenditure in education which furnishes the skills for management all become goals set by the technostructure.

While Baran and Sweezy see such "organized" capitalism as still driven by a single economic law toward its demise, Galbraith asserts (1972: 291):

> …reputable social science no longer has overtones of revolution…The revolution was to be catalyzed by the capitalist crisis…But the industrial system has, as an integral requirement, an arrangement for regulating aggregate demand which, while permitting it to plan, gives promise, with minimal management, of preventing, or at least mitigating, depression. So the danger of an apocalyptic crisis seems more remote.

What is most illuminating in Galbraith's work is that whereas Baran and Sweezy largely reduce socialism to resolution of a technical problem in "organized" capitalism of suboptimal utilization of the so-called economic surplus, Galbraith sees a convergence of the two systems. Galbraith works with the widely accepted definition of socialism as an "organized" or planned economy with public ownership of the means of production. First, the old enemy of socialists, the capitalist, has already been rendered a "casualty of organization…The technostructure in cases of both public and private ownership assumes similar powers and uses the same group methods for arriving at decisions" (Galbraith 1972: 100). While socialism held out the promise of democratic or "social control" of the publicly owned economy, such a possibility has been outstripped by history, according to Galbraith. Those same forces of technological complexity, the sheer scale of planning tightly coupled multiplant industrial operations which pried effective power from hands of the entrepreneur also removed such potentialities from "social control", lodging them in hands of the technostructure (Galbraith 1972: 104). Second, the nexus of technostructure membership and goals of the technostructure in managing the modern corporation finds its corollary in the relationship of the technostructure to the state. Interests of the state in fostering economic stability and growth, education, scientific, and technological advancement are those of the corporation and the technostructure. This similitude manifests itself most specifically in relation to the national goal of defense. For Galbraith, the military in its ethos of technological advancement and practices of government procurement is a paragon of economic planning. In this way public goals are "adapted" to goals of the technostructure (Galbraith 1972: 311–2).

To sum up, while mass public sentiment may be swayed to believe in an impending conflict between two systems—capitalism and socialism—

"much of what is believed turns out to be fanciful", declares Galbraith. Leaving no ambiguity, Galbraith observes (1972: 334):

> The reality in the case of the United States and the Soviet Union is of two large industrial nations…
> There is a large and unquestioned difference in the two systems in the role of politicians, writers, artists and scientists…But it is less clear that the contrast in the systems of economic management is so great. Both systems are subject to the imperatives of industrialization. This for both means planning…Instead of contrast leading to implacable conflict, a more evident economic tendency is convergence.

Little that is not glaringly self-evident needs to be offered by way of critical review of Galbraith's work. Though Galbraith, to be fair, disparages the field of neoclassical economics at multiple points throughout his book, he nevertheless suffers from a fatal conceit of bourgeois thought. This being that "regulating" or "governing" the capitalist market, as human beings may, negates the causal force of the fundamental contradictions of the capitalist mode of production. Nothing could be further from the truth. As we shall see, the enthusiasm which attended "Keynesian" economic management in the post-WWII era along with Galbraith's faith in the technostructure, which the course of history cruelly dashed, was again refurbished around a new neoliberal "god" at the close of the twentieth century. And such faith faces an even greater dire end.

In fact, the "quaint" idea of the US economy being managed by Wall Street humored by Galbraith would, as later discussion of "financialization" reveals, become an unfortunate reality. If Marxist work suffered to that juncture of being far too beholden to the belief in economic laws playing themselves out in history with an "iron necessity", Galbraith's work gets caught out by a blind faith in the technocratic powers of states and managerial classes akin to that human beings held around the mastery of nature.

Finally, Galbraith's grasp of an impending "convergence" of capitalism and Soviet-style socialism unwittingly corroborates an important though unheralded critique of the kind of socialism the Russian Revolution materialized. This being that in its basic modeling, socialism in the Soviet style remained far too great a prisoner of capitalism (Westra 2018). Thus,

Baran and Sweezy could claim the building of socialism simply entails resolution of a technical problem in capitalism of utilizing the so-called economic surplus. And Galbraith conversely asserts how technological imperatives bring socialist dreams down to earth. Unfortunately, neither the prognosis of Baran and Sweezy, nor that of Galbraith, withstands the test of time.

Long Wave Theory and Late Capitalism

It is the work of Ernest Mandel in his major book, *Late Capitalism*, which offers the first widely read and debated, systematic Marxian periodization of capitalism from its inception through to the 1970s and beyond. While in my view Mandel persists with the tendency in Marxian political economy to "chain link" capitalist change to a specific constant or prime mover, his work differs from that of theories of imperialism or monopoly capital in its eclecticism, and attempt to draw in multiple causal forces, both economic and non-economic, into his explanation.

Mandel sets out the problem of periodizing capitalism as follows. He asks why the "integration of theory and history which Marx applied with such mastery…has never since been repeated…to explain [the] …successive stages of the capitalist mode of production" (Mandel 1978: 23). The tasks he explains are twofold. On the one hand, capitalist history over the past century must be shown to be a history of the development of the "internal contradictions" of capitalism. That is "as determined in the last resort by its 'abstract' laws of motion". This requires demonstrating the "intermediate links" operating between the abstract laws and concrete historical elements. On the other hand, modern history of capitalism must be "traced back" to the "laws" of capitalism in a way that explains the expansion of capital accumulation in relation to precapitalist parts of the world "conquered" by capital (Mandel 1978: 22).

Because profit is fundamental to capitalism, for Mandel, not only profit but the search by capital for above average or "surplus profit" is at the root of capitalist dynamics. However, though fluctuations in the rate of profit constitute the "seismograph" of change across capitalist history, it correlates with other variables, according to Mandel. These include the organic composition of capital, relations between "Department I" (production of producer goods) and "Department II" (production of consumer goods), and the rate of exploitation (Mandel 1978: 39–40). The latter, for example, is a "function" of class struggle and its varying potential outcomes in different periods of capitalism. Mandel, in fact, in a follow-up work to *Late Capitalism*, emphasizes how class struggle adds the all-important "subjective" or "exogenous" element to the "objective" or "endogenous" laws of capital in explaining periods of capitalist change (Mandel 1995: 36–7).

Yet, what distinguishes Mandel's periodization of capitalism is his incorporation of an early, though initially unsung, schema of explaining capitalist change—"long wave" theory. In fact, when at the outset of this chapter I stated that a paucity of new thinking in Marxist theory sprung from the Soviet Union following the revolution, long wave theory is a contribution which bucked the trend. Its primary architect is Nikolai Dimitrievic Kondratiev. Arguably, long wave theory was developed less as a perspective on periodizing capitalism *stricto sensu*, and more as an explanation for capitalist breakdown. This, of course, was a pressing concern in the aftermath of the revolution because Lenin initially believed that, while Russia was the "weak link" in the imperialist chain, only if the most advanced economies joined it in revolution and transitioning to socialism would the revolution succeed. Where long wave theory enters the picture is to show that Marx's analysis of decennial business cycles in *Capital* do not explain epochal capitalist crises. That, instead, required recourse to a theory of major, half-century long, economic cycles or waves based on comprehensive renewals of fixed capital and corresponding built infrastructure (Screpanti and Zamagni 2005: 314).

We have discussed Marx's basic theory of the capitalist business cycle in its bare bones above in relation to monopoly capital and, in Chap. 2, with our treatment of Hilferding and imperialism. Its complete elaboration outstrips the bounds of this chapter (for a succinct summary, see Westra 2012/2013). Mandel, by way of comparison, is not clear on the need, in Marx's basic or pure theory of capital, to bring to bear both the "micro-equilibrium" and "macro-dynamic" parts of Marx's theorizing of capital on understanding the decennial business cycles. The former entails the tendency of capital accumulation to reach a point of relative price stability, an "optimal" allocation of available productive labor power in society and average rate of profit across all spheres of production. The latter demands account be taking of the specific theory of population in capitalist economies which involves questions of the absorption and reconstituting of the industrial reserve army. It is through this process in the course of business cycles that capital maintains its relations of production with the commodification of labor power as their sine qua non (Sekine 2013: 193–6).

But where Mandel is correct in his analysis of the decennial business cycles Marx analyzes in *Capital* is that the revolutionizing of the forces of production Marx adverts to brings about incremental changes in productive technologies which do raise the organic composition of capital. And the cyclical oscillations occur within the ambit of market forces and operate as a basic tendency of capital accumulation. However, Mandel explains that Marx's elaboration of business cycles was never intended to cover the seismic transmutations of capital which occasion the wholesale remaking of its technological infrastructure and rise of new commanding heights industries (Mandel 1978: 110–4). Hence, it is to address that question that Mandel incorporates long wave theory into his study of capitalist change.

According to Mandel, capitalist history is marked internationally by four cyclical periods of approximately 50 years in length. Except the first, each of the periods is characterized by thoroughgoing technological revolutions and the incorporating of new available power and energy sources. The first period then stretches from the eighteenth century to the 1840s. It saw the generalizing of the handicraft or manufacture-made steam engine. Next is the long period beginning in 1847 and culminating in the 1890s. This is the first technological revolution where machine-made steam engines spread across the advanced economies. The period of the second technological revolution runs from the 1890s to WWII. It is characterized by general application of electric power and combustion engines throughout major economies. Beginning in the 1940s is the long wave of the third technological revolution. What distinguishes it, are generalized control of machines by electronic apparatuses and the application of nuclear energy (Mandel 1978: 120–1). Mandel dubs the periods of the three technological revolutions respectively "freely competitive" capitalism, "classic" imperialist capitalism, and "late capitalism".

As "historically distinct periods" of capital accumulation, each long wave is punctuated by a roughly two-decade run of rising profit rates and robust capital accumulation to be followed by an economic downswing, a spell ending in a new upswing of another long wave. "Freely competitive capitalism" experienced its upswing, according to Mandel, during the period 1848–1873. Its downswing was 1873–1893. Classic imperialism's upswing occurred 1893–1913: its long downswing, 1914–1940. Late capitalism, according to Mandel, arises from the detritus of war, delay of the world revolution anticipated by creation of the Soviet Union, depression, fascism and defeats of the working class, and ultimately the decomposing of the capitalist system with the added exit from it by China. Its upswing is the period 1940–1967 (Mandel 1995: 82–3).

In *Late Capitalism,* Mandel provides an extended table outlining the purported ways the variables he sets out, which we introduce above, concatenate with the rise and fall in profit rates across long wave stages of capitalism (Mandel 1978: 130–2). These will not be reviewed here partly due to the fact that their treatment outstrips the bounds of this section and such a job is best left to readers of Mandel's book. Partly too, because as critics of Mandel explain, the enormity of the explanatory task Mandel undertakes in their sketch is never actually completed by him. Thus, at the end, it leaves the reader with more questions than answers, a criticism with which I concur (see Rowthorn 1976: 61). Mandel's work is replete with multiple rejections of competing theories including, mono-causal approaches to capitalist change, underconsumption, and disproportionality (between the Departments) theories of capitalist crises and breakdown. However, in various places he invokes variants of these, leading one commentator to quip that Mandel "*always* wants to have his theoretical cake and eat it" (Harman 1978).

Yet the landmark contribution Mandel makes to the specific enterprise of periodizing capitalism should not be overlooked or summarily dismissed. Nor should Mandel's robust argument for the specific crisis of late capitalism necessarily be conflated with his overarching, far less precise, multicausal explanations for long wave oscillations across capitalist history. Let us explore key features of the late capitalist era treated by

Mandel en route to examining his view of crisis which brings the prosperity phase of the "wave" to an end.

First, in opposition to Baran and Sweezy's notion of "carefully" orchestrated technological change, Mandel argues for late capitalism as a stage marked specifically by technological dynamism of the third technological revolution. This technological revolution spreads rapidly across all industries. Core innovations include: automatic continuous flow processes in chemical and petroleum industries, for example; semiautomatic and computer-controlled manufacturing and numerically controlled machine tool industry; and, tighter coupling of production systems and coordinated movement of parts between these as occurs in automobile production (Mandel 1978: 193–4). Second, Mandel emphasizes the rapidity of technological innovation and increased incorporation by businesses of research and development (R&D) facilities. Mandel, like Baran and Sweezy, along with Galbraith, recognizes the substantial role scientific and technocratic managerial classes play in capitalism in the "late" era. Third, Mandel sees international concentration and centralization of capital exacerbating a tendency of classic imperialism where "several imperialist formations harden in their mutual antagonism" (Mandel 1978: 338). Fourth, the expansion of monopoly capital into the service sector which itself is greatly enlarged is dealt with by him. This includes food production and distribution, retail operations, the substitution of services once undertaken within the division of labor within proletarian families involving precooked meals, canned goods, and so forth. Fifth, Mandel treats what he describes as the "permanent arms economy", something we will return to momentarily. Sixth, the role of the state in late capitalism is visited. Seventh, Mandel covers dynamic idiosyncrasies of the period including the changed operation of the business cycle and the role played "permanent inflation", points we also address below.

Military production as a "permanent" feature of the post-WWII economy is something also covered by Baran and Sweezy as well as in a non-Marxist way by Galbraith. The latter emphasizes the nexus of military production and technological advancement as binding the goals of the technostructure to those of the state. The former treats it as an avenue for monopoly capital to absorb the so-called rising surplus which ultimately is destined in their schema to bring about the demise of capitalism.

Mandel explains it drawing on variations of both elements. On the one hand, military production spurs technological innovation which is only accelerated by ideological compulsions of the Cold War. On the other hand, permanent arms expenditure illustrates the "parasitic" nature of late capitalism as a feature outlined by Lenin where profits not easily absorbed by civilian industry, despite the latter's growth, find an investment home to the benefit of some capitals.

There is certainly a truth to the argument that military investment by the state not only contributes to technological innovation but also shapes its development in relation to society in significant ways (Molina 1989). However, Mandel's arguments for it on the basis of state military spending impact on rates of profit and the organic composition of capital are as difficult to defend as a general "law". Ditto for Harman's critique of Mandel that military spending raises rates of profit even as its "workers produce nothing of benefit to the rest of the economy" (Harman 1978). The fact is military spending is directed toward large monopoly capitalist corporations' divisions of which also produce consumer producer and goods for the civilian economy. In this way, during the post-WWII period, it provided a "floor" under the civilian economy for effective demand which the state can rely on with its countercyclical spending. Whether military spending, in the case of the US economy at least, raises profit rates may be beside the point. Already from the 1950s US security establishment policymakers realized that access to the world's vital raw materials was necessary for the very survival of US power into the future and potentially, even the survival of global capitalism that the US deemed itself "indispensable" to lead. And a robust international military posture offered a guarantee of this whatever the cost (Westra 2012: 45–8).

Finally, Mandel's explanation of the transformed business cycle in late capitalism confirms the charges of eclecticism leveled against him by critics such as Rowthorn (1976: 67ff). Mandel mixes elements of his adaptation of long wave theory into the discussion of the truncated decennial business cycle of post-WWII capitalism. His basic starting point is, however, correct. Pace Galbraith, as long as private ownership of the means of production, commodification of labor power, and a modicum of capitalist market operations exists, so cyclical oscillations of capital will persist notwithstanding monopoly pricing strategies and state economic management. The rudiments of the transformed nature of the business cycle in post-WWII capitalism have been set out. Mandel touches on the tendency toward maintenance of overcapacity in monopoly capitalist business, though without explicitly dealing with its relationship to the reconfiguring of the decennial business cycle as his analysis trails off onto its implications for the long wave of late capitalist expansion (Mandel 1978: 457ff).

Mandel's nuance with respect to Baran and Sweezy, which also reflects his temporal orientation to the development of post-WWII capitalism, is his attempt to theorize the phenomenon of "permanent inflation" in relation to capitalist crises. According to him "permanent inflation" is a "specific mechanism" deployed under late capitalist conditions of rapid capital accumulation and low levels of unemployment to maintain high rates of profit (Mandel 1978: 422). Its possibility as tool in the foregoing regard arises with the decommodification of money in "national" economic spaces following abdication of the gold standard. The post-WWII Bretton Woods monetary system, which substitutes for the gold standard internationally, enshrined the US dollar as world money but with the value of the dollar itself anchored in gold. It facilitated post-WWII trade liberalization with the metric it offered for exchangeability among national currencies. However, the restriction on speculative international flows of funds Bretton Woods mandated provided a cocoon for national fiscal and monetary policy autonomy.

Such policy autonomy entailed a coalescing of monetary policy which tightly regulated interest rates, fiscal policy of countercyclical Keynesian management of effective demand, and rising wage and benefit package offered by large corporations. Mandel, in a somewhat different language, captures this as well as the expanded role of the credit system responding to it. But there is more to the phenomenon of inflation in the post-WWII period corresponding to late capitalism. What economist Hyman Minsky shows is that corporations themselves, notwithstanding their ability to draw upon internal resources for fixed capital investment, nevertheless incurred growing amounts of short- and medium-term debt. While Minsky was never explicit here, the reason this happens relates to the "roundaboutness" of the post-WWII production of consumer durables bringing to bear layers of interconnected businesses producing inputs into final products the completion of which involves significant time lags. Corporations, thus, were impelled into the business of "money management". Banks got "bigger". And the sheer weight on the economy from the multiple sources of money injections fomented a persistent mild inflation (Westra 2016: 147–8). Inflation, of course, favors borrowers over lenders. Yet this was tolerated by all economic stakeholders as long as investment opportunities and profitability were guaranteed.

Late Capitalism as the End of Capitalism

For Mandel, as adverted to above, long waves are expressions of both the endogenous variables revolving around the fundamental "law" of capital to seek surplus profit and exogenous variables such as class struggle. Setting in of a downswing in a long wave, according to Mandel, is function of endogenous forces. However, the upswing is more dependent on historical and geospatial exogenous conditions. Class struggle, here, has a "relative autonomy" in that the working class ultimately may succumb to defeat as an outcome of extended crisis or victory which presumably means the dawn of socialism. Mandel is not so sanguine as Marxist theorists of imperialism that capitalist crisis will be followed by socialism. Reloaded capitalism, or unresolved crisis, degenerating into barbarism, is also an option (Mandel 1995: 42).

Late capitalism falls into crisis, according to Mandel, at that point where the third technological revolution reaches its limit in terms of gains in profitability deriving from rapid innovation raising the organic composition of capital in the face of the given level of wages. Though innovation continues, the absorption of the industrial reserve army, which had been proceeding apace in major capitalist accumulators, meant that increasing the rate of exploitation faced strong opposition (Mandel 1995: 63ff). Mandel is skeptical whether rejuvenating rates of profit is possible even anticipating a long "cleansing" period of crisis and depression into the 1970s, 1980s, and 1990s. He accepts that a technological foundation for this is on the horizon with radical restructuring of economies by the information and computer technology revolution where so-called robotism will accelerate automation to replace living labor. But the costs of this in terms of mass unemployment Mandel sees as essentially unsustainable. In a fashion quite prophetic given his temporal emplacement, Mandel also suggests a dramatic expansion in the global capitalist market, drawing in the Soviet Union and China as well as an increasingly industrialized underdeveloped world portends the possibility of a new sustained capitalist boom (Mandel 1995: 83–8).

With critique of long wave theory and debates over the roots of the crisis which besets the post-WWII golden age receiving treatment in later chapters through the prism of elaborating on other theories, it is worth bringing the chapter and the discussion of Mandel to a close with a point he makes that is not readily appreciated in most other periodizations. Mandel asserts "that the concept of a fundamental turning point in the history of capitalism occurring in 1914 is quite relevant from an economic and political point of view". He further maintains this turning point prefigures "the decline of bourgeois society…of what one could call bourgeois civilization" (Mandel 1995: 51). Mandel cites the extraordinary depth and duration of the Great Depression as the first indicator of this point. What is ironic in this is not the truth value of the claim. Rather, it is the fact that despite his insight, Mandel does not question whether periodizing capitalism in the later stage of late capitalism is best served by extrapolating basic "laws" of capitalism following what he believes constitutes a watershed in the very existence of capitalism as a mode of production. Or, by extension, that "laws" of capitalism continue to drive it toward demise even as they gestate "organized" socialist forms within capitalism. Indeed, as Screpanti and Zamagni observe, "only [Japanese Marxist Kozo] Uno had the courage to make explicit, that the history of capitalism had ended in 1917; then began the history of the transition to socialism" (Screpanti and Zamagni 2005: 449).

References

Baran, P. 1957. *The Political Economy of Growth*. New York: Monthly Review Press.
Baran, P., and P. Sweezy. 1966. *Monopoly Capital*. New York: Monthly Review Press.
Brewer, A. 1990. *Marxist Theories of Imperialism: A Critical Survey*. London: Routledge.

Foster, J.B. 2014. *The Theory of Monopoly Capitalism*. New ed. New York: Monthly Review Press.
Galbraith, J.K. 1972. *The New Industrial State*. Rev. ed. London: Andre Deutsch.
Harman, C. 1978. *Mandel's Late Capitalism*. https://www.marxists.org/archive/harman/1978/07/mandel.html. Accessed 5 Aug 2018.
Howard, M.C., and J.E. King. 1992. *A History of Marxian Economics: Volume 2*. Princeton: Princeton University Press.
Mandel, E. 1978. *Late Capitalism*. London: Verso.
———. 1995. *Long Waves of Capitalist Development: A Marxist Interpretation*. Rev. ed. London: Verso.
Marx, K. 1977. *Capital Volume I*. New York: Vintage Books.
———. 1991. *Capital Volume III*. London: Penguin Classics.
Molina, A.H. 1989. *The Social Basis of the Microelectronics Revolution*. Edinburgh: University Edinburgh Press.
Rowthorn, B. 1976. Late Capitalism. *New Left Review* I/98: 59–84.
Screpanti, E., and S. Zamagni. 2005. *An Outline of the History of Economic Thought*. Oxford: Oxford University Press.
Sekine, T. 2013. General Equilibrium and the Dialectic of Capital. In *Towards a Critique of Bourgeois Economics: Essays of Thomas Sekine*, ed. J. Bell. Berlin: Owl of Minerva Press.
Westra, R. 2012. *The Evil Axis of Finance: The US-Japan-China Stranglehold on the Global Future*. Atlanta, GA: Clarity Press.
———. 2012/2013. *Capital* as Dialectical Economic Theory. *Journal of Australian Political Economy*, Special Issue on *Capital* against Capitalism: New Research in Marxist Political Economy, 70.
———. 2016. *Unleashing Usury: How Finance Opened the Door to Capitalism Then Swallowed It Whole*. Atlanta, GA: Clarity Press.
———. 2018. *Socialism in the Twenty-First Century*. Hauppauge, NY: Nova Science Publishers.

4

Periodizing Really Existing Capitalism of the 1980s and 1990s

In comparison with periodizations of capitalism treated in Chaps. 2 and 3, the writings this chapter explores constitute an eclectic mix of anti-Marxist, non-Marxist, and neo-Marxist work. Yet the reason for selecting such an apparent mishmash of diverse theories for inclusion in a single chapter is their shared orientation to and in time. That is, in Chap. 3, Baran and Sweezy Galbraith and Mandel (at least in his *Late Capitalism*) sought to theorize capitalist change in the post–World War II (WWII) era largely through the 1960s with Mandel, alone, offering some insight into transformations of the 1970s and beyond. In this chapter, while work by sociologist cum futurist Daniel Bell extrapolates from trends just discernible from the early 1970s, Scott Lash and John Urry, as well as Michael Piore and Charles Sabel, theorize those tendencies as they play out in the 1980s. If Mandel had left us with observations over the potential impact upon his late capitalism of new elements such as a burgeoning service sector or on what the looming information and computer technology (ICT) revolution portended for the reorganization of work, Bell, Lash and Urry, and Piore and Sabel in their own way argue such transmutations usher in a new stage of capitalism in its own right. What is most significant about the three sets of perspectives on this purported new

R. Westra, *Periodizing Capitalism and Capitalist Extinction*, Palgrave Insights into Apocalypse Economics, https://doi.org/10.1007/978-3-030-14390-9_4

stage is that they maintain contra Marxist theory, that capitalist change now vitiates whatever claims had been made of a capitalist telos of "socialization" leading to a post-capitalist future. This fact, it is further argued by these authors, has far-reaching methodological implications for social science to the detriment of Marxist theory.

While the foregoing exude a sense of finality in their periodizing of capitalism, in that sense exhibiting their orientation *in* time, the writings of Giovanni Arrighi and Carlota Perez indirectly offer a corrective of sorts. Their efforts situate the kinds of transformations captured by Bell, Lash and Urry, and Piore and Sabel within an overarching and ongoing historical dynamic of capitalist change which, in the case of Arrighi, does not necessarily forestall the transformatory collective action that socialists believed the persistence of capitalism would ultimately foment. Though Arrighi's grasp of what constitutes a post-capitalist society is significantly different from Marxist views on this.

Importantly, this chapter provides an opportunity to critically examine and contrast two very different epistemological strategies in the periodization of capitalism and theorization of capitalist change. These strategies were initially summarized in general terms in the introductory chapter of this book. The contrast pits the strategy of stylized facts deployed by Bell, Lash and Urry, and Piore and Sabel against the reliance upon a constant or prime mover of capitalism in the hands of Arrighi and Perez. Our discussion here provides a bridge to the periodizing of capitalism in the hands of a very different family of theory elaborated in Chaps. 5 and 6.

Post-Industrial Society

In his book, *The Coming of Post-Industrial Society*, Daniel Bell begins with a clear epistemological proviso. This being how his work seeks to build a "conceptual schema" which "selects particular attributes from a complex reality" to then impose a "logical order" upon the "factual order". While conceptual schemas offer space to draw in multiple perspectives in understanding social change, they simultaneously enable concentration upon key principles, according to Bell. Bell maintains that as Marx developed conceptual schemas around principles of property relations in feudalism, capitalism, and socialism, so he operates with conceptual schemas of pre-industrial, industrial, and post-industrial society built around the principle of production with its attendant form of knowledge. Bell then proceeds to the analytical claim that society is divisible in three parts: its "social structure", political system, and culture. Each is founded on an "axial principle" with "economizing" being that currently in force for the social structure. It is then the transformation of the social structure in terms of the economy and occupational system with attendant change in the relation between science and technology that Bell's concept of post-industrial society treats (Bell 1973: 11–3).

As Bell puts it:

> The concept of a post-industrial society is not a picture of a complete social order; it is an attempt to describe and explain an axial change in the social structure (defined as the economy, the technology and the stratification system) of the society. But such a change implies no specific determinism between a "base" and a "superstructure"; on the contrary, the initiative in organizing a society these days comes largely from the political system. (Bell 1973: 119)

Bell then sets out five dimensions of post-industrial society. For the economic sector, change entails a shift from production of goods to the service sector. In terms of occupations, professional and technical classes attain preeminence over workers and capitalists. Its "axial principle" is "the centrality of theoretical knowledge as the source of innovation and policy formulation". The orientation of post-industrial society to the future is its need to "control" technology and "technological assessment". And post-industrial society requires a transformation of decision-making with creation of a new "intellectual technology" (Bell 1973: 14).

Echoing, in some ways, Galbraith's conceptualization of a "techno-structure", Bell places great emphasis upon the centrality of technology in shaping the trajectories of society. Marx's vision of communism, according to Bell, was wrongly proffered as a post-capitalist "stage" of history when, in reality, it captured but "one of a number of alternative modes of industrialization" (Bell 1973: 74). And, both Soviet society and advanced capitalist economies find themselves confronted by the rapid pace of change brought about by new technologies in the technical requisites of decision-making. According to Bell, a revolution in knowledge and its systematizing in science, R&D, and so forth are currently in process (as of the 1970s). This, in turn, serves to elevate a "technical intelligentsia" of scientists and economists to the forefront of public policymaking (Bell 1973: 43).

If Mandel, in Chap. 3, picked up on the increased role of services in his theorizing of late capitalism, explaining the tendency in terms of capitalist commodification encroaching on new spheres, Bell views the burgeoning of the service sector as an economic turning point. Advanced capitalist economies plus the Soviet Union, Bell states, were material "goods-producing societies". In their historical progression, "raw muscle" power is increasingly replaced by energy as the coupling of energy and technology reduces workers to cogs between machines until even those functions are replaced. Bell opines: "The manual and unskilled working class is shrinking in the society, while at the other end of the continuum the class of knowledge workers is becoming predominant" (Bell 1973: 343). Post-industrial society, on the other hand, is based upon services. Rather than raw muscle power and energy, it is information that counts most. Its "central person", Bell maintains, is the "professional", the education and training of which supply the skills demanded in post-industrial society. The service "skills" Bell is talking about include finance, insurance, and real estate or the FIRE sector in current parlance as well as the personal services discussed by Mandel (Bell 1973: 126–7).

Bell, interestingly, describes post-industrial society as a "communal" society. By this he means a society where social or public decisions grow in importance over that of the aggregation of individual decisions at the center of mainstream economics. Thus, in economic terms, Bell sees a communal society as one where "public mechanisms" displace the market as an allocator of goods, while "public choice" determines distribution of services. Through public mechanisms, then, the rights of community members—children, students, minorities, and so on—are expanded as the recognition of externalities (effects of private actions on parties other than those involved in a transaction) compels social regulation and public redress. In Bell's post-industrial world, it is no longer "quantities" of goods which define success but quality of life (Bell 1973: 128, 159).

Finally, a coalescing of the above changes portends a new architecture of rule and government for Bell. Decisions over production and business generally, Bell claims, are shifting to government which, in turn, avails itself of the new "technical intelligentsia". These are "the scientists, the mathematicians, the economists, and the engineers of the new intellectual technology" (Bell 1973: 344). While Bell recognizes that the process here envisioned will take on various forms in different contexts, a "central fact is clear: The autonomy of the economic order (and the power of the men who run it) is coming to an end, and new…control systems are emerging. In sum, the control of society is no longer primarily economic but political" (Bell 1973: 373).

Disorganized Capitalism

The End of Organized Capitalism by Lash and Urry sets its goal as correcting deficiencies in theretofore periodizations of capitalism. It points to the periodizations emanating from the non-Marxist literature a-la-Bell: pre-industrial, industrial, and post-industrial society; and to periodizations in Marxist writings: competitive capitalism, monopoly capitalism, and late capitalism. Lash and Urry claim periodizations from both currents miscarry in several ways: first, they are economically reductionist; second, analysis of capitalist relations in each nation-state as a whole tends to be occluded; third, there is scant attention paid to class struggle and class politics or the "spatial scale" of such politics within nation-states; and fourth, the role of the state in "structuring" politics and society is not considered. Instead Lash and Urry advance an alternative periodization, suggesting that each "Western" advanced capitalist society has proceeded historically through three stages: liberal, organized, and disorganized capitalism (Lash and Urry 1987: 301–2).

What centrally interests Lash and Urry is updating Marx's arguments building on tendencies he discerned from the latter decades of the nineteenth century toward the "socializing" or organizing of capitalism which purportedly constitutes an antechamber for socialism. If Bell's theorizing of post-industrial society holds implicit the view that society somehow is becoming post-capitalist though not socialist, Lash and Urry defend the position that capitalist social relations persist along with capitalist class dominance notwithstanding the expansion of professional and service cohorts. Yet Lash and Urry agree with elements of the post-industrial thesis that reductionist claims over working-class politics and class struggle for socialism have been outpaced by historical change. Succinctly put, "transformations of time and space, of economy and culture…disrupt and dislocate patterns that Marx and Engels so brilliantly foresaw" (Lash and Urry 1987: 2).

Much of what Lash and Urry assemble as an "ideal type" or stylized facts of organized capitalism recapitulates what we have summarized in writings of Hilferding and Bukharin and on the theory of monopoly capitalism. After all, both Marx and Hilferding initially developed the notion of the organizing of capitalism. And both Marx and Hilferding distinguish those facets of capitalism in its "organizing" mode from what Lash and Urry dub "liberal" capitalism, particularly in terms of capitalist macrodynamics in altered modalities of the business cycle and technological change. Organized capitalism for Lash and Urry, however, is a state of the world economic and political order predicated upon centralized power, business gigantism, and governing of markets. Lash and Urry do not offer constituents of an ideal type for what they dub liberal capitalism. Where Lash and Urry develop the concept of organized capitalism with implications for their treatment of so-called disorganized capitalism revolves around questions of culture and ideology and the effects of these on politics. As Lash and Urry admit, in that endeavor they develop lines of argument advanced by Bell in a succession of books (Bell 1960, 1976). We will return to this.

Lash and Urry's argument for the making of disorganized capitalism is constructed upon a mountain of comparative national empirical data on the US, UK, Germany, France, and Sweden. A breakdown of their key stylized facts for disorganized capitalism is as follows: (1) the deregulation of national markets (both financial and production) and deconcentration of capitalist business in the face of an expanding global market resulting in deindustrialization of capitalist heartlands; (2) enlargement of the "white collar" service class of professionals leading to growth of "new social movements" which disrupt class politics and undermine class-based political parties; (3) numerical diminution of the manufacturing working class and subsequent decline of union membership; (4) spread of capitalist manufacturing to the third world which expands the number of states implicated in capitalist production in turn accelerating the hollowing out of manufacturing industry as labor intensive processes are transferred abroad; (5) a new spatial division of labor which deconcentrates industry globally, regionally, and even locally in the shrinking of "industrial cities"; and (6) advent of so-called time-space distanciation creating a "global village" of mass disseminated cultural tropes and a "postmodern" condition of fragmented narratives and identities which undermine working-class solidarity (Lash and Urry 1987: 5–7).

As with Bell's post-industrial society, Lash and Urry's claims for disorganized capitalism carry significant ramifications for the Marxism. Pulling together threads of discussion from earlier chapters there are two dimensions of "socialized" or organized capitalism which factor into the case for socialism as the telos of history. From the perspective of historical materialism outlined in the famous "Preface", the "ripeness" of socialism purportedly stems from the concentration of capital in ever larger units and the centralization of capital in hands of fewer big capitalist magnates. It is this process, as alluded to at multiple places above, which Marxists believe offered the foundation for "rational" socialist planning in future societies. On the other hand, the same tendencies toward concentration and centralization of capital supposedly fostered the collectivization and ultimate cooperation of the working class in the giant, integrated units of capital engendering, in turn, a working-class consciousness of shared laboring identity and struggle. Subsequent ups and downs of capitalist economies in which workers bore the brunt in terms of impoverishment and regular bouts of unemployment were expected to catalyze organized working-class opposition to capitalism. Whether this proceeded to manifest itself in mass electoral class politics and ascendance of socialist parties or in direct working-class action is, of course, a matter still debated. But that the periodizing of capitalism was bound to this telos, such that stages of capitalism served as signposts on the road to socialism, largely shaped thinking about capitalist change in Marxism.

While conservative critics of Left politics such as Bell might be summarily dismissed on ideological grounds, Lash and Urry's analysis springs from the Marxist fold making its challenge to periodizations of capitalism rooted in a telos of socialism all the more significant. They recognize the way the Marxist narrative or "metanarrative" (in the language of postmodernism) of historical materialism held Marxists worldwide in thrall. However, even without buying into much of the arcane claims of postmodern culture discussed by Lash and Urry (1987: 298–9), the disintegration of mass production structures and dispersal of ever more components of manufacturing processes across the globe have proved more devastating than they perceived for cultivating working-class solidarity: Though this is not because a postmodern cultural trope of "classless" society pervading current thinking as Lash and Urry suggest (1987: 14–5).

In fact, working-class organizations in advanced economies share some of the responsibility for what ultimately befell workers everywhere. After all, the "organized" capitalism of production-centered economies which reached its apogee in advanced economies of the post-WWII period did so within an international context of "economic nationalist" capitalist development projects. As Lash and Urry recognize (1987: 203), the international political settlement of the Bretton Woods monetary system, which we advert to in Chap. 3, established a protective "cocoon" of sorts that provided space for war-torn advanced economies to rebuild. Its demise would carry repercussions for all world economies hoping to blaze similar development trails. As we also discuss briefly in relation to Mandel, the domestic dimension of this development model brought to bear the accouterment of the welfare state with its countercyclical macroeconomic policy apparatus of fortifying effective demand and guaranteeing of the social wage. Central to the "national" settlement were so-called tripartite "class accords" where both commanding heights corporations and the state welcomed labor union leaders to the policy table. However, the catch was that this welcome was accorded to the extent labor organizations concerned themselves with rising wages and benefit packages but muted radical political dissent and questioning of private property and capitalist relations of production.

This model was held out by development experts as the road to be traveled by the third world if it got with the "free world" capitalist program during the Cold War decades. As the possibilities for the third world to blaze such a trail appeared ever more remote year by year through the

1960s, a major group of such economies called for a "new international economic order" (NIEO). The NIEO demanded corporations make cutting-edge technologies available on favorable terms and revamp global terms of trade in ways amenable to raise prices for third-world commodities. Yet, as major advanced economies descended into a prolonged economic slowdown from the mid-1970s, they looked at the prospect of an NIEO where the third world received their support to become industrial competitors as anathema. However, if then still powerful labor unions in advanced economies had not traded political quiescence for increased consumption benefits and simultaneously defended their own positions against capital even as they lent their strong support to the NIEO, the potential existed for deepening social democracy and strengthening "organized" class-based political action in ways that challenged capitalism notwithstanding the technological transformations Bell and Lash and Urry allude to (Westra 2018: 69–72).

Though Lash and Urry criticize other approaches to periodizing capitalism for, among other things, ignoring class struggle, they also occlude crucial elements of it from their analysis. On the one hand, and we will develop this analysis further in examining the periodization of capitalism of the Uno approach in Chap. 6, is that superimposed upon the extensive organizing or even socializing of capitalism in the post-WWII era was a capitalist class ideology of anti-communism (Westra 2012: 46–7). Thus, arguably, the basis for the emergent so-called fragmented, "schizophrenic," or "decentered" identities of postmodernism, remarked on by Lash and Urry, has very "modern" roots. These reside in the way actions of mass working-class collectivities were paradoxically oriented away from genuinely collective interests toward consumption benefits which, in the world of the frenzied "sales effort" of mass advertising for superficially differentiated products noted in the 1960s by Baran and Sweezy, reduced ostensibly collective interests to the satisfying of supposedly unique, individual consumption choices on the market.

On the other hand, there is something that had concerned the theorists of imperialism; this is the role advanced economies have played ensuring the world beyond "Western" advanced society is rendered pliable to advanced economy capitalist interests. Notions of post-industrial society are alluring, but it is necessarily on the back of some able-bodied people somewhere in the world that the burden of manual work falls to this day. Led by US capital, there was a concerted counterattack against whatever aspirations third-world economies held for their development along lines of prosperous "material goods producing societies", to paraphrase Bell. As just noted, neither mass labor collectivities nor social democratic parties representing them in advanced economies defended the third world against this. What the counterattack yielded, as will be treated in later chapters, is neither a post-industrial nor disorganized world economy. Rather it established a radical reconfiguring of work and industry globally with a degree of "organization" in terms of transportation, logistics, communication, and connectivity unimaginable before the ICT revolution revved up. It is thus in China, today, for example, that we find the "industrial cities" that Lash and Urry set out in their stylized facts as vanishing. However, Lash and Urry, given the orientation in time of their writing, had no inkling of the global carnage that working people everywhere would face through the late 1980s and into the neoliberal globalization decades. A question we will thus address below is whether working with the theorizing of a constant of capitalism rather than "stylizing" facts from the empirical environment is productive of knowledge that is not as time bound.

Flexible Specialization

Writing of MIT theorists Michael Piore and Charles Sabel offers the final perspective treated in this chapter on changes taking place in major economies by the early 1980s. At the core of their framework of periodizing capitalism is the view that economic development across the ages flows from human "experiments" in organizing production around existing technologies. Seismic breakthroughs in utilizing labor and technologies which drive periods of economic development, Piore and Sabel dub "industrial divides". As they put it,

> ...in the world of possible worlds, relatively short periods of technological diversification punctuate longer periods of uniformity. The technical knowledge that is accumulated during interludes of diversity creates the

> possibility of divergent breakthroughs…At these technological divides, the different political circumstances in different regional or national economies moves technology down correspondingly different paths. But competition eliminates some of these technological experiments, and bends others toward a common goal. (Piore and Sabel 1984: 39)

Such periods, in the schema of Piore and Sabel, then, are characterized by episodes of expansion followed by crises that reveal the limitations of the existing technological development path. Subsequent crises, according to them, assume two major forms: In the first, a mismatch arises between the institutional ensembles within which technological development takes place. It is reflected in dysfunctional arrangements of income or matching of supply and demand, along with power distributions, within the ambit of a given technological system. The second form of crisis stems from the technology *itself* in terms of available choices given the configuring of markets and political circumstances. Resolution of this latter form of crisis is what ushers in a new industrial divide (Piore and Sabel 1984: 4–5).

According to Piore and Sabel, the first industrial divide emerged in the nineteenth century. Their claim is that in Western Europe production was characterized by "flexible" craft systems where "general purpose" machinery managed by a skilled laboring cohort produced changing assortments of goods for shifting markets. This craft-based production was marked by cooperative relations and sharing of costs between business owners and workers, and was embedded in an ensemble of institutions which provided protection for vulnerable members of the communities where such production was based. The first industrial divide originated in the US and the UK, Piore and Sabel argue. In contrast to "flexible" craft systems, it was characterized by "rigid" mass production technologies (we will have the chance to more deeply explore the question of "rigidity" of mass production technologies in Chap. 5, particularly as it allegedly factors into crisis of the system). Piore and Sabel weave a historical narrative through national strategies of industrialization to explain the great global joust which pitted the two "technological paradigms" against each other until, by the early twentieth century, the paradigm of mass production won out in both the realm of production and that of ideas (Piore and Sabel 1984: 44–7). Craft production, however, according to Piore and Sabel, was never completely vanquished. It persisted within select industries and industrial districts in various advanced economies in the interstices of the mass production dominated world (Piore and Sabel 1984: 28–31).

Piore and Sabel then elaborate upon how the successful paradigmatic evolution of mass production technologies engendered appropriate microeconomic and macroeconomic institutional fixes. On the microeconomic side, they argue, the pricing system of economic coordination or "regulation", as captured by neoclassical economic theory, proved increasingly deficient in the face of the growing size of mass production business units with attendant high fixed investment costs and their subsequent need to integrate and coordinate specialized manufacturing processes. It is this deficiency which called forth the business form of the modern corporation. Treading similar conceptual and empirical terrain as Baran and Sweezy along with Mandel, Piore, and Sabel argue the large corporate form of enterprise was then confronted by two major challenges relating to the stabilizing or "regulating" of the market. On the one hand, given price competition was anathema for all the reasons we have outlined, the corporation necessarily sought to govern its market. It accomplished this, as others above also suggest, through strategies such as market segmentation, product differentiation, and the empowerment of corporate management by ensuring corporate self-financing.

However, as the efficiencies and economies of scale in mass production progressed, the corporation turned to macroeconomic stabilization as the necessary complement to its efforts at microeconomic coordination. In line with Baran and Sweezy, Piore and Sabel offer an underconsumption argument (1984: 73ff). Mass production, they aver, rendered investment increasingly sensitive to the level of consumer demand so as to maximize capacity utilization of expensive technologies. Following WWII, what businesses had in many cases struggled against—mass labor unions—were not only welcomed to the policy table (though unions were safely depoliticized, as just discussed), but corporations, beginning in the auto sector, acceded to union demands for wage raises tethered both to productivity and cost of living increases. Accompanying corporate wage settlements as a macroeconomic regulatory device was a ratcheting up of government spending. This, as several authors in the present book concur, entails rampant military spending in the US along with social wages in the US and elsewhere. The third macroeconomic stabilizer, according to Piore and Sabel, is government fiscal and monetary countercyclical demand management which brings in direct government investment as needed.

If Mandel, in Chap. 3, had explained the economic crisis which unraveled late capitalism or, in the framework of Piore and Sabel, the first industrial divide largely in terms of endogenous travails of capital accumulation and class struggle, Piore and Sabel view exogenous factors exacerbated by policy fumbles as the catalyst. These include swelling US and global social unrest at the end of the 1960s, the US abdication of Bretton Woods, oil shocks, and the US dollar interest rate hike from 1980. Nevertheless, Piore and Sabel, as per their underconsumption perspective on capitalist crises, also cite as a major contributing facet of the crisis the endogenous advent of market saturation of core consumer goods, such as the automobile, aggravated by international competition from Europe and newly industrializing countries (Piore and Sabel 1984: 184–9). This fosters a mismatch within the mass production paradigm in major economies between supply and consumer demand that investment and innovation are so closely attuned to.

Corporations responded to the confluence of the foregoing travails in part by seeking out alternative dynamic sectors replacing automobiles and, most importantly, by internationalizing production. Initial benefits of this strategy, particularly as capital embarked to low-wage third-world economies which could be "played off" against each other in a race to the bottom, were the advantage to be gained from global economies of scale. But its lacuna, according to Piore and Sabel, was the absence of a global macroeconomic regulatory mechanism which could bring global demand into sync with expanding global supply of mass-produced commodities (Piore and Sabel 1984: 200–2).

For Piore and Sabel, the world economy is therefore brought to a crossroads. Resolution of the economic crisis in terms of Piore and Sabel's first crises scenario of fashioning an institutional response within the ambit of a given technological system, in this case the mass production paradigm, would necessitate a "multinational Keynesianism". Its central pillars, according to Piore and Sabel, are the increased integration of advanced economies into regional blocs tied to trade with groups of developing economies; emplacement of an institutional mechanism to coordinate private corporate decision-making to ensure fruition of long-term investment without fear of fomenting industrial overcapacity; and to rationalize capacity among advanced and newly industrializing economies. Bringing such a macroeconomic regulatory edifice into existence could be undertaken within the context of existing multilateral institutions of the Bretton Woods monetary system, including the International Monetary Fund and General Agreement on Tariffs and Trade. Piore and Sabel, though, do recognize here that the acceding by the US to this settlement, given its global power and influence, would be a vital ingredient for the success of the proposal (Piore and Sabel 1984: 252–7).

As touched on in discussion above on Lash and Urry, however, the US had no intention of ever countenancing what a "multinational Keynesianism" entailed for its position in the global driver seat established following WWII. As argued at length elsewhere (Westra 2012: 74ff), the closing of the gold window to effectively end the Bretton Woods monetary system was in fact the first step in the US gambit to change its orientation to the world as its economy faltered. Both Lash and Urry and Piore and Sabel bemoan earlier periodizing of capitalism for occluding discussion of divergent national strategies, but both are guilty of failing to probe deeply into US national intentions. The time for a global social democratic solution to international travails of the world economy which enlisted the supranational institutions created as part of the Bretton Woods system was the 1970s. But it necessarily demanded replacement of the US dollar as hub currency with an alternate monetary unit along the lines of other options which were floated at the time of the original Bretton Woods conference. Yet limitations placed upon US policy autonomy and global adventurism in line with such limitations adopting a neutral international hub currency unit placed on all other states is something the US capitalist class and its political mouthpieces find abhorrent. Thus, the interest rate hike of the early 1980s by then US Federal Reserve Chair Paul Volcker was not simply a policy fumble as is implicit in Piore and Sabel's analysis. It was the final move in a global gambit to dollarize the world economy in a way the ensured US preeminence even as its trade, budget, and capital account fell into mounting deficit. Whatever pretentions third-world countries had to construct full-scale integrated industrial economies as set out in the call for an NIEO were also dashed by that interest rate hike. And it simultaneously accelerated the disintegration of US manufacturing industry which led to evisceration of the US mass commodified labor force.

For Piore and Sabel, the other potential resolution to the economic crisis of the mass production paradigm follows from apprehension of the crisis as one stemming from the technology itself. Hence, this mandates humanity making an alternative technological choice that crystallizes a new industrial divide. Piore and Sabel call this future new industrial divide "flexible specialization". Thematic in their writing is that craft production, upon which flexible specialization is purportedly based, has always persisted as the "mirror image" of mass production, as we note. Its "flexibility", they claim, derives from the adaptability and changeability of its material accouterment. Computer technology is offered as an example given the way the same hardware can be repurposed by reprogramming or replacement of the software. It is akin, so Piore and Sabel assert, to Marx's "artisan tool" (1984: 261). Flexible specialization as it exists in sectors of the fashion industry, metalworking, carpentry, and so forth is attuned to "small batch" production and tacit skills of its workers. It also cultivates artisanal "community" culture as envisaged by the likes of Pierre-Joseph Proudhon who opposed the alleged Promethean proclivities of Marx.

Piore and Sabel make clear that microeconomic stabilization or regulation of spreading flexible specialization as the route to renewed national and global prosperity does not involve the simple resurrection of neoclassical pricing which the evolution of mass production suppressed. Rather, microeconomic stabilizing of craft production requires removing from competition wages and conditions of work to foster interdependence among producers. Further, in the nature of work itself, the sundering of conception and execution characteristic of mass production must be reversed. With short production runs, workers will require broad sets of skills enabling on the spot problem solving and the ability to collaborate and multitask. Finally, if it fell to the corporation in mass production to organize flows of materials and financing, in flexible specialization this task is undertaken by the community and its institutions. Piore and Sabel opine,

> ...flexible specialization works by violating one of the assumptions of classical political economy: that the economy is separate from society...By contrast, in flexible specialization it is hard to tell where society (in the form of family and school ties or community celebrations of ethnic and political identity) ends, and where economic organization begins. (Piore and Sabel 1984: 275)

Finally, according to Piore and Sabel, flexible specialization largely obviates the need for macroeconomic regulation and will thrive in an open global economy where stabilization mechanisms are internal to each of the units and their communities. Though it is never made clear why separate communities or the flexibly specialized production units within them will suddenly reverse the ethos of winner take all business competition existing among nation-states in the global economy today.

The Poverty of Bypassing Theory

Several important issues have been raised by these three perspectives on periodizing the economic transmutations of the 1970s and early 1980s. Questions of the *causa causante* of the crisis which brought down the post-WWII golden age of prosperity will be deferred once again to the following chapter. There we will have the advantage of being able to compare arguments of all the main schools. Those on the ICT revolution and its ultimate impact on changes in the geospatial reorganizing of work, disarticulating or "disorganizing" capitalist production, and hypertrophying of the service sector to realize a "post-industrial" society form part of the subject matter of Chap. 8. Though Perez, mentioned later in the chapter, also delves into this. Contrasting of mass production and flexible production as industrial paradigms, however, is undertaken in the context of debate over so-called *fordism* and post-*fordism* in Chap. 5. And issues of ideology of consumption reflected in postmodernism are dealt with in Chap. 6. Debate across many of the approaches to periodizing capitalism that are covered in this book accrues around similar questions as we will discover in our treatment of all the major schools. Therefore, issues are repeatedly dealt with from different angles at multiple points in the present work.

Yet, at this juncture, a pivotal elision in the foregoing three perspectives must be singled out. This is the problematizing of capitalism. As we have noted several times above, periodizing of capitalism has drawn upon two broad research strategies. One is the systematizing of empirical history in stylized facts or ideal types. The other is the setting out of a constant or prime mover as a firm constitutive marker of capitalism as a society and driver of capitalist change. However, we have already shown how the second strategy miscarries in our critical review of theories of imperialism and monopoly or late capitalism when understanding historical transformation is circumscribed by the view of it being impelled by an inexorable telos. But the case of systematizing empirical history of capitalism in lieu of clarity over an invariable substance which marks an economy out as capitalist notwithstanding its transformations involves another problem.

Marx, in our Chap. 2 discussion of his own formative periodizing of capitalism and Kautsky's interpreting of that, had crucially explained that in every form of existing human society one kind of production or economic principle predominates and determines the scope of operation of others. His point here was that, for example, while market activities are found in antiquity, their influence is delimited by the paramount constellation of socioeconomic relations of mastership and slavery through which the main basic staple goods for material reproduction were furnished and distributed. In the feudal era markets did exist. However, their operations were also exogenous to core principles of material reproduction in that historical society. As we argued in Chap. 2, both from the perspective of Marx's economic theory and that of the historical record, an economy based solely upon privately owned craft goods production with dedicated skilled labor, whether conceived in terms of Kautsky's so-called petty commodity society or Piore and Sabel's "flexible specialization" society of craft "traders" would be an economy of shortage unless superimposed upon by either interpersonal redistributive relations of production or the impersonal principle of the capitalist market.

Piore and Sabel's reference to Proudhon as a critic of Marx's purported views on organized production and the state passes over discussion of Marx's trenchant critique of Proudhon and other "utopian socialists" who sketched out plans for future non-capitalist societies; but did so without clearly understanding how the then only gestating capitalist economy worked. Because, to paraphrase Marx from Chap. 1, "bourgeois society is the most highly developed and most highly differentiated historical organization of production" such that "comprehension of its categories and organization" enable us "to gain insight into the organization and the conditions of production" in precapitalist historical societies, it was from his in-depth study of capitalism that Marx arrived at the conclusion that private labor is never directly social. The sort of economy Piore and Sabel allude to, where "economic organization" is placed in the hands of communities rather than markets (Bell's "communal society"), to ensure supply of basic goods adequately meets social demand would, if realized historically, be a form of socialism!

Piore and Sabel confuse the issue through their thematic contrasting of two technological systems. But, identifying technological structures does not tell us anything about the kind of historical economy with its signal economic principle that these are embedded in. To the extent the economy is capitalist, production is necessarily oriented to profit making or value augmentation in Marx's specialized economic lexicon. Here, it is the self-regulating market that constitutes the central operating system. While we will elaborate upon the theoretical dimensions of this issue in Chap. 6, there is a general recognition among the approaches to periodizing capitalism dealt with hitherto, from theorists of imperialism to Piore and Sabel, that markets operate in close to "pure" form only in the twentieth century. Lash and Urry recount the historical steps in the organizing of capitalism. But, unlike theorists of imperialism, they do not attempt to explain why capitalist economies, which paradigmatically begin life with the subsumption of material life by systems of self-regulating markets, ultimately evolve political and economic structures that increasingly govern markets. Piore and Sabel, similarly, offer a historical account of the ascendency of what they refer to as mass production. Yet their work omits discussion of the capitalist specific compulsions for this. In fact as we will see, while production of standardized material goods is a general characteristic of capitalism from the industrial revolution in mid-nineteenth-century Britain, the mass production of consumer durables is a historically particular feature of post-WWII capitalism and it is to that period of capitalism that the crisis elements they cite apply. If material goods producing (to paraphrase Bell) or production-centered economies constitute hallmarks of the capitalist historical era, then questions must be asked as to whether a post-industrial or "disorganized" flexibly specialized craft production–based society can be a capitalist economy? And if not, from the perspective of human material reproduction, how are we to understand the disintegration of production-centered societies which follows in the wake of the crisis of post-WWII mass production economy?

Flexibility as the Goal of Capital in Systemic Cycles of Accumulation

Writings of Giovanni Arrighi controvert the methodological focus of the foregoing three perspectives in the chapter. Its claim is that grasping the "world dynamic" of capitalism entails much more than the adding up of "national dynamics". Rather, it can be understood only when we take "as unit of analysis, not individual states but the *system* of states in which world capitalism is embedded" (Arrighi and Moore 2001: 56). For Arrighi those tendencies captured by Lash and Urry toward "disorganizing" of capitalism or by Piore and Sabel in the direction of a renewed "flexible specialization" akin to craft economies of old are hardly novel. They only appear so in absence of a long-run perspective on world capitalist transformation.

Arrighi believes he discovers in Marx's theory, via French historian Fernand Braudel's copious historical studies of capitalism in its *longue durée*, the specific capitalist constant upon which capitalist change in its historical vicissitudes may be explained. It resides, according to him, in a restating of Marx's general formula of capital we touch on in Chap. 2—M-C-M′. In Arrighi's restatement, M or money "capital" represents "liquidity, flexibility, freedom of choice". C or commodity capital "means capital invested in a particular input-output combination in view of a profit". As such, it involves "concreteness, rigidity, and a narrowing down of [choice]". M′ "means expanded liquidity, flexibility, and freedom of choice". Importantly, according to Arrighi, investment in the "input-output combinations" is not an end in itself. It is but a means for capital to secure "even greater flexibility and freedom of choice at some future point". Arrighi opines, capitalists "prefer" liquidity (Arrighi 1995: 4–5).

Inhering in M-C-M′, according to Arrighi, is the key to deciphering recurring patterns of capitalist historical development as a "world system". Marking this pattern are phases of material expansion reflected in MC periods of capital accumulation and CM′ phases of financial rebirth and expansion. In the phase of material expansion, money "sets in motion" a growing mass of commodities including commodified labor power. On the other hand, in the phase of financial expansion a burgeoning mass of money capital "sets itself free" from the commodity form with accumulation proceeding through "financial deals". In Arrighi's terms, combination of the two phases in M-C-M′ constitutes a "full systemic cycle of accumulation". The import for Marxism of analysis of systemic cycles of accumulation, Arrighi asserts, is that contrary to Kondratiev's long wave theory his cycles "are inherently capitalist phenomena". But, while systemic cycles of accumulation establish the "continuity" of "world-scale" historical trajectories of capital accumulation, they also show how phases of discontinuous change alternate with these. That is, MC entails a process of continuous change where the world economy grows "along a single developmental path". CM′ phases of financial expansion involve a process of discontinuous change where growth along the previous path reaches its limit. The world economy then experiences a "shift" with "radical restructurings and reorganizations" setting it onto another path (Arrighi 1995: 8–9).

There is, however, one further ingredient Arrighi adds to his framework for periodizing capitalism. This is the fact that paralleling the emergence of a world economic "system" through interlinking of markets has been a "world system of processes of state formation". Superimposed upon the "market" dynamic of the world system in his framework, Arrighi sets competition among states. Such competition has largely been over coveting available "mobile" financial "capital". Phases of accord and then discord to remake the world economy occur under the auspices of agencies of particular states. Therefore, in his words, "inter-state competition has been a critical component of each and every phase of financial expansion and a major factor in the formation of those blocs…that have led the capitalist world-economy through its successive phases of material expansion" (Arrighi 1995: 9ff).

To lend further specificity to his understanding of competitive leadership within the international state system Arrighi introduces the notion of "world hegemony" to capture the specific nature of power exercised by leading states. Hegemony conceptualizes power in the Gramscian sense, Arrighi explains, where leadership combines "consent and coercion", such that leadership never implies direct "dominance". Instead, while states pursue power, hegemonies are consolidated when that pursuit is combined with the role leading states play in remaking the world system on an expanding foundation. Arrighi opines: "recurrent fundamental restructurings" of the world system have been "led and governed by successive hegemonic states" (Arrighi 1995: 30–1).

With this framework in place Arrighi periodizes capitalism in terms of "long centuries" and systemic cycles of accumulation which evidence hegemonies of particular states. The combining of the political and institutional hegemony with the specific nature of the expansion of the world system in its thrall Arrighi dubs a "regime of accumulation". Four successive regimes, according to him, have shaped the world system from 1400 to 2000. These are as follows: the Genoese systemic cycle of accumulation across the long fifteenth and sixteenth century; the Dutch systemic cycle of the long seventeenth century; the British systemic cycle over the long nineteenth century; and US hegemony in the systemic cycle of the long twentieth century (Arrighi and Moore 2001: 64ff).

What Arrighi displays with his schema is that from the 1980s where the CM′ phase of the US hegemonic regime of accumulation allegedly begins, there unfolds all those tendencies of disorganizing production and emergence of flexible business models that in the hands of Lash and Urry or Piore and Sabel are grasped as elements of a new stage of capitalism. In Arrighi's narrative on historical change and the emergence of new hegemonies, each historical regime of accumulation is presaged by a phase of CM′ commencing with the historical prelude to Genoese hegemony. It resides precisely in the advantage gained by managing financial accumulation, Arrighi argues, that states other than preeminent military powers as was the case with Genoa accede to hegemonic status in the phase of MC in a systemic cycle of accumulation. Looking forward to the future from his vantage point in the 1990s Arrighi notes how in the CM′ phase of the long twentieth century, with the US economy succumbing to various crisis maladies, it is East Asian economies led by Japan supplanting the US as global creditors. And Japan, in particular, which is the progenitor of new flexible forms of internationalization of production. Arrighi queries whether this heralds a shift of financial power from the West to the East to uniquely gestate a new hegemonic regime of accumulation there (Arrighi and Moore 2001: 74; Arrighi 1995: 341ff). Though, for Arrighi, the possibility exists for either a "post-capitalism" or demise of the "world system" and descent of humanity into chaos (Arrighi 1995: 356).

While Arrighi serves up an interesting and provocative periodization of capitalism which appears to contain a sought-after capital-centric constant that he then combines with a state system dynamic to explain transmutations of capitalism across capitalist history it misfires in several directions.

First, Marx, in *Capital*, discusses two antediluvian forms of capital as an inroad into exposing the differentia specifica of capitalism as a historical society. M-M′ for Marx constitutes the formula for usurers or "loan capital". In precapitalist society, where social wealth is bound firmly to land and the useful goods materialized from it by the labor and production process, and "exchange" of goods predicated upon their useful, qualitative properties, the notion of money "breeding" with interest payment viewed as satanic (Westra 2016: 65–8). That is, the social use of money was to be "spent" in the concrete act of "exchange" the end purpose of which is consumption. Both the hoarding of money and its use for other than its spending in exchange for the purpose of consumption held no socially redeeming value in precapitalist society. M-M′ as usury or "loan capital" is indifferent to what the money is used for as it is indifferent to how loan plus interest is repaid. The latter may be set in a fashion that destroys the debtor (as in Shakespeare's *Merchant of Venice*) or forces them to strive for others ruination. Usury, hence, corrupted princes and kings, forcing them to bleed their populations. It fueled cycles of indebtedness through the wars it compelled. Lending to merchants spread the commercial economy that increasingly mediated between producers and consumers to impel populations into debt which dispossessed them of their land. In short, while M-M′ corroded staid precapitalist social relations it carried no principle for ensuring the material reproduction of any kind of human society.

M-C-M′, first introduced by Marx as the formula for merchant capital, expands M-M′, as "money making money", to capture the merchant practice of using money to "buy cheap and sell dear". As touched on in our discussion of Marx's periodizing of capitalism in terms of formal and real subsumption of the labor and production process, merchant capital initially intervenes in the reproduction of precapitalist economic life. It also helps, alongside "loan capital", to corrode staid precapitalist social relations, particularly in the competition it offers to urban guilds with their restrictions on craft quality and expectation of a "just price" (Westra 2016: 59–60). But ultimately, merchant capital in its fundamental practice of buying and selling, brings to bear no substantive principle to guarantee the economic reproduction of a human society. Like money, wages, profits, money lending, trading, and so forth, merchant activities constitute forms of capital which have existed benignly across varying modes of historical economy with their discrete principles of material reproduction. It is only when human labor power is commodified, that the "C" in M-C-M′ reflects the capitalist subsumption of human material life and Arrighi's investment "in a particular input-output combination in view of a profit" representative of capitalism.

Put differently, neither M-M′ as usurers "capital" nor M-C-M′ as merchant capital, generate new wealth. They rather shift it from hand to hand. As discussed at points above, the historical specificity of capitalism is its wielding of the labor and production process of society for the purpose of augmenting abstract mercantile wealth. Mercantile wealth or value is augmented when the wellspring of all social wealth, human labor power, is converted into a commodity, "freed" from its access to means of livelihood except via wages paid by capital. Through the production process itself, as explained in our critique of Baran and Sweezy's notion of "economic surplus", surplus labor is performed by commodified labor power which is then materialized as surplus value. M-C-M′, as capital in the form of money invested in means of production and labor power which produces commodities that are then sold at profit with the latter reinvested, constitutes the capitalist circuit of value augmentation as a whole. Capital does not exist as any part separately. When profits in the form of money are not invested in the capitalist production-centered circuit but withdrawn to be deposited in the banking system or used for any "financial" purpose, they no longer function as capital.

What Arrighi has allowed himself to be unwittingly duped by is the "fetishism" of capital residing in the category of interest. We see in Chap. 2 consideration of Hilferding, depreciation and contingency funds as well as monies set aside for shorter periods according to investment horizons of business operations are withdrawn from the capitalist production-centered, profit-making circuit and deposited in the banking system. Such monies rendered idle in this fashion cease to be capital. In the hands of banks, this idle money becomes a commodity or "asset" the "ownership" or custody of which entitles banks to the income stream of interest. Banks, in capitalist economies assume and transform the activity of money lending. Banks, of course, unlike usurers, do not lend their own money. They perform a capitalist social, socially redeeming role in capitalist economies in their lending to other profit-making businesses for determinate purposes and lending to commercial capital, which takes over the function of merchant buying and selling for industrial capital to rapidly return profits to it for reinvestment in its production-centered circuit.

In bourgeois calculus, the borrowing of money on the part of both industrial and commercial capital leads to a peculiar "reconceptualizing of itself" by capital. As profits return to commercial capital, accounting divides them between return on investment minus interest paid and "entrepreneurial profit" seemingly gained from savvy marketing. Similarly, industrial capital divides its profits onto return on investment minus interest paid plus entrepreneurial "reward" for wily business acumen. In both cases, all vestiges of surplus value and exploitation of commodified labor power in the production process subsumed by capital are effaced. As with antediluvian M-M′, whether monies are lent to merchants to realize M-C-M′, or not, capital by virtue of its status as "property" appears to automatically attract an income stream for its owner to "breed" (Westra

2016: 105–7). In this sense, the "dream" of capital is always to "free" itself from its metabolic dependence upon value augmentation through the labor and production process of society. Yet, while Arrighi strives to consummate the "dream" of capital with his schema of "freedom and choice" enjoyed by capital in "liquid" M form, the purported preference of capitalists, without investment in the value augmenting labor and production process of capital, Arrighi's world may be left with "capitalists" but no capitalism as Chap. 8 demonstrates.

Second, with a crafty sleight of hand, Arrighi divides M-C and C-M′ into two historical phases. Yet in specifically capitalist economies, even within short business cycle oscillations, "C" in Arrighi's second phase is a "C′" with commodities produced in the capitalist labor and production process, M-C, now "pregnant" with yet unrealized surplus value. However, what Marx makes crisply clear in *Capital*, C-M is always the salto mortale or "deadly leap" for the commodity for which there is never a guarantee that it will be sold thus frustrating in perpetuity its realization as M′ (Marx 1977: 200–1). Therefore, if capital is ever to enjoy such "freedom" or "choice" Arrighi ascribes to it, capital must first complete its production centered circuit of M-C-M′. Yet, in the context of decennial business cycles theorized by Marx, the failure of C-M′ confirms for capital that crisis has befallen it and it best scurry to salvage what liquidity it can before the capitalist credit and financial system seizes up. It is precisely to explain the crises factors which disrupt M-C-M′ over longer phases of accumulation and how, if at all, capital potentially emerges from such cataclysms that brought into being the periodization of capitalism research agenda in the first place. With his self-styled division of M-C and C-M′ as two phases of a "long century", Arrighi leaves the very page on capitalist crises, which always originate in limits reached by capitalist production, largely blank. In some way, Arrighi attempts to overcome this gap with his notion of a recurrent "signal crisis" marking a "turning point" in every systemic cycle where financial debts build up around the existing hegemonic state prompting it to shift to speculative endeavors globally in ways that open the door to hegemonic contenders coveting the spigot of international liquidity (Arrighi and Moore 2001: 64–6). However, this still leaves the question unanswered of what foments the demise of the production system in a dominant capital accumulator which turns its economy toward global arbitrage in the first place. Arrighi cannot answer that question because his analysis, except for a few gratuitous references to Marx, elides what Marx grasped as distinctive about capitalism as a means of reproducing human material life and the role commercial banking plays in this. In fact, the very roots of what is elaborated in Chap. 7 as financialization grow here not at the "level" of a so-called world system.

Third, notwithstanding his claim to provide a capital-centric explanation for systemic cycles of accumulation, Arrighi in fact displaces questions of the catalyst of their continuities and discontinuities onto struggles among states during his purported financial expansions. This is the unfortunate case because Arrighi is trying to squeeze the transmutation of capitalism into a prefab world system box that has little to do with capitalism. Arrighi's problem, of course, as with most world system theorists, begins with reliance upon Braudel who conflates capitalism with the existence of interlinked "market" trade networks (Arrighi 1995: 10–2). Arrighi follows Braudel here to claim this market-based "world system" originates in the fifteenth century. However, as we have repeatedly emphasized at varying points in this book, there is nothing very systemic or capitalist market oriented about world trade until the late eighteenth and early nineteenth century which in Arrighi's schema is where the British systemic cycle purportedly gestates. But Arrighi ignores Marx's elaboration upon subsumption of the labor and production process of society by capital and the centrality of the commodification of labor power to this by blithely dismissing it as "Marx's focus on the domestic aspects of capital accumulation" (Arrighi 1995: 13). However, the question is not "domestic" versus "international" but the differentia specifica of capitalism as a historical society. And the mere appearance in a society of trade, market exchanges, money, and so forth is no signpost of that.

Long Waves and Techno-Economic Paradigms

If Ernest Mandel had drawn meticulously upon Marx in integrating Kondratiev's theory of economic long waves into Marxian analysis of capitalist trajectories of profit-making booms and crises, the tradition

Carlota Perez works in combines long wave theory and work by Joseph Schumpeter. Schumpeter is an ardent follower of neoclassical economics equilibrium theory. However, while he was satisfied with neoclassical explanations for periods of economic stability, Schumpeter sought to extend the theory to account for times of economic dynamism and major transformation. Though the "monadic" behavior of agents in neoclassical models accounted for economic reproduction, Schumpeter believed dynamic economic changes followed upon the anomalous behavior of the heroic, "innovating entrepreneur" in search of "profit". Entrepreneurial action on this ground spurs technological and business innovation in a competitive process Schumpeter famously dubs "creative destruction". Such seismic change, according to Schumpeter, is not limited to economic factors but demands broader "psychological" and "social" shifts within society at large. Finally, Schumpeter brings issues of finance and credit into his framework of "creative destruction" given the dependence of entrepreneurs on access to available funds in society (Screpanti and Zamagni 2005: 262–6).

Carlota Perez weaves all the foregoing ingredients of Schumpeter's grasp of capitalist transmutation into her theorizing of "technological revolutions" as ushering in new historical periods of capitalist development. As she puts it, "the sequence *technological revolution-financial bubble-collapse-golden age-political unrest* recurs about every half century and is based on causal mechanisms that are in the nature of capitalism" (Perez 2002: 5). This sequence is thus shaped by the facts of technological change occurring in "clusters" which radically modernize the production system; the separation of financial and production capital with their diverging profit pursuits; and, the resistance of the "socio-institutional" framework to techno-economic change (Perez 2002: 6). Thus, for Perez, if the notion of a technological revolution captures the reshaping of economic eras by adoption of the full gamut of "clustering" innovations, that of "technological paradigm" refers to the condition by which the technological and institutional changes become the best practice, commonplace order of a given period of capitalism.

From the close of the eighteenth century to the opening decade of the twenty-first century, five successive technological revolutions have occurred; each commencing in a core state or group of states. First is the industrial revolution in Britain from 1771; second is the "age of steam and railways" originating in Britain and then spreading to continental Europe from 1829; the third is the "age of steel, electricity and heavy engineering" sparked in the US and Germany in 1875; fourth comes the "age of automobiles and mass production" emerging in the US and transferring to Germany and Europe from 1908; and fifth is the "age of information and telecommunication" spreading from the US to Europe and then Asia from 1971 (Perez 2002: 11). Perez emphasizes that there always exists a time lag between the technological revolution in terms of the discovery of the innovative technologies and their widespread adoption. Initially, Perez maintains, technological innovations are received as a "shock". Thus, diffusing them both encounters resistance within the economy and society as it also carries initial discombobulating impacts for economies. Ultimately, technological revolutions elicit not only a revamping of production structures but "a transformation of the institutions of governance, of society and even of ideologies and culture, so deep that one can speak about the construction of successive and different *modes of growth* in the history of capitalism" (Perez 2002: 24–5).

Four phases in the "surges" of economic development manifested in installment of a new techno-economic paradigm are set out by Perez (2002: 47ff). The "irruption" phase follows the "big bang" where key innovations are apprehended. Irruption and its potential wealth effects are what attract finance in the guise of "venture capital" to the propagation of the innovations. Financial exuberance is stimulated by the fact that the "big bang" occurs at a juncture where the older technological paradigm with its leading firms languishes at the tail of its "maturity" phase (Perez 2002: 33). It is the incidence of the "frenzy" phase, which follows the "irruption" where finance, with its speculative goals for the "idle money" in its hands, becomes increasingly intoxicated with wealth potential vastly outstripping the actual instatement of the new technological paradigm. This foments the bubble and crash as finance "decouples" from productive capital. Re-coupling financial and productive capital and controlling the ethos of speculative gain engendered during the frenzy entails a process of "adaptive regulation" (Perez 2002: 97, 99ff). Yet, given the fact that not all frenzied financial gamesmanship is displaced from the productive economy, a "synergy" phase takes root which establishes the flourishing of the new techno-economic paradigm. Finally, with the setting in of the maturity phase, finance capital, according to Perez is once again impelled on its hunt for yield, encouraged by the emergence of a potential new revolutionary technological cluster of innovation on the horizon. Thus, both the "frenzy" phase and that of "maturity" hold out the greatest possibilities for the business internationalization and opportunities for developing economies.

However, it is the "maturity" phase of the wave where the crises tendencies of the technological paradigm play out. In her own words (Perez 2002: 30):

> [T]he core industries that had served as engines of growth begin to encounter market saturation and decreasing returns to technological innovation. This announces the approaching maturity of those industries and the gradual exhaustion of the dynamism of that whole [technological] revolution…
>
> When the potential of a paradigm begins to reach limits…productivity, growth and profits are seriously threatened.

Perez thus summarizes her perspective: "Technology is the fuel of the capitalist engine" (2002: 155). Yet it resides in the way technological innovations are absorbed and assimilated which compels the raft of socioeconomic changes which manifest themselves in consolidation of a new technological paradigm. All the changes toward "decentralized" networks, market segmentation, economies of "scope" and specialization, and so on touched on by Lash and Urry and Piore and Sabel reflect, in the account of Perez, the settling in of the new "microelectronic paradigm" of the late twentieth and early twenty-first century. Perez opines, "'flexibility' is probably the most important key-word within the new paradigm" (Perez 1985: 449). What Perez then refers to as the "installation period" for technological paradigms, which encompass the "irruption" and "frenzy" phases, had neared completion for the "microelectronic paradigm" as of the 2002 point of completing her writing in her major book. For the US economy, this historical juncture is the immediate aftermath of the bursting of the tech bubble marked by the NASDAQ collapse.

Thus, the question Perez leaves open is that of what she refers to as the current "turning point". This is where the decoupling of financial capital and productive capital comes to an end and recoupling in the technological "deployment period", which combines the phases of "synergy" and "maturity", commence. Looking forward, Perez points to resolution of three "tensions": the bringing of paper values in line with real wealth; realizing the global and domestic expansionary potential of the new ICT products and services; and reducing political and social pressures of the vast wealth asymmetries, particularly between advanced economies and the third world, that the microelectronic paradigm accelerated (Perez 2002: 168–70). From our present historical vantage point, it is only the second tension that in some way has been addressed though likely not as Perez envisioned.

Brief Retrospective on Theory and the Close of the Twentieth Century

Theories of imperialism, monopoly capitalism and to some extent, late capitalism, which claimed to be extrapolating "laws" or "logic" of capital into the future according to the view of socialism as the historical telos all appear to have run aground on the empirical conditions of economic change occurring from the 1980s. If, in fact, Marx's theorizing of capitalism in its most substantive sense is tied to the consummating of this telos as per readings of historical materialism qua Marxism as a master theory of historical directionality, the empirical challenges to Marxism posed by capitalist change as theorized by Bell, Lash and Urry, and Piore and Sabel would be devastating.

We will return to questions of the apprehension of Marx's theorizing of capitalism in later chapters. Here our concern is with the readings of empirical trends themselves. Approaches based upon the epistemological strategy of stylizing facts seemed attractive for their ability to free "facts" from the perceived deterministic framework of Marxism. Yet they miscarry in eliding the problematization of capitalism. Categories such as organizing and disorganizing, or rigid and flexible, for example, refer to the nature or arrangements between parts of a structure. They say little about the specific mode of economy as the deep undergirding of that structure. Thus, many of the fundamental questions that humanity should be asking about economic trends burgeoning from the demise of the golden age, which we ultimately find euphemized as "globalization" or referred to in terms of neoliberal policy, were never asked. And, for example, questions such as whether such a thing as a post-industrial society can even be a capitalist society are still not being asked.

On the other hand, the non-Marxist (and this includes Arrighi) refashioning of long wave theory into systemic cycles of accumulation or technological revolutions and paradigms fares no better than both the above genres of theory. Of the two, Perez's account of technological revolutions is more sophisticated as it brings into the analysis important dimensions of broad-based institutional, cultural, and ideological change which accompanies a revamping of the production structure within societies, according to her. In this way, Perez may be upheld as extending the frontier of long wave theory to its limit as an "endogenous" theory of periodizing capitalism (Went 2014: 414). Arrighi, however, who for some oblique reason felt the need to refer to Marx's general formula for capital, yet offers everything but a Marxian analysis, ends up producing a convoluted explanation for seismic economic change across the modern era. Though Arrighi and Perez may be seen as attempting to address issues of technological and organizational transformations highlighted by Lash and Urry or Piore and Sabel, their theories are saddled with the same sort of determinism the latter sought to escape from.

In many ways, the Marxist variant of determinism is preferable to that of Arrighi's systemic cycles and Perez's technological revolutions because it held to the important notion of Marx that capitalism is a historically delimited society. Its problem is that, in closely following Marx's approach to human history in toto set forth in the pithy theory of historical materialism, the delimitation argued for is drawn from Marx's very general schema of the course of human history rather than from Marx's specific elaboration upon the contradictions of capitalism. And this has fossilized Marxist thought on periodizing capitalism in the belief that whatever the economic changes wracking societies what remains must still be a form of capitalism until socialist revolution ends the march of capital in history. But in Arrighi's systemic cycles and Perez's adaptation of long wave theory there is scant attention paid to whether capitalism as a historical mode of economy is amenable to further transformation. Arrighi's systemic cycles and Perez's long waves of technological paradigms proceed with a determinate automaticity notwithstanding their "radical restructurings" or "turning points" which purportedly punctuate their long periods. And the emergence of a successor cycle or paradigm is assumed to be essentially a fait accompli.

References

Arrighi, G. 1995. *The Long Twentieth Century*. London: Verso.

Arrighi, G., and J. Moore. 2001. Capitalist Development in World Historical Perspective. In *Phases of Capitalist Development: Booms, Crises and Globalizations*, ed. R. Albritton, M. Itoh, R. Westra, and A. Zuege. Basingstoke: Palgrave Macmillan.

Bell, D. 1960. *The End of Ideology: On the Exhaustion of Political Ideas in the Fifties*. Glencoe, IL: Free Press of Glencoe.

———. 1973. *The Coming of Post-Industrial Society*. New York: Basic Books.

———. 1976. *The Cultural Contradictions of Capitalism*. New York: Basic Books.

Lash, S., and J. Urry. 1987. *The End of Organized Capitalism*. Cambridge: Polity Press.

Marx, K. 1977. *Capital Volume I*. New York: Vintage Books.

Perez, C. 1985. Microelectronics, Long Waves and World Structural Change: New Perspectives for Developing Countries. *World Development* 13 (3): 441–463.

———. 2002. *Technological Revolutions and Financial Capital: The Dynamics of Bubbles and Golden Ages*. Cheltenham, UK: Edward Elgar.

Piore, M., and C. Sabel. 1984. *The Second Industrial Divide: Possibilities for Prosperity*. New York: Basic Books.

Screpanti, E., and S. Zamagni. 2005. *An Outline of the History of Economic Thought*. Oxford: Oxford University Press.

Went, R. 2014. Capitalism and Stages of Accumulation. In *The Enigma of Globalization*, Chapter 5. London: Routledge. Reprinted in McDonough, T., D. Kotz, and M. Reich. *Social Structure of Accumulation Theory*. Vol. I. Northampton: Edward Elgar.

Westra, R. 2012. *The Evil Axis of Finance: The US-Japan-China Stranglehold on the Global Future*. Atlanta, GA: Clarity Press.

———. 2016. *Unleashing Usury: How Finance Opened the Door to Capitalism Then Swallowed It Whole*. Atlanta, GA: Clarity Press.

———. 2018. *Socialism in the Twenty-First Century*. Hauppauge, NY: Nova Science Publishers.

5

Regulation School, Social Structures of Accumulation, and Intermediate Theory

To recapitulate, periodizing of capitalism from theories of imperialism forward has appeared in two overarching forms. One, largely of Marxist persuasion, has tethered its periodizing of capitalism to a constant or prime economic mover which drives capitalist change toward building the foundations for socialism. Non-Marxist variants of this genre of periodizing capitalism theorize a succession of capitalist stages according to operation of a constant but, while maintaining this succession unfolds with a determinate automaticity, do not make any teleological claims with regard to a socialist future. The second approach to periodizing capitalism is predicated upon the systematizing of empirical history in "ideal types, or stylized facts. Such stylizing and ideal-typical analysis purportedly offers a "flexible" method to grapple with nationally diverse and flexible forms of production and economic change generally which advocates of this perspective on capitalist change argue best fit the new economic realities of the 1980s onward, in particular.

In this chapter, our analysis changes course to treat two innovative theoretical traditions on periodizing capitalism. These approaches to periodizing capitalism deal, in many ways, with empirics already covered. But they do this through a very different theoretical lens which brings to

R. Westra, *Periodizing Capitalism and Capitalist Extinction*, Palgrave Insights into Apocalypse Economics, https://doi.org/10.1007/978-3-030-14390-9_5

bear new conceptual infrastructures and epistemological provisos. To some extent, these epistemological provisos attempt to combine insights and research potentialities of both of the foregoing separate strategies of producing knowledge of capitalist change and stages of capitalism marking capitalist history. And, as will be discussed later, this theoretical tendency brings Marxist thought back to focus upon questions of the ontology of capital and capitalism which had concerned Marx.

Finally, given the emphasis the theories treated in this chapter place upon the "embedding" of capitalist markets in institutional support structures to "regulate" capital accumulation over relatively longer periods of stable economic expansion, the theorists find themselves at pains to set out those factors that bring such stability to an end. Thus, this chapter offers an optimal point in the book to deal with a long-running debate over what caused the post–World War II (WWII) period of organized, welfare state capitalism, to fall into crisis. Answers to this question enable us to draw out the most fundamental insights emanating from Marx's theory of capitalist crises elaborated in *Capital*. And, as well, to build on work commenced in theories of imperialism to distinguish between crisis within the context of the "pure" operation of markets and business cycle oscillations Marx deals with in his basic theory of capital, and those crises which punctuate intervals between seismic transmutations of capitalism and emergence of successive stages of accumulation.

From "Homogenous" Value to Intensive Accumulation

In his groundbreaking introduction to French *Regulation School* (RS) periodizing of capitalism, Michel Aglietta opens discussion by highlighting the tensions inhering in development of Marx's theorizing of capitalism between delineating laws of capitalism and the actual historical course of capitalist development.[1] Aglietta is unequivocal:

> The way forward…means a collective effort to develop a theory of…capitalism which isolates the conditions, rhythms and forms of its social transformations…The study…cannot be the investigation of abstract economic

> laws. It is the study of the transformation of [capitalist] social relations as it creates new forms that are both economic and non-economic, that are organized in structures and themselves reproduce a determinate structure, the mode of production...In this perspective, history is no longer an alibi designed to justify certain abstract schemas. (Aglietta 1987: 15–6)

Further, while it will be shown that Aglietta does not necessarily deny the workings of basic, "abstract" tendencies of accumulation, the class struggles capitalism generates carry no teleological impetus toward a socialist historical outcome in his view. Such struggles, he declares, are "beyond any 'law'". And, as he explains, social science, in any case, is tasked with theorizing that which is "already initiated"; history, however, "*is initiatory*" (Aglietta 1987: 67–8).

With this said, Aglietta turns in his attention to the central question he believes Marxist theory must address. Because, as he declares (1987: 47), "not all economic problems can be treated at the same level of abstraction", the specific "level" of abstraction where theory strives to "identify stages in the development of capitalism and...interpret the structural crises of this mode of production" needs to be settled upon (Aglietta 1987: 17). Though he is not completely clear in his explanation, Aglietta sets out what he understands constitutes Marx's project in *Capital*. Aglietta does not use the term "pure" theory but, rather, alludes to the "space of measurement" in *Capital* "as the homogenous field of value" (Aglietta 1987: 53). He thus enters the thorny epistemological and ontological thicket here in noting that the possibility of abstraction in theory resides in the fact of the "process of homogenization", which Marx purportedly elaborates upon, existing in "reality" (Aglietta 1987: 38). Yet, Aglietta offers but a fuzzy claim for why this is the case, asserting that it derives from the process of exchange which renders the "quantities...measurable" (1987: 53). From there Aglietta incorporates what he had earlier set out axiomatically as the "invariant kernel" of capitalism—"the concept of *surplus-value*" (1987: 37)—which directs attention to the "fundamental relation" within the homogenizing space of value that "defines" capitalism, "the *wage relation*" (1987: 45).

For Aglietta, the operation of the wage relation effects the "division in the space of value" according to the degree of complexity of work that, in turn, involves questions of the technological composition of capital and the rate of surplus value. It is such determinations that constitute the basis of macroeconomics, according to Aglietta. And it is in specifying these determinations through which theory moves from the abstract to the concrete (Aglietta 1987: 46). The key determinations for Aglietta flow from the distinction between absolute and relative surplus value.

Text Box 5.1

Marx's basic theorizing of surplus value is as follows: Surplus value from which profit is derived reflects the augmentation of value in the capitalist production process. Its condition of possibility along with capitalism, for that matter, is the commodification of labor power as we discussed. Let us, for example, take a small capitalist textile business which invests $100 in machinery or means of production, $50 in raw materials, and $50 in wages for commodified labor power. If in 4 hours of working for the capitalist the worker can produce commodities equal in value to the $50 in wages which is the money measure of the laborers necessary labor then, supposing means of production are depreciated and raw materials exhausted in a day, factoring in the $150 of value these transfer to the product and the $50 worth of value added by the laborer as equivalent to his/her necessary labor, we end up with the $200 with which we began. In other words, following our assumption—labor power purchased in the market for its abstract quality of being amenable to indifferent application in producing any use value in demand, then set into motion by capital to produce one such good—*value* has been created but not *surplus value* or profit. For surplus value to be created, and the augmenting of value characteristic of the capitalist economy to be realized, workers must toil for more time than is simply required to produce the equivalent of their necessary labor. This is precisely what occurs in capitalist society where the capitalist owners of the social means of production set the time of the *working day*. So, in fact, with an 8-hour working day, where in 4 hours the worker produces $50 of value equivalent to his/her necessary labor, in 4 further hours of surplus labor, the worker produces $50 of surplus value or profit for the capitalist as $250 ultimately emerges, like magic, from the capitalist production process.

Aglietta builds upon Marx's distinction between absolute and relative surplus value in terms of the "extensity" and "intensity" of the labor and production process subsumed by capital. The magnitude of absolute surplus value depends upon the time the laborers work over and above the time required to produce the equivalent of their necessary labor, assuming that technology remains constant. Its extension, here, is possible only by increasing the surplus labor time worked. The magnitude of relative surplus value refers to the intensifying of work such that, if the technology is revolutionized increasing the productivity of labor, while the time of the working day is held constant or potentially diminished, a greater number of commodities will be produced in which value is materialized. It is the dynamic tendency of capital to "economize" on labor. Not, of course, for the flourishing of workers. But to reduce the proportion of the working day devoted to necessary labor which reproduces the workers livelihood in order to increase surplus labor time and surplus value produced for purposes of value augmentation.

According to Aglietta, if the foregoing constitutes the abstract principles of accumulation, in moving to analyze the process of economic change in the US economy, which is Aglietta's illustrative case for his periodizing of capitalism, it is necessary to introduce an "intermediate concept" or level of theory (Aglietta 1987: 68). The key intermediate range concept in his framework is that of the *regime of accumulation*. Boyer and Saillard succinctly explain (2002: 38): an accumulation regime captures "the social and economic patterns that enable accumulation to occur in the long term between two structural crises". It is this fundamental understanding of crises germinating in societies necessarily beset by conflicts which the very concept of "regulation", as per the name of this Marxist school, is elaborated to address. Lipietz puts the question thus: "how can conflictual social practices be reproduced with sufficient regularity to form...systems of relations" (Lipietz 2001: 215)? The answer resides with the *mode of regulation*. Modes of regulation, in turn, bring to bear ensembles of socially and historically constituted "institutional" or "structural forms", including the cardinal wage relation, type of economic competition, the monetary system, form of state, and position of the state within the international order; all which coalesce to "regulate" the economy of a given regime of accumulation (Lipietz 2001: 227).

It then falls to the third level of theory, as Boyer and Saillard summarize it, that a specific, really existing regime of accumulation in a given geospatial locale and historical period is treated (2002: 39). As Aglietta phrases it, with the "law of capital accumulation" formalized, and intermediate concepts set out to grasp the "overall perspective on its historical movement", investigation then turns to "stylized facts" building upon "results already produced by historians". This cements the "dialectical relationship between different aspects of scientific procedure...as a passage from the abstract to the concrete" (Aglietta 1987: 65–6).

Again, though Aglietta himself, along with other RS theorists, is not completely clear on what "level" the following conceptualization refers to (an issue we will return later), RS claims capital accumulation across capitalist history bifurcates into two regimes of accumulation. One is the "extensive regime of accumulation" revolving predominately around the extraction of absolute surplus value for capital accumulation. In it, as capital subsumes the labor and production process of society, it subjects it to a reorganization which may still preserve elements of traditional production processes. Two is the "intensive regime of accumulation". There, capital not only decisively transforms the labor and production process but fully integrates consumption of the working class into the process of value augmentation.

In Aglietta's case study, which arguably constitutes his attempt to bring to bear abstract and intermediate theory in order to animate his third level of theory, where historically constituted "structural forms" coalesce to "regulate" a particular economy in its specific regimes of accumulation, three "stages" of capitalist development are identified. First, the US economy in the period from 1846 to 1919 reflects the gestation and entrenchment of the "extensive" regime of accumulation with its "competitive" mode of regulation. It supposedly falls into crisis as productivity in Department I (Marx's production of the means of production) outpaces the absorptive capacity of Department II (production of the means of consumption), the latter saddled by constricted effective demand or underconsumption of workers. Underconsumption in this instance reflects the persistence of precapitalist patterns of consumption with the direct producing class mired in petty commodity production (Aglietta 1987: 78).

While the period 1919–1945 ushers in a new regime of intensive accumulation, it fails to develop its capitalist potential due to an innate crisis tendency. The specific trends of US capitalism which mark the initial shift toward intensive accumulation in this period are the rapid expansion of heavy industry in the closing decades of the nineteenth century and the rise of the new capitalist production sector of consumer durables in the aftermath of World War I (WWI). Its innate crisis malady stems from the tendency toward underconsumption of the working class. This time, however, underconsumption does not follow from precapitalist modalities of consumption as these are now supplanted by commodity relations. Rather, it arises in the continuance of competitive regulation that forestalls a general rise in wage levels which expansion of the production sector of consumer durables requires (Davis 2001: 91–103). Aglietta argues that for capital to emerge from the subsequent deep crisis it faced during the Great Depression of the 1930s, the consolidation of the intensive regime of accumulation demanded a reset of the wage relation by a new mode of regulation. In his own words, "when the accumulation of capital finds its content no longer simply in a transformation of the labour process, but above all in the transformation of the reproduction of labour power, a new stage in capitalist development has arrived" (Aglietta 1987: 80).

Before proceeding to what, in fact, is the signature RS analysis of the post-WWII era, it is important to note that Aglietta's underconsumption arguments have been subject to persuasive critique in their theoretical dimension similar to that leveled against Baran and Sweezy and, further, in their empirical dimension regarding the evolution of the US economy (Brenner and Glick 2001). What Brenner and Glick importantly add with regard to the theoretical critique is that notwithstanding the fact that stunted effective demand can potentially emerge as a problem for capital in specific contexts, the cause of the problem is not the disproportional growth of Department I. A welter of possibilities exists to counteract this including demand for new capital goods across the economy generated by technological change, the demand of labor forces employed in capital goods production of the new productive forces, rising wages in the technologically advanced sectors, and mounting unproductive expenditure. On the empirical front, Brenner and Glick show that wages in manufacturing actually rose in the years preceding the Great Depression (2001: 377, 379). In fact, one of the lessons learned by capital from the Depression period, which would influence its policies post-WWII, is that from 1929 to the onset of WWII, among large oligopolistic corporations in manufacturing profits were made even as real wages climbed 40 percent (Westra 2012: 35).

Fordism and Golden Age Capitalism

It is largely through its conceptualization of *fordism* as the signifier for the post-WWII intensive regime of accumulation that RS periodizing of capitalism is most widely known. Though major RS adherents claim theorizing *fordism* evolved as a "result" of their research program rather than as its central problematic (Boyer 2002: 2). The RS appellation for the post-WWII period of capitalism or regime of accumulation—*fordism*—is the institutional form around which the mode of regulation crystallizes. That is, within the constellation of institutional forms contributing to the relative cohesion or relatively long-term stability of capital accumulation characterizing a given regime the force of a particular institutional form, the wage relation, predominates and constitutes the anchor for other institutional or structural forms.

Fordism, in RS periodizing of post-WWII capitalism, encapsulates the following: First, semiautomatic assembly-line mass production of consumer durables and upstream components facilitated by the electronicizing of industry. Semiautomation and continuous flow of assembly-line work revamp the labor process, effectuating a greater intensity of work, fragmenting of tasks, and specialization of functions. Such reorganizing of the labor process, Aglietta argues, accompanies mechanization of industry and is first adopted by capital in its imbibing of "taylorist" time and motion strategies of work process control. Taylorism seeks to tether movement of workers to the machines and minimize the "gaps" in the working day so as to rivet worker activity to their immediate jobs (Aglietta 1987: 113–9). Second, *fordism* generates a "norm" of mass consumption in which worker demand for mass-produced goods emerges as integral to accumulation. This fosters the congruence between accumulation of Department I and Department II to increase the rate of surplus value across the economy even as the organic composition of capital rises in an intensive regime of accumulation (Aglietta 1987: 154).

Third, the norm of mass consumption induces a major shift in the social function of consumption which accords "status" to individuals with regard to the dimensions of their commodity ownership. For this, the key commodities, Aglietta explains, are the standardized family home as the privileged site of consumption and the automobile which underpins the separation of workplace and residence for the working class. Complementing these is the new range of consumer durable goods the consumption of which takes place in the private family home. Ongoing mass consumption is ensured by planned obsolescence. The latter acts to more rapidly devalorize capital while suppressing the contradictions of accumulation by supporting high rates of surplus value. This assemblage materializes the "golden age" of capital accumulation over the first two decades following WWII (Aglietta 1987: 158–61).

Fourth, galvanizing of the golden age economy demanded alleviating capitalist insecurity over employment and wages. One central element of this was the "socializing" of consumption through the varied accouterment of the social wage including insurances for unemployment, old age, health care, welfare, and so forth, superintended by the state. Another key element of the *fordist* wage relation is the instatement of collective bargaining between capital and labor. Unions acceded to intensity and control demands by capital, in return receiving large wage increases and benefit packages for member workers. The latter were indexed, ostensibly, to productivity gains and corporate profitability. Aglietta claims the role collective bargaining plays in fortifying the wage relation cements it as a "structural form" ensuring the cohesion of the *fordist* mode of regulation and intensive regime of accumulation (Aglietta 1987: 188–98).

Fifth, Aglietta traverses terrain we have covered in earlier chapters as he makes his case for *monopoly regulation* subduing price competition among the new, *fordist* commanding heights corporations. His intervention, quite simply, is that the surplus profit innovating capitalists garner in the upswing of the business cycle under competitive regulation persists as a condition of capitalism yet does so in an altered form. Rather than through the route of price competition, which guarantees innovating capitalists a greater market share, with monopoly regulation surplus profit accrues to innovators that improve their market shares by coveting increased demand at a given price (Aglietta 1987: 304–5).

Finally, according to RS, as the US where *fordism* initially gestates emerges as the globally hegemonic power in the post-WWII period, it remakes the international order of states in its likeness through promotion and fortifying of an international institutional edifice composed of the Bretton Woods monetary system, Marshall Plan to reconstruct war-torn foes and allies alike in Western Europe, the General Agreement on Tariffs and Trade, and two new supranational institutions—the International Monetary Fund and World Bank—to "regulate" global capitalism and foist *fordism* on the world. As RS maintains, it is ultimately the internalizing of the *fordist* regime of accumulation by Western Europe and Japan which constitutes the lynchpin for the post-WWII golden age of "free world" capitalist development (Glyn et al. 1990).

What brought this golden age to an end, according to RS analysis, is a crisis rooted at bottom in flagging productivity (Davis 2001: 114; Lipietz 2001: 233). The crisis, declares Aglietta, "is first of all a crisis of the mode of labour organization" (1987: 162). How it unfolds stems from what is described as the "rigidity" of *fordist* semiautomatic machine systems which encounter limits to the fragmenting of tasks and intensifying of labor upon which the high surplus value-high wage and benefit bargain is predicated. Because Department I, producing means of production, is no longer capable of delivering those technological transformations which mechanize the labor process so as to effectuate sufficient savings in labor time to offset increases in the organic composition of capital, disproportionality between the two Departments arises once again. From the juncture of the compromised wage relation, the crisis cascades down through the *fordist* mode of regulation as a whole undermining the norm of mass consumption and welfare state support for it leading to renewed class struggle (Aglietta 1987: 162–7; Glyn et al. 1990: 88–97). With *fordism* soon facing challenges across its heartlands, RS claims, "market" competition is revived in domestic spaces and the world economy at large as captured under the rubric "globalization". Finally, the process of financial centralization which Aglietta theorized in terms of "contractual savings" that channeled available funds in society toward productive investment and state provision of the social wage unravels (Aglietta 1987: 227ff). This, in turn, unleashes the trend toward international "financialization" which serves to perpetually undermine restorative efforts for the golden age (Lipietz 2001). We will return to questions of what follows *fordism* below.

Before critically assessing the adequacy of the RS conceptual framework and, as promised, explore the landscape of proposed causes of the post-WWII golden age period of capitalism degenerating into crisis, let us examine an approach to intermediate or mid-range theorizing of capitalist stages originated in the US at a similar temporal point as RS.

Theorizing Social Structures of Accumulation

Paralleling the work of RS, in terms of both its location in time and decrying of teleological extrapolations of historical outcomes from purported laws of capital accumulation is a theoretical tradition on periodizing capitalism spawned in the US: the Social Structures of Accumulation (SSA) school. In what constitutes the founding work of the school, David Gordon, Richard Edwards, and Michael Reich set the SSA position out forcefully (Gordon et al. 1982: 21–2):

> Marxists...generate mechanical theories of historical inevitability in which the emergence of a class-conscious proletariat always lurks around the next corner...Marxists have corrected this mechanical determinism by adding...a variety of complicating factors... [But] analysis of capitalist dynamics...remains indeterminate when it is pursued *only* on this abstract level... [M]any [Marxist] historians...have placed virtually singular emphasis on concrete and specific analysis... [Yet] these studies are usually quite divorced...from more abstract theoretical formulations; consequently, their broader meaning remains ambiguous...
>
> We propose that an intermediate level of analysis, focusing on the logic of long swings and stages of capitalism, is necessary for an understanding of capitalist development.

It is at the intermediate level of analysis that the concept of "social structure of accumulation" is deployed. SSA theory outlines what it conceives as the basic premises of capital accumulation: tendencies of capital to expand into remaining non-capitalist environments; enlargement of the magnitude of capital concentrated and centralized in fewer hands; proletarianization of populations to replenish the reserve army of capital; transformation of the labor process with technological development to intensify work; and the gestating and strengthening of working-class oppositional action. However, such abstract analysis of capitalism, SSA maintains, must be complemented by analysis of "long swings" and stages of capitalism the foundational building block of which is the social structure of accumulation. In a nutshell, the social structure of accumulation "consists of all the institutions that impinge upon the accumulation process". Among such institutions the financial system provisioning the economy with money and credit, the pattern of state involvement in the economy and the form class struggle assumes are paramount (Gordon et al. 1982: 23–5).

Recognizing the criticisms heaped upon long wave theory since its inception, the SSA perspective seeks to underscore their divergence from earlier renditions of the long wave approach. Where long wave theories largely misfire, according to Gordon, Edwards, and Reich, is over their mono-causal explanations. What is required is a multidimensional approach that takes account of both the basic process of capital accumulation and the "macrodynamics" of capitalism. It is precisely the macrodynamics that play out in the context of the institutional environment set by the social structure of accumulation. If its institutional matrix is stable, accumulation will proceed apace. When the institutional structure falters, accumulation slows and capitalism descends into crises. Economic crises, thus, punctuate intervals between remaking of the social structures of accumulation. This pattern produces "a succession of social structures of accumulation within the capitalist epoch". Such periods with their respective social structures of accumulation constitute stages of capitalism, according to SSA (Gordon et al. 1982: 31–2).

Where SSA theory most diverges from RS at the level of institutions is arguably over the emphasis it places upon international capital. Gordon et al. claim that because accumulation operates as a "world capitalist system…one should analyze its contradictions and social structures of accumulation on a world scale" (1982: 37). In the three stages SSA claims mark capitalism across its history, two stages are dominated by a hegemonic power which fostered a stable institutional environment for capital accumulation. The existing capitalist stages SSA propose are based on the historical course of US capitalism but are maintained as indicative of stages of capitalism experienced internationally, at least among advanced capitalist economies. The first social structure of accumulation holds from the 1840s to 1890. The second, dubbed the "monopoly SSA"

(McDonough 1994: 103ff), is consolidated between 1896 and 1904 and persists until WWII, though with its institutional structure unraveling prior to the Great Depression. Finally, the post-WWII social structure of accumulation, also referred to as the "postwar corporate system", comes into being following WWII and commences its degeneration in the late 1960s. Let us explore the social structure of accumulation of the postwar corporate system.

Drawing upon Bowles et al. (1984), three cardinal institutional structures of the post-WWII SSA or corporate system are as follows: First, *Pax Americana* is treated as the international institutional glue which bound US hegemony with the economic reconstruction of Western Europe and Japan along lines of the post-WWII form of accumulation. US global economic dominance is cemented by the Bretton Woods international monetary system based upon the US dollar and its convertibility to gold. Accompanying Bretton Woods are the global institutions headquartered in the US which supranationally superintend the world economy. Of course, for Bowles, Gordon, and Weisskopf, the role the US plays in remaking the world order in the aftermath of WWII is hardly an exercise in altruism. With the dollar as hub currency, the US created virtually ex nihilo demand for its manufactures which fostered domestic full capacity utilization among its commanding heights corporations as it gave access to global primary products at extremely favorable terms of trade. The US state supported the internationalization of US capital through changes in the US tax code allowing the US increasingly transnational corporations (TNCs) to postpone payment of US taxes if their earnings are held offshore and to credit foreign tax payments against domestic obligations. Internationalization of US capital also received strong support from the US state with its ratcheting up of military spending—a direct generator of effective demand—and through US military interventions to pacify recalcitrant third-world countries that sought to restrict US TNC access to their natural resources (Bowles et al. 1984: 65–9). In short, SSA analysis puts greater weight on the international dimension of the institutional support system for capital than RS.

The second institutional pillar of the post-WWII SSA is the *capital–labor accord*. SSA analysis here echoes RS emphasis upon the *modus vivendi* forged between capital and labor. We have also treated this issue in Chap. 4. At its core, the capital–labor sees organized labor trade political quiescence for a rising wage and benefit package where wage increases are ostensibly tied to productivity gains. Through the golden age era, into the late 1960s Bowles, Gordon, and Weisskopf show, productivity gains were shared as both job security for workers and industrial safety improved. Yet this "carrot" is paired with the "stick" of elevated levels of shop floor supervisory control and monitoring to ensure intensity of labor in production is maintained. This led to mounting TNC costs as a stratum of supervisory personnel grew in proportion to productive labor (Bowles et al. 1984: 70–4).

Third is the institutional structure of the *capital–citizen accord*. Again, SSA analysis deals with questions addressed in other periodizations of capitalism including: state macroeconomic countercyclical demand management to dampen negative, recessionary impacts of business cycle oscillations; social wage provisioning along with direct state infrastructure and military spending topped up by indirect business subsidies; and a commitment to "full employment" which engendered employment insurance programs to assist those rendered unemployed by remaining cyclical economic vagaries, though the unemployment was deemed in the golden age to always be a temporary phenomenon (Bowles et al. 1984: 75–9).

If RS had its attention riveted upon its signal structural form—the *fordist* wage relation—as the locus of stability and potential crisis progenitor, SSA views both the source of capitalist stability and the unraveling of that in the institutional cohesiveness of the SSA. As Terrance McDonough explains, unlike long wave theories that deduce successive stages of capitalism from this or that prime mover, the SSA views the emergence of a coherent institutional matrix for long-term capital accumulation as historically contingent. Thus, if successful capital accumulation in a given SSA depends upon a historically contingent ensemble of institutions, capitalist crises follow upon the disintegration of that specific SSAs institutional cohesiveness making causes of capitalist crisis a multidimensional, contingent event (McDonough 2014: 237–8).

In the case of the post-WWII SSA, while it is evident that declining productivity is an integral aspect of the breakdown of the SSA, theorists of the school set out four explanatory factors for its erosion. First is the point that the success the US achieved in rebuilding the post-WWII order, particularly its support for reconstructing Western Europe and Japan, was ironically greater than expected leading to heightened competition from their corporations in both international and the US domestic market. US decline in competitiveness was exacerbated by increased military spending into the 1960s. Bowles, Gordon, and Weisskopf suggest there was no way out as US international military adventures composed the flip side to the role of the dollar as hub currency given the need to keep markets open to US dollar economic penetration. Costs for this rose incessantly due to uppity third-world states and movements among them that wanted out of the system in lieu of a better deal (Bowles et al. 1990: 63–6). We dealt with this New International Economic Order challenge in Chap. 4.

Second, the capital–labor accord began to fray partly under the impact of its own exclusions argue Bowles, Gordon, and Weisskopf. Growing cohorts of laborers in jobs outside of the unionized sector were women and minorities. Their increasingly vociferous demands for equality of income and opportunity led to the US state expanding its welfare programs to accommodate the "new social movements" that were engendered. Yet the costs of such programs weighed heavily on government at a time of diminishing economic vibrancy. Further, union members themselves began to rebel against the heightened degree of supervisory control they had been saddled with as part of the high wage bargain and increasingly chose "exit" strategies to deal with it. Such rebellion against corporate control led to falling productivity even as real wages in the unionized sector remained high (Bowles et al. 1990: 67–71).

Third, rising social costs related to environmental concerns, worker safety, and so on concatenated with higher energy costs surrounding the belief that nuclear energy would provide a cheap, easily implementable alternative to petroleum. However, this proved a chimera as political opposition to it mounted. Finally, picking up the thread from the first institutional erosion, imports into the US of goods produced by major capitalist competitors fostered a new imperialist rivalry. In sum, according to SSA, the account of institutional erosion is corroborated by statistical analysis of falling profit rates among major corporations occurring at the point of the post-WWII institutional unraveling (Bowles et al. 1990: 72–9).

Anatomy of the Golden Age Crisis

The predominating mainstream "liberal" view as the golden age period proceeded, to paraphrase Galbraith from Chap. 3, "was danger of an apocalyptic crisis seems more remote". In a sense, if the cataclysm of the Great Depression is taken as the touchstone for what constitutes an "apocalyptic crisis", there is some truth to mainstream perceptions. After all, there is a unifying theme across all heterodox and Marxist economic perspectives on periodizing capitalism which has been explored heretofore, that the combined accouterment of the welfare state, armature of government macroeconomic management and governing of markets by commanding heights TNCs forfend such an occurrence. While RS adherents claim theorizing of *fordism* springs from a broader research program on the "regulating" of capitalism by a complementary ensemble of institutions, the historical evidence for this pattern of heavy capitalist reliance upon extra-market supports is a feature largely of the post-WWII period. Though theorists of imperialism recognized the organizing of capitalism by monopoly combines and finance capital in an effort to cushion business cycle downturns, as well as the role of the state in pursuing imperialist policies both domestically to protect home markets with tariff walls and internationally to covet "economic territory", they would never have envisioned the panoply of direct extra-market economic programming tools being applied in the golden age outside of socialist economies.

But there is also a broad concurrence among heterodox and Marxist economic theories that major economies, at varying temporal points, experienced economic slowdowns, and stagnation from the early 1970s. Not to be dismissive of the human carnage that resulted from economic stagnation in societies which had enjoyed relative prosperity and raised standards of living for almost three decades, there is, however, no single Great Depression–like event which signals the golden age demise. Yet, that the golden age did unmistakably meet its demise has led to contentious debates over what the *causa causante* of its crisis was.

Below we will summarily treat explanations of the crisis of the post-WWII economy offered by Mandel, Lash and Urry, Piore and Sabel, Perez, RS, and SSA. Let us begin with Lash and Urry. These authors diverge from the perspectives which follow in that they do not actually maintain the golden age came to an end due to a particular crisis condition. Rather, given their itemizing of key features of what they dub organized capitalism, the changes which strike major economies from the 1970s entail seismic shifts across the spectrum of economic and political institutions along with supporting cultural practices of "organization" to yield a new, disorganized socioeconomic reality. Internationalization of production and deregulation of finance importantly enter into the equation, though more as descriptions of the transmutations toward disorganization than as causal claims.

In the view of Piore and Sabel, what is referred to as the mass production paradigm meets its demise through impacts of both exogenous and endogenous factors. Exogenous, contingent occurrences include the US and global social tumult of the 1960s, the US exit from Bretton Woods, 1970s oil shocks, and, finally, the US unilateral dollar interest rate hike of 1980. Their endogenous explanation traverses familiar terrain of underconsumption theories which hold that the cause of capitalist crises is inadequate demand of the direct producers. This is particularly the case for the mass production economy of the post-WWII era where mass consumption of expensive consumer durables both stimulated investment in innovation as well as ensuring maximum capacity utilization in industries with high upfront investment costs.

Carlota Perez's theoretical edifice on successive long waves of capitalist development is predicated upon technological innovation as the lifeblood of capitalism. The combined impact of revolutionary innovations that appear in clusters has far-reaching effects across society, renovating not only the economy in a new technological paradigm but transforming its social and political system in their wake. As the production innovations and new products are generalized across businesses economy-wide competition intensifies, markets become saturated, returns on investment slow, thus curtailing business spending, leading to falling productivity which diminishes profits. It is worth noting that, as touched on above, it is in the "maturity" phase of the long wave where internationalization of production further generalizes the innovations and new product production process thus exacerbating competition and tendencies toward market saturation. For the golden age economy, the technological breakthroughs occur in the early twentieth century in Perez's formulation thus, by the 1960s, the automobile and oil technological paradigm is exhausted.

According to RS, as covered above, the crisis germinates in the wage relation of the *fordist* mode of labor organization where high rates of surplus value sufficient to offset increases in the organic composition of capital derived from intensified work rhythms according to continuous flow semiautomatic mass production technologies. When "rigid" technologies in semiautomatic mass production systems proved incapable of delivering further labor time savings productivity fell, undermining the high wage high mass consumption class compromise. Lipietz explains how the productivity slowdown unfolds from the end of the 1960s as "'technical' problems of the scientific organization of labor" metastasize (Lipietz 2001: 233–4).

Keeping in mind McDonough's intervention above on the multidimensional and contingent nature of crises in SSAs, Bowles et al. nevertheless maintain the cause of the golden age US "economic crisis was the slowdown in the rate of productivity growth…This not only explains why people worked more and earned less from the mid-1960s…it also helps explain the spiraling stagflation of the 1970s" (1990: 97). They argue, however, that fully understanding the slowdown requires a "social model of productivity" through which struggles of people against institutions of social control, as per the fraying of the capital–labor accord treated above, is factored into analysis (Bowles et al. 1990: 99). But, again, as per the disintegration of other elements in the post-WWII SSA discussed above, resistances to TNC power were bolstered by popular struggles to compel business to compensate for social costs (health, environmental, and so forth), as well as costs of corporate power brought to bear on countering such struggles and resistances (Bowles et al. 1990: 100ff).

We have left Mandel's explanation for the crisis of the post-WWII golden age to last on this list because, among the foregoing, Mandel uniquely does not theorize the *causa causante* of the crisis in terms of falling productivity, underconsumption, market saturation, and the like. Mandel constructs his argument around Marx's position of crisis breaking out at the peak of the prosperity phase of business cycles with the absorption of the industrial reserve army at a given level of technological development. Mandel further incorporates aspects of what Hilferding, in Chap. 2 had adduced: that is, as fixed capital becomes "heavier" and more costly, innovation in business cycle troughs, where capital economy-wide has been devalued, becomes anathema. Thus, as a result of market power, monopoly business, and later corporate capital dealt with by Mandel, innovate selectively and potentially more frequently at various points chosen by them throughout the business cycle. Under conditions of Mandel's third technological revolution, high TNC profitability derived from rapid technological innovation and depreciation of fixed capital across the business cycle. While this raised the organic composition of capital, high wages were nevertheless maintained given the offsetting factor to a rising organic composition of capital of high rates of exploitation and surplus value extraction. With the third technological revolution proceeding apace, its spread continuing to raise the organic composition of capital across industries, the industrial reserve armies within major capitalist economies of the US and Western Europe were simultaneously absorbed.

In this sense, Mandel deals with points made by both Aglietta on the necessity for high rates of surplus value to offset a rising organic composition of capital and Perez on the spread of technological revolutions. Yet, for Mandel, pace RS, technological innovation persists and, pace Perez, the lifeblood of capital is not technology, but profit. And it is precisely because of the absorption of the industrial reserve army that the possibility of increasing the rate of exploitation faced strong opposition therefore confronting capital with a falling rate of profit which signals an overaccumulation of capital in relation to the size of the working population.[2]

By way of summary critique, it is apropos to begin with an interrogation of the productivity slowdown hypothesis as it tends to be the most widely adopted view, though with diverging explanations given for it. Taking Aglietta and RS as representative of part of that position, there is what we may qualify as a "qualitative" argument against its case for the exhaustion of the *fordist* regime of accumulation. On this, Brenner and Glick query why tendencies toward industrialization and mechanization which, as Marx shows, from the dawn of the capitalist era had operated to deskill labor processes, fragment tasks, and intensify labor should, somehow in the mid-1960s, meet a limit that throws the capitalist economy into crisis. It is true, Brenner and Glick recognize, that the tethering of worker movements to the rhythms of electronic semiautomatic machine systems, which weakens the power of labor on the shop floor even as unions strengthened worker bargaining power over wages and benefits with capital, sharpens significantly in the golden age era. However, the sheer extent of mechanization has brought to bear often "incalculable" explosions in productivity through its incorporating of scientific and technical advances which continue to this day as in robotics, for example (Brenner and Glick 2001: 395–8). Indeed, in Mandel's discussion in Chap. 3, technological rents from such advances play a large part in the golden age profitability equation.

Yet, there is an even more robust "quantitative" argument against productivity slowdowns as the ultimate cause of the golden age malaise. It is certainly the case that assessing productivity of labor, and the technological transformation which increases it, in disaggregated fashion to gauge the effects of technical change in a single sector (Webber and Rigby 2001: 253–4), or in aggregate terms (Glyn 2001: 196–7), is a complicated endeavor. Nevertheless, what the best data compiled demonstrates is, first, besides the variance in productivity changes among major economies, productivity in manufacturing did not fall continuously or significantly prior to the 1970s which suggests contra RS that it was not the "rigidity" of mass production systems from which the productivity slowdown and golden age crisis originated (Glyn 2001: 198). Second, in US manufacturing, diminution of business profits commenced from the mid-1960s as economic growth began its downward trend from the 1970s, yet productivity growth continued into the later 1970s as the oil price hike compelled labor-saving technological development (Webber and Rigby 2001: 254–6).

Internationalization of production and finance is latched onto by Lash and Urry and Piore and Sabel as a central cause or condition of the economic shifts of the 1970s. Internationalized production purportedly exacerbates market saturation in relation to underconsumption propensities in the account of Piore and Sabel which then fosters the bifurcation of supply and demand in the mass production paradigm. In the scheme of Lash and Urry, both internationalized production and deregulation of finance set economies and polities off on the course of disorganization. Yet the evidence on international financial flows which supported the internationalization of production and contributed to the newly industrialized economy phenomenon in parts of Latin America and Northeast Asia, only ratchet up after major golden age economies experience an economic slowdown (Webber and Rigby 2001: 257–8).

Both SSA and Perez take their eye off capital. The former trains it on the institutional dimensions of stability. The latter trains it upon technology with instabilities of the broader institutional and sociocultural edifice following from exhaustion of technologies at the root of the long wave paradigm. Mandel, with eyes trained firmly upon capital, correctly grasps that it is, in fact, the falling rate of profit in major golden age economies, beginning in the US and Canada from the mid-1960s, that constitutes the *causa causante* of the golden age demise. Notwithstanding the fact that technological innovation and rapid depreciation of capital continued to raise the rate of exploitation, capital ultimately reached a barrier with its overaccumulation in relation to the size of the industrial reserve army which is absorbed in major economies. As succinctly summarized by Webber and Rigby (2001: 259–60):

> [I]n a largely closed economy the market into which firms could sell depended on wages paid to workers, and corporations at large had an incentive to raise wages…For both reasons, the real wage was bid up and the rate of capacity utilization approached its effective upper bound. Under these circumstances, demand and supply grow at the same pace and the rate of profit is subject to the classic constraints. Productivity change raises the capital-labour ratio. But if all the output that is produced is to be sold then the real wage must rise, for otherwise some capital has to shift into unproductive uses. In practice, both effects occurred: real wages continued to rise, limiting corporations' capacity to raise the rate of exploitation, and some capital became surplus. Therefore rates of profit began to fall under the impetus of increases in the technical [organic] composition of capital.

It falls to Chaps. 7 and 8 to explore the impact on the capitalism and the global economy of both the strategy of commanding heights TNCs of major and newly industrialized economies to raise rates of exploitation as well as the tendency for what Webber and Rigby refer to as "capital becoming surplus" accelerating from the 1980s. In some ways, the latter is exacerbated by the former strategies in the context of changes toward what Perez labels the microelectronic paradigm; the broader repercussions of the information and computer technology revolution, though, are not fully grasped by Perez given the temporality of her writing. Before we turn to these problems, however, some pressing theoretical loose ends need to be tied up.

Theorizing Capitalist Change Back to the Future

This chapter commenced with recognition of the theoretical impasse of periodizing capitalism where one set of theories endeavor to "chain link" explanations of capitalist change to a single "essence" or prime mover. While another genre of theory periodized capitalism according to systematizing of empirical history in stylized facts or ideal types. Where the promise of the former resides is in seeking to problematize a fundamental element of capitalism which helps identify the specifically capitalist nature of changes across the course of capitalist history notwithstanding the complex empirical nuances of different capitalist eras. What the latter offered, so its proponents maintain, is an escape from the constrictions of historical diversity and potential historical paths of change the theorizing of capitalist transformation in terms of a prime mover or constant of capitalism mandates. Marxist theories, in particular, are pegged in the latter genre as "totalizing", where all facets of change throughout society are placed analytically within the context of a "type" of capitalism (Hirst and Zeitlin 1991). Of course, if the theories examined in the first part of Chap. 4, including Bell, Lash and Urry, and Piore and Sabel are indicative of the opposing strategy of systematizing empirical history to periodize capitalism, then, as we emphasize, they miscarry by playing fast and loose with history to generate forecasts for the emergence of imaginary economies that would never have been viable in any case. And none of the models, as these are set out, including post-industrial society, disorganized capitalism, or flexible specialization, ultimately come to pass, according to their forecasts, in actual history.

It is to avoid apparent contradictions of the foregoing research strategies, and to generate concepts adequate to the task of capturing both the forms in which capitalism congeals in bouts of growth and stability over relatively long periods, as well as its processes of change, that the RS and SSA research agendas are crafted. RS and SSA concur over the issue of capitalism as a mode of production manifesting some basic, abstract trans-capitalist "laws". Where they part company with the preceding Marxist currents, which also hold that view, is over whether these can be directly applied to charting the historical course of capitalism. What is novel in the RS and SSA approach to periodizing capitalism is the claim that to apply basic or abstract theorizing of capital to history demands an intermediating step of mid-range theory. To be fair, Mandel, as discussed in Chap. 3, had called for theory to construct "intermediate links" between the abstract laws of capitalism and concrete historical elements but never developed this. For RS and SSA, part of the argument for intermediate or mid-range theory is that it brings to bear the institutional dimension of capitalist economies. Intermediate range theory, therefore, does not just seek to confront the problem of abstract economic laws winning their way through history, but that of market economic forces themselves requiring some degree of institutional support to ensure the material reproducibility of capitalist society. And in theorizing the interplay of basic inner workings of capital and the institutional structure that these function within at a mid-range level of theory, it is then possible to explore the variety of actual historical cases of this type of economy in a given period.

Where the difficulties for the RS and SSA periodizing of capitalism at an intermediate range level of theory originate is with the foundation for their arguments that capitalism manifests basic, abstract tendencies or operates according to abstract laws at one level, and the kind of theory needed to demonstrate this. SSA posit four constituents of what they claim constitute abstract capitalist dynamics, but offer no ontological argument on what it is about capitalism or capital as an object of theory that produces these dynamics in the first place.

RS provides a foundational argument with reference to Marx. To paraphrase Aglietta from our quote at the beginning of the chapter, RS research agenda aims to "study the transformation of capitalist social relations that are both economic and non-economic and that are organized in structures". In this endeavor, Aglietta further maintains RS will "elucidate the general lesson of historical materialism: the development of the forces of production under the effect of class struggle". He adds how his perspective will "draw on the results of contemporary debates within historical materialism" of which "the Marxist conception of the capitalist system… [and] articulation of the laws of capital accumulation" are central (Aglietta 1987: 16–7). Aglietta, then, makes two major points: that class struggle set off by "laws" of accumulation carries no teleological impetus toward socialism; and, economic problems cannot be dealt with at the same "level" of theoretical abstraction.

While Aglietta states revisiting past debates over historical materialism would outstrip the bounds of his book, I agree with the conclusion he claims to draw from them, that history is a social science which is non-predictive. This settles the matter for RS on historical materialism foreordaining the capitalist historical outcome. But we are still left with the question of what "lesson" of historical materialism leads Aglietta to argue for problems of economic theory being treated at different levels of abstraction? Aglietta does declare that he is building his analysis on "the general theory of capitalism founded by Marx" (Aglietta 1987: 380). However, Marx's "general" or basic theory of capitalism is set out most systematically within his corpus in *Capital*. And nowhere does Marx maintain that *Capital* elucidates any "lesson" of historical materialism. In fact, the latter is a general theory or approach to human history in toto. Its fundamental argument which Aglietta alludes to is that modes of production succeed one another under the impetus of a contradiction between the forces and relations of production. When the latter in a given mode of production become "ripe" (in the sense of developing beyond what can be managed under existing social class relations), a period of social revolution follows. If anything, this is what historical materialism contributes to "articulation of the laws of capital accumulation" in Aglietta's expression. Yet this purported general contradiction of human history is not what animates *Capital*. In *Capital*, Marx commences with what he argues is the *specific* contradiction of capital in its most fundamental incarnation from which he educes the economic categories for its study.

Why Marx's beginning in *Capital* and elaboration of the economic categories of capital are important for the research agenda of periodizing capitalism is that it focuses analysis upon what is historically distinct about capitalism. There are two important elements of this. First, Marx's pithy theory of historical materialism offers insight into what Marx suggests constitutes a general historical process of succession of modes of production common to all class societies, including capitalism. However, Marx undertakes a sustained, in-depth analysis of only one mode of production, capitalism. The import of Marx's elaboration of the categories of capital based upon what he sets out as the germ or "cell form" of capital (Marx 1977: 90) is thus to first provide a touchstone for distinguishing the capitalist from the non-capitalist. And in this fashion, to advance a key to the understanding the transmutability of capitalism which is the concern of the periodization research agenda.

RS and SSA present what they see as determinate facets of capitalism. Yet they do this with little reference to Marx and his effort to define capital in *Capital.* Of, course, developing Marx's ideas does not mean slavishly accepting everything Marx says. But neither RS nor SSA clarifies at the outset, where and on what grounds it revises Marx. This impoverishes their analysis not only because they do not show where differences with Marx reside but because they elide much of what Marx elaborated as the touchstone for clearly differentiating the capitalist from the non-capitalist.

Aglietta asserts that the wage relation and its generating of surplus value is the "invariant kernel" of capitalism. However, in Marx's *Capital*, these categories are themselves derived from more primary categories. In fact, for Marx, the sine qua non of capital is the commodification of labor power. However, Marx does not simply assert this but unfolds it in a logical order of exposition which Aglietta ignores. The wage relation is thus only a form of the deeper capital–labor relation and would not be able to account from what Marx, as discussed in Chap. 2, theorized as the formal subsumption of labor by capital which existed in the merchant putting out system, for example (Albritton 2001: 425).

Indeed, it is on the grounds of Aglietta picking and choosing categories from Marx in a largely ad hoc fashion that Albritton maintains that, though RS makes constant reference to "levels" of theory, it never develops this in terms of what is genuinely distinct about each level, or how interconnections among them may be established, in any systematic way. Rather much of what RS delivers is simply "preliminaries" to a single level of theory that is dubbed intermediate range (Albritton 2001: 432).

It is true that RS and SSA offer an escape route for Marxist theory from theorizing capitalist change in terms of a constant that "chain linked" periods of capitalism in a historical telos, the end which is seemingly forever delayed. However, replacing this with another level of theory the concern of which is study of alternating bouts of capitalist stability and instability and the institutional matrices functional to maintaining the former, the very question Marx began with which is to counter bourgeois theory by confirming capitalism as a historically delimited society is lost. Even the RS account of why institutional stability is required to regulate capitalist economies, for example, is vague. Lipietz, above, had phrased it roughly in terms of answering "how conflictual social practices are reproduced with sufficient regularity to form systems of social relations". But what these "conflictual social practices" are and what the "system of social relations" reproducing the practices with "regularity" is, beyond at least the implicit notion of class division in modes of production set out in Marx's pithy theory of historical materialism, is never addressed specifically for capitalism.

Marxist critics of RS and SSA thus pounce on mid-range periodization from two directions (Westra 2009: 59–62). On the one hand, they accuse the mid-range project of imbibing elements of postmodernism that dwells in the realm of stylized facts which are simply plucked from history with abandon without any reference to deeper structural forces like capital. On the other hand, critics suggest that because RS and SSA build their edifices largely on single cases, their intermediate range projects prove as incapable of capturing historical diversity as Marxist precursors on abstract laws of capitalist history (see Fig. 5.1).

The second important element of Marx's specific beginning of *Capital* for periodizing capitalism brings to bear key ontological and epistemological provisos. RS and SSA refer to things like abstract theory or abstract laws in regard to theorizing capitalism and its process of historical change.

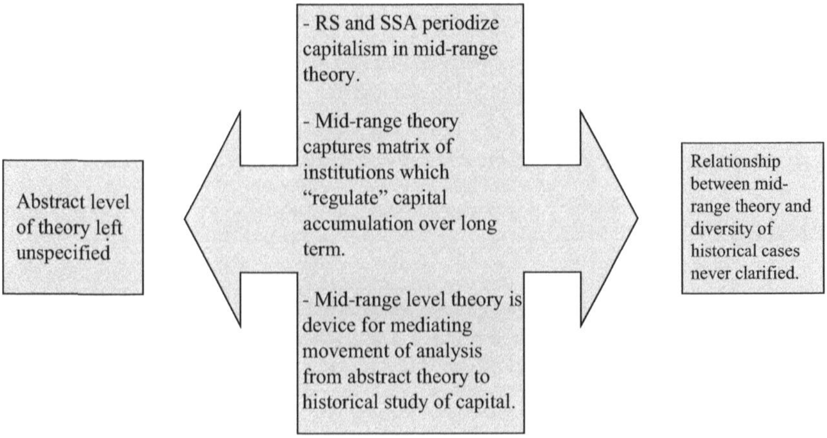

Fig. 5.1 RS and SSA mid-range theoretical project (Source: Author)

Yet they never answer the ontological question of what it is about capitalism that enables thought to grasp workings of capitalism in terms of abstract theory that then studies these systematically. After all, Marx never talks about "abstract" laws or "inner logic" for other modes of production—primitive communism, slavery, feudalism, or even socialism—the latter which he argues liberates human beings from "extra-human" compulsions of the market with material life being organized by a superstructure of free associations of free human beings for their concrete purposes of human flourishing.

Aglietta veers in the direction of problematizing the ontological basis for abstract theorizing of capital with his claim that the possibility of abstraction in theory resides in the fact of the "process of homogenization" existing in "reality". But beyond his assertion that the phenomenon of "homogenization" derives from the process of exchange which renders the "quantities…measurable" Aglietta goes largely silent and makes no reference to Marx's *Capital* the "general theory" of which he is supposedly guided by. And what the "reality" is that foregrounds the epistemological approach of abstraction Aglietta also never offers an answer. This, of course, is not just about philosophical hair-splitting. Being clear on what something is in its basic ontological incarnation so that we can determine what is scientifically knowable about this aspect of "reality" is central to our grasp of the limits of its transmutability and very existence which, in the case of capitalism, is what the periodization research project is ultimately all about.

Notes

1. Michel Aglietta's book may be taken as the foundational work of RS. Yet, as Jessop explains in his "Preface" to a five-volume edited research survey of Regulation theory writings (Jessop 2001: xiv–xv), Aglietta and other prominent RS theorists such as Robert Boyer and Alain Lipietz are pegged as members of the "Parisian" variant of the theory. Other French "schools" of the theory exist as do other European genres of RS. Nevertheless, given that the conceptual infrastructure was initially set out by Aglietta and followed up on by Boyer and Lipietz, the discussion of RS in this chapter will largely treat only the writings of the foregoing along with commentaries and critical reviews of that work.
2. For interested readers, the best schematic summary I am aware of for the main positions of debate on the demise of the post-WWII golden age is found in Webber and Rigby (1996: 76–80).

References

Aglietta, M. 1987. *A Theory of Capitalist Regulation*. London: Verso.

Albritton, R. 2001. Regulation Theory: A Critique. In *The Parisian Regulation School: Regulation Theory and the Crisis of Capitalism 1*, ed. B. Jessop. Northampton: Edward Elgar.

Bowles, S., D. Gordon, and T. Weisskopf. 1984. *Beyond the Wasteland*. London: Verso.

———. 1990. *After the Wasteland*. Armonk: M.E. Sharpe.

Boyer, R. 2002. The Origins of *Regulation* Theory. In *Regulation Theory: The State of the Art*, ed. R. Boyer and Y. Saillard. London: Routledge.

Boyer, R., and Y. Saillard. 2002. A Summary of *Regulation* Theory. In *Regulation Theory: The State of the Art*, ed. R. Boyer and Y. Saillard. London: Routledge.

Brenner, R., and M. Glick. 2001. The Regulation Approach: Theory and History. In *The Parisian Regulation School: Regulation Theory and the Crisis of Capitalism 1*, ed. B. Jessop. Northampton: Edward Elgar.
Davis, M. 2001. Fordism in Crisis. In *The Parisian Regulation School: Regulation Theory and the Crisis of Capitalism 1*, ed. B. Jessop. Northampton: Edward Elgar.
Glyn, A. 2001. Productivity and the Crisis of Fordism. In *Regulationist Perspectives on Fordism and Post-Fordism: Regulation Theory and the Crisis of Capitalism 3*, ed. B. Jessop. Northampton: Edward Elgar.
Glyn, A., A. Hughes, A. Lipietz, and A. Singh. 1990. The Rise and Fall of the Golden Age. In *The Golden Age of Capitalism*, ed. S. Marglin and J. Schor. Oxford: Clarendon Press.
Gordon, D., R. Edwards, and M. Reich. 1982. *Segmented Work, Divided Workers: The Historical Transformation of Labor in the United States*. Cambridge: Cambridge University Press.
Hirst, P., and J. Zeitlin. 1991. Flexible Specialization versus Post-Fordism: Theory, Evidence and Policy Implications. *Economy and Society* 20 (1): 1–56.
Jessop, B., ed. 2001. *The Parisian Regulation School: Regulation Theory and the Crisis of Capitalism 1*. Northampton: Edward Elgar.
Lipietz, A. 2001. Accumulation Crises, and Ways Out: Some Methodological Reflections on the Concept of 'Regulation'. In *The Parisian Regulation School: Regulation Theory and the Crisis of Capitalism 1*, ed. B. Jessop. Northampton: Edward Elgar.
Marx, K. 1977. *Capital Volume I*. New York: Vintage Books.
McDonough, T. 1994. The Construction of Social Structures of Accumulation in US History. In *Social Structures of Accumulation: The Political Economy of Growth and Crisis*, ed. D. Kotz, T. McDonough, and M. Reich. Cambridge: Cambridge University Press.
———. 2014. The Resolution of Crisis in American Economic History. In *Social Structure of Accumulation Theory: Volume I*, ed. T. McDonough, D. Kotz, and M. Reich. Northampton: Edward Elgar.
Webber, M., and D. Rigby. 1996. *The Golden Age Illusion: Rethinking Postwar Capitalism*. London: Guilford Press.
———. 2001. Growth and Change in the World Economy Since 1950. In *Phases of Capitalist Development: Booms Crises and Globalizations*, ed. R. Albritton, M. Itoh, R. Westra, and A. Zuege. Basingstoke: Palgrave.
Westra, R. 2009. *Political Economy and Globalization*. London: Routledge.
———. 2012. *The Evil Axis of Finance: The US-Japan-China Stranglehold on the Global Future*. Atlanta, GA: Clarity Press.

6

The Japanese Uno–Sekine Approach to Marxian Political Economy

It has never been widely appreciated or interpolated into debates over Marxism raging in Western academies, the extent to which Marxism in Japan emerged "as a virtual synonym for social science" to make groundbreaking contributions to Marxist theory (Barshay 2004: 50). Where Marxism initially influenced a broad cross-section of thinking in Japan over social science was through its contribution to so-called modernist thought on Japan's development trajectory in the world. Marxism entered Japan in the 1890s, following the consolidation of the Meiji "revolution", and gained influence after the Russian Revolution and the labor strife that struck Japan during the same period. Marxism's synonymy with social science was cultivated through perceptions of it as offering the first, major coherent "world view" of the transformation of social systems. The importance of such a world view is underscored by Japan's own travails at capitalist modernization and industrial development and the way this process was apprehended. Understanding of Japan's development in the context of theories of capitalist change was not simply an academic exercise but a question of political practice. Thus, Marxism sought to prove its mettle as synonymous with social science in its analysis of Japan's own

R. Westra, *Periodizing Capitalism and Capitalist Extinction*, Palgrave Insights into Apocalypse Economics, https://doi.org/10.1007/978-3-030-14390-9_6

development trajectory. This would provoke a major debate within the field of Marxist studies in Japan.

Two "factions" of Japanese Marxists ultimately went to battle over the nature of capitalism in Japan. The Koza-ha faction followed the dictums of the Comintern from Moscow, which claimed that before Marxists in Japan turned toward issues of building socialism, it was first necessary to purge Japan of significant feudal remnants that continued to retard Japan's full capitalist and democratic development. The Rono-ha faction, on the other hand, maintained that while capitalist development in Japan got off to a belated start in comparison with Western European economies, it was nevertheless proceeding apace, allowing Japan to take its place as a rival capitalist imperialist power. And, while residues of pre-capitalist class structure lingered in Japan, because Meiji Restoration amounted to Japan's version of a bourgeois revolution, feudal remnants along with capitalism will be extirpated by the socialist revolution that Marxists should strive for immediately. While the Koza-ha faction attained a position of dominance within Japanese Marxism, both its view and that of Rono-ha had been challenged as early as 1935 by Kozo Uno. What Uno contended is that Japan's capitalist development reflected neither a strong persisting feudal system a-la-Koza-ha nor one where proletarianization of its rural hinterlands was proceeding seamlessly a-la-Rono-ha, but specific characteristics of a stage of "late development" (Barshay 2004: 55–6).

Impending war and the galvanizing of a police state in Japan soon silenced the Marxist debate. However, following World War II (WWII), it all sprang back to life with a vengeance, with Marxian economics becoming de rigueur in many Japanese universities. And it was the Marxist school associated with Kozo Uno that became the "most influential" at that time (Barshay 2004: 69). Why the Uno approach attained the status it did in Japan owed much to its original intervention in staid Marxist debates. Studying in Germany in the 1920s, Uno first read Marx's *Capital* in German along with writings of Marx's prominent followers such as Lenin and Hilferding. Uno was also exposed in Germany to work of Max Weber and the "Historical School" of Friedrich List. However, Uno was unimpressed with both: Weber, because his ideal type strategy of systematizing empirical history produced essentially groundless, subjective constructs; and List, on the one hand, because he could not clearly explain what it is about capitalism specifically that compelled its transformation through the development "stages" List sets out, and on the other hand, due to List's propensity to simply rationalize existing state policies, such as "protectionism" in his theories.

But Uno was also critical of Marxists, including Hilferding, for attempting to extrapolate directly from elements of Marx's basic theory of capitalism in *Capital* to explain the changes capitalism undergoes in its imperialist stage. Notwithstanding Uno's recognition of Hilferding's landmark contribution to Marxian political economy, it was the tension he discerned between the need to grasp the logic of the capitalist commodity economy and simultaneously examine the discrete paths of capitalist historical development that drove Uno to formulate what was the first "levels of analysis" approach to Marxian political economy (Barshay 2004: 98–100). Before we explore the particularities of this, two points need to be made. First is the historical issue of Uno's temporal location in the refinement of Marx's research program. As remarked upon earlier in the book, Regulation School's (RS's) and Social Structures of Accumulation's (SSA's) intermediate range theoretical contributions appear in the later 1970s and early 1980s. Hence, it is fair to say that language barriers prevented both RS and SSA progenitors from recognizing and accrediting Uno with his path-breaking interventions as RS and SSA research programs were in their own period of gestation. However, from the mid-1970s, scholars working in the tradition of Uno's theories and writing in English were publishing in major "Western" academic journals and recognized presses, but have been ignored by RS and SSA proponents with few exceptions.[1] Uno's views on levels of analysis in Marxian political economy had crystallized by the 1950s. The attempts undertaken to integrate insights among the approaches to produce the most robust Marxian political economic analysis of capitalism have been extremely one-sided in the hands of scholars working in the Uno tradition, as will be discussed later.

The second point is that Uno's deep immersion in Marx's *Capital* during his days in Germany coalesced with his exposure to the interwar debates surrounding the German Historical School in a fashion that drove him to consider rewriting of *Capital*. In this sense, Uno recognized that a Marxian mid-range theory that periodized capitalist stages of development would offer little more than a subjective, Weberian ideal type if crisp clarity over what constitutes the touchstone for defining capital in the abstract level of theory is not arrived at. It was to be *Capital* reconstructed and completed that would ultimately constitute this abstract theory for Uno. And, it is in answering the question that Lenin and Hilferding wavered over, whether or not *Capital* could be extended to treat the historical transmutations capitalism undergoes by the early twentieth century, which leads Uno to formulate his method of political economy that takes a "three step" approach to the social scientific study of capitalism (Sekine 1975: 853; Barshay 2004: 107).

Ideology and Science in Marxist Theory

Nothing has subverted Marxist creative political economic thought across over a century than the codification by Kautsky of Marxism as an overarching theory of historical directionality or historical materialism. It was this view, notwithstanding varying interventions and qualifications of Marxist theoretical positions, which bound the early periodization of capitalism research program to supporting the position of socialism as the telos of history and end state of capitalist change. Even more destructive for unleashing the potential of Marxist analysis is the perspective of the *cognitive sequence* cemented in Marxism where Marx's pithy theory of historical materialism is claimed to endow the other regions or research spheres of Marxism with scientificity. That is, in the last instance, where the idea is hatched that Marx's economic studies in *Capital* are but a subtheory of historical materialism. This hackneyed view is repeated again and again, even by those who have taken great strides in developing Marx's economic thought. For example, Hilferding, in the "Preface" to his book, declares (1981: 23):

> Marxism…is only a theory of the laws of motion of society. The Marxist conception of history formulates these laws in general terms, and Marxist economics then applies them to the period of commodity production. The socialist outcome is a result of tendencies which operate in the commodity producing society.

Lenin avers: "[Marx's] *historical materialism* was a great achievement in scientific thinking...[It] shows how, in consequence of the growth of productive forces, out of one system of social life another and higher system develops...Marx [then] traced the development of capitalism... from simple exchange...to large-scale production" (Lenin 1913). Aglietta, as we quoted in the previous chapter, stated that his periodizing of capitalism in levels of theory "will elucidate the general lesson of historical materialism: the development of the forces of production under the effect of class struggle" (Aglietta 1987: 16).

For Uno, however, the most basic conception of historical materialism which we quote from Marx in Chap. 1, that humans "enter into definite relations that are indispensable and independent of their will...The sum total of these relations of production constitutes the economic structure" of society (Marx 1904: 11),[2] is verifiable only in a limited case. That is, prior to the dawn of the capitalist era, there was no ontological warrant for even thinking about a thing called "the economy" separate from a gamut of social practices—religion, culture, politics, ideology, and so on—with which human material existence was entangled and indistinguishable in itself. Polanyi (1957) famously described this condition of capitalist society as one where the economy or "economic" seemed to "disembed" from those social practices that it had been intermingled with in precapitalist societies. Marx had a far more precise explanation of why economic life first appears "transparently" in capitalist society so as to be amenable to disciplined study. What concerned Uno, here, it may be preliminarily stated, was the following: If the very existence of an economic substructure or base separate from the political and ideological superstructure is verifiable only in the study of capitalism, which is the only mode of production Marx explores exhaustively, the cognitive sequence in Marxism runs from the study of capitalism to historical materialism.

Uno thus viewed historical materialism as a theory of historical directionality foretelling a socialist historical outcome in terms of an ideological hypothesis, though an ideology informed by the science of *Capital* and Marxian political economy (Sekine 1975: 873). To Marx, the importance of the ideological hypothesis extracted from his approach to human history in toto is that it protected him from falling prey to more insidious ideological traps set by bourgeois economics. As Uno asseverates, "ideology serves science…only when it criticises the dominant ideology of the age, which passes for the unquestioned *pre*supposition of science, not when its own espousal demands the name of science" (Uno 2016: 30).

But what makes the study of capital in *Capital* a science? Building on frontier debate in the philosophy of science,[3] science per se is the endeavor to arrive at truth about the causal mechanisms and structures of this world, making connections between what these things are ontologically and how they act in the world, and the kind of knowledge about them we are able to produce. The epitome of science is for a correspondence to be reached between the logical structure of our theories about the world and the causal structure of those mechanisms or forces the theories purport to explain (Westra 2018).

When Aglietta, in Chap. 5, in his discussion of Marx's economic theory in *Capital*, maintains that the possibility of abstract theory in economics resides in a "process of homogenization" that exists in "reality", he is referring in a rather oblique fashion to the foregoing scientific procedure. For Marx, the "reality" that provided the scientific ground for his theorizing of capitalism is the process of marketization that subsumes human economic life with the spread of capitalism. Marx refers to capitalism and its process of marketization as an "alien", "upside-down", imposition on human economic existence. He cites its tendency to convert individuals into "bearers" of "economic categories" (Marx 1977: 92), or convert concrete interpersonal social relations of production into abstract impersonal "relations between things", such "things" as commodities and money then taking on a "life of their own" (Marx 1977: 165), as "fetishistic". Marx, therefore, had well in advance provided an explanation for Polanyi's observation of the economic appearing to "disembed" from the social. This is the fact that while capitalism is socially and historically constituted, as its market relations meditated by "things" subsume human economic life, its causal power of *reification* sets "the economy" "above" the social as a separate "sphere" for the first time in human history, making disciplined, scientific, study of economic life possible. And, if the very possibility of economic theory rests with the historical existence of capitalism, the cognitive sequence in Marxism necessarily runs from the study of capitalism to other regions of the Marxist research agenda.

Marx's *Capital* as the Theory of a Purely Capitalist Society

If Marx's pithy theory of historical materialism offers a general approach to historical change rooted in a "contradiction" between the productive forces of society and the relations of production corresponding to these, Marx provides a far more pointed theorizing of the constitutive force of capitalism in *Capital*. Marx commences *Capital* with the most elemental indicator of capitalism—the commodity. He justifies this on the grounds of "*the commodity* as the universally necessary social form of the product [which] can only emerge as the *consequence of the capitalist mode of production*" (Marx 1977: 949). Marx, in this fashion, problematizes the commodity as the "cell form" or most basic economic category of capital in terms of its dual properties as both a *use value* and *value*. Use value, according to Marx, is the substantive foundation of all human material existence. No human society could survive without the metabolic interchange between human beings and nature through which the labor and production process of society furnishes the concrete, qualitatively heterogeneous, useful goods human beings require for their economic sustenance and flourishing. Value, on the other hand, is the historically delimited, abstract, quantitative, homogenizing principle of capital.

Marx's economic thinking is thus predicated upon his apprehension of the manifest tension or conflict existing in capitalist economies between the substantive reproduction of human use value existence and the peculiar, commodity-economic subsumption of human material life by capital and the dictates of value augmentation. It is precisely this tension existing at the heart of capitalist economies, between the reproduction of substantive material life and its subsumption by the reifying force of capital, which Marx captures with his notion of the "contradiction between value and use value". This basic contradiction that pervades capital is detected by Marx in the economic form of the commodity. Indeed, if any determinate locus in capitalist economies is to be found for what Lipietz, in Chap. 5, fuzzily refers to as "conflictual social practices", it is precisely the contradiction between value and use value.

While the field of mainstream economics from classical to neoclassical economics begins with the idea of "exchange" of use values for purposes of consumption as memorialized in Adam Smith's description of barter between a mythical deer hunter and beaver trapper in "rude society", for Marx, such a methodological presupposition naturalizes capitalism. It does so by presenting capitalism as simply an extension of barter for purposes of consumption. Because consumption of use values is a transhistorical facet of all human societies, the "contradiction" Marx detects in a society of generalized commodity production is exorcized. Marx, fortunately, was no fool and we need not be made ones. In *Capital*, Marx approaches the commodity in capitalism from the perspective of the seller as selling for the purpose of profit making is the most fundamental activity of capitalist society. Hence, a use value or good becomes a commodity due to the fact that its owner is not interested in its use value as an object of consumption. Commodity owners bring their good to market because they are indifferent to the concrete, heterogeneous, useful qualities of these as objects of consumption. Rather, they are interested in the abstract, homogenous, quantitative aspect of commodities as value objects. Such indifference to use value pervading the most basic act of "exchange" in capitalist economies reflects the reifying tendency of capitalist market operations to suppress the qualitative, heterogeneous attributes of goods in order to differentiate commodities according to homogenizing, quantitative criteria of market pricing.

In this sense, the scientific procedure of abstraction deployed by Marx follows the real-world material action of buying and selling on the capitalist market, which abstracts from the concrete qualities of things to relate them in abstract, quantitative terms. Capitalism is in fact a society where the fundamental social goal—the augmentation of mercantile wealth—is itself quantitative and abstract. Recalling our discussion in Chap. 2, the real subsumption of the labor and production process of society by capital demands the direct producers be "freed" from the means of production and land which then confronts them as capital and private property. What they have to sell on the market is their labor power that capital then buys and sets in motion producing *any* good for which there exists social demand and opportunities for profit making. Put differently, capital is *indifferent* to use value except as a byproduct of value augmentation. Marx's intention in conceptualizing the commodity (from the perspective of the seller) as the "cell form" of capitalism is to expose the idiosyncratic operation of capitalist profit making. And the commodity *already* contains within it the basis for the logical unfolding of all the economic categories of capital. As summarized by Albritton (2007: 24):

> Just as simple cells divide and differentiate in the formation of biological organisms, so does the commodity form divide and differentiate in the formation of capital as an integrated system of self-valorizing value....The theoretical starting point for Marx...is the...commodity form, through whose development and differentiation the necessary inner connections of the basic categories of capital can be derived.

But the "kind" of economic theory Marx produces in the three volumes of *Capital* is a major point of contention within the field of Marxist studies. Such contention in many ways flows from Marx's own ambiguous statements on this. Marx is certainly methodologically correct to seize upon the study of capital as providing the ontological grounds for a science of economic study of the capitalist mode of production. Marx's methodological procedure of tracing capital's own self-movement of abstraction, from the contradiction between value and use value in the commodity, to draw out all the categories of capital in their logical immanence, is also sound. It is this procedure from which Marx's claim to produce a pure, basic, or general theory of capital in *Capital* stems.

Yet Marx passed away before completing *Capital*. And Marx's statements in his writings, such as in the *Communist Manifesto*—"All fixed, fast-frozen relations...are swept away...[capital] compels all nations to adopt the bourgeois mode of production" (Marx and Engels 2018)—or in *Capital* as adverted to in the introduction to this book, "capitalist production begets, with the inexorability of a natural process, its own negation" (Marx 1977: 929), lend credence to the view of the logic of capital in its substantive operation and historical course of capitalism as synonymous. For Marx, it appeared from his historical vantage point of capitalist development in nineteenth-century Britain that the logic of capital was purging material life of all non-economic, non-capitalist encumbrances or "impurities". And, if the organized working class, increasingly immiserated by this did not rise up to overthrow the reign of capital, the horror of capital subsuming human material life across the globe would be realized as a historical fact.

What Uno's study of the theorists of imperialism taught him, however, was that imperialism entailed a qualitative transformation of capitalism that obstructed the tendency capitalism had exhibited to the end of the nineteenth century toward its self-purification. This demanded for him, on the one hand, that Marx's project in *Capital* be completed by extrapolating the logic of capital to conclusion in the self-contained theory of a purely capitalist society. And, on the other hand, that the study of capitalism in its imperialist form as undertaken by Lenin and Hilferding be treated in the separate level of analysis of stage theory (Uno 1980: xxii, 2016: Forward to the Revised Edition of 1971; Sekine 1975).

Though Uno's 1950/1952 two-volume completion of Marx's project in *Capital* as the theory of a purely capitalist society has never been translated into English, Uno's single-volume abridged version of *Principles of Political Economy* (Uno 1980), and subsequent two-volume reconstructions of *Capital* building upon Uno's *Principles* by his student Thomas Sekine (1986, 1997, forthcoming), along with single-volume abridgements of Uno's two-volume *Principles* (Itoh 1988; Bell 2009), and article summaries of the theory of a purely capitalist society (Westra 2012/2013) make Uno's ideas available to an English readership.

Succinctly put, the theory of a purely capitalist society is an economic theory of an "economic society" par excellence wherein human material life is reproduced as a byproduct of value augmentation. From the analysis of the contradiction between value and use value in the commodity as the "cell form" of capital, the theory unfolds all the circulation, production, and distribution categories of capital in three "doctrines".

The doctrine of circulation captures the contradiction between value and use value in terms of value seeking to escape its qualitative use value constraints to express itself quantitatively in terms of "price". Further specification of the circulation forms of capital explores the functions of money as a measure of value or social connector in a capitalist society, money as means of exchange or active money, and money as store of value or idle money. It concludes with an analysis of the forms of capital as in M-M′ (money that makes more money in the form of antediluvian usurers or “loan capital”), and the formula for merchant capital, M-C-M′, where C denotes the commodity and M′ the sale of a commodity for profit.

It is in the doctrine of production where the contradiction between value and use value undergoes further elaboration in terms of the contradiction between the operation of capital as a process of self-augmentation of value and the production of use values in general. What is revealed, first, is that in contrast with activities of antediluvian forms of capital, the modalities of which are captured in the doctrine of circulation through interrogations of the commodity form, only the paradigmatic form of capital, *industrial capital*, frees capital from remaining use value constraints under specific historical conditions where the wellspring of social wealth, human labor power, is commodified. For capital can then purchase that commodified labor power on the market and set it in motion producing *any* good for its abstract purpose of mercantile wealth augmentation. Second, the doctrine of production shows how the validity of the law of value and fundamental material economic reproducibility of capitalism as a historical society imply each other. That is, while use value constitutes the transhistorical foundation of human existence, as commodities goods are not produced by capital for their use value, but for the production of surplus value commodities contain. This, in turn, necessitates the specifically capitalist mode of production characterized by manufacturing operations of industrial capital. Finally, the doctrine of production explores the material Marx had set out in Volume II of *Capital*. What is demonstrated is the circulation process of capital involving the coordination and non-interruption of capitalist operations across all its units in the economy as a whole. With the reproduction process of capital, the doctrine of production traces the self-expansion of aggregate social capital to confirm the possibility of capitalism as a historical society.

In the doctrine of distribution, the theory of a purely capitalist society treats the contradiction between value and use value in the operation of capital on the capitalist market. There, capital must reconcile its fundamental indifference to use value in its process of surplus value production and value augmentation with the heterogeneity of use value that, then, compels capital to adopt varying production techniques to produce divergent use values. The contradiction between value and use value thus assumes the form of the contradiction between capitalist indifference to use value and the unavoidability of technical variations in use value production. In overcoming this contradiction, capital distributes the surplus value it produces to each individual capital in proportion to the magnitude of their initial investment. As per the material in Volume III of Marx's *Capital*, the doctrine of distribution deals with mechanisms of capitalist competition, formation of an average rate of profit, divergence of production-prices from values in the capitalist market, and the oscillations of capitalist business cycles through prosperity and depression phases. Finally, in examining the way capital distributes surplus value among individual sectors and units of industrial capital, the theory of a purely capitalist society treats questions of claimants on surplus value other than the industrial capitalist—private landed property with the category of ground rent and capitalist banking and finance with the category of interest. Marx explains interest as the most fetishistic concept of capital given its reflection of capital itself becoming a commodity or "asset" the ownership of which commands an income stream. Interest thus extirpates all traces of the value augmentation in the labor and production process of society subsumed by capital.

Animating Uno's recasting and completion of Marx's *Capital* as the theory of a purely capitalist society is his understanding of the way Marx's *Capital* "mixes" what he sets out as "the purely theoretical position" he employs in *Capital* (Marx 1977: 99), with analysis of the form capitalism takes on in mid-nineteenth-century Britain, along with historical-descriptive material on capitalism in Britain, Europe, and the world. As touched on above, influenced by his study of writings by the major Marxist theorists of imperialism, Uno concluded that the form or "type" of capital and characteristic form of use value production referred to by Marx in his example of nineteenth-century cotton manufacturing by industrial capital in Britain be treated at the mid-range level of analysis. In the theory of a purely capitalist society that seeks to capture capitalism in its most fundamental incarnation, Uno argues it is necessary to assume a world in which capital gets things all its own way. This demands holding use value per se in all its qualitative heterogeneity and innate recalcitrance to the dictates of capital and value augmentation implicit.

Thus, in the theory of a purely capitalist society, all inputs and outputs of society's material production and reproduction process are specified only in terms of the fact that they are all subsumable by capitalist production. Even the technology of industrial capitalist manufacturing is materially specified in the theory solely as a capitalistically operable industrial technology complex. Subject positions are personifications of economic categories as human agency is subjected to the logic of capital. Of course, according to Uno, this was actually Marx's own methodological assumption in *Capital.* It is just the case, to repeat what is emphasized above, that given Marx's temporal emplacement he accepted industrial capital in its nineteenth-century British capitalist form as a manifestation of the logic of capital purifying the world of non-capitalist, non-economic distortions in history. With no grasp of the momentous changes capitalism undergoes in the era of imperialism, which followed his passing, Marx saw no need to separate the components of *Capital* that he mixes. However, for Uno, the seismic shifts of imperialist capitalism confirmed the necessity of reformulating Marxian political economy in three levels of analysis: an abstract level of the Marxian economic study of capital or the theory of a purely capitalist society, a stage theory of capitalist development and empirical-historical analysis of capitalism (Uno 1980: xxii–xxiii).

Let us explore what is distinct about the mid-range level of analysis of stage theory in the Uno–Sekine approach to Marxian political economy and how the theory of a purely capitalist society connects to stage theory and informs its construction.

Stage Theory and Periodizing Capitalism

To momentarily take a step back in our analysis to material presented in Chap. 2, Marx importantly observed how "[i]n all forms of society there is one specific kind of production which predominates over the rest, whose relations thus assign rank and influence to the others" (Marx 1973: 106–7). What Marx is referring to is the fact that while this or that economic form such as sale of a commodity for money is observable in pre-capitalist economies, the impact of these is external to the primary economic principle at the core of human material reproduction of these societies. Similarly, while economic forms associated with precapitalist economies, like slavery, or post-capitalist forms such as cooperatives, appear in capitalism, their impact is external to the core principle of capitalism. Therefore, the very purpose of the theory of a purely capitalist society, in Uno's perspective, is to expose each and every facet of the operation of capital, as the core principle of capitalist society, in its most fundamental incarnation. Knowledge of what capital is, as such, constitutes a timeless touchstone or constant informing our judgments over the historical dawning of the age of capital and its potential passing. In short, it is the ultimate metric for differentiating the capitalist from the non-capitalist.

Theorists of imperialism, monopoly, and "late" capitalism, who continued to believe the transition from organized capitalism to socialism was nigh, ignored the potential embedded in Marx's *Capital* for consummating Marx's "purely theoretical position" to define capital in a timeless fashion. What interested Uno, on the other hand, was to explain the constant of capitalism in terms of how an "upside-down", "alien" society, as Marx saw it, can actually exist in history to reproduce human material life in the first place. Hence, when we use the above expression, of capital reproducing a human society as a byproduct of value augmentation or profit making, it captures Uno's insight into the need for economic theory to demonstrate how capital, as an economic principle or "one specific kind of production" in Marx's purview, meets what Uno refers to as the "general norms of economic life" (Uno 1980: xix). These general norms of economic life are not discoverable empirically through observing all historical societies because it is only in capitalism where the economic emerges "transparently" as a separate "sphere" amenable to disciplined study. The general norms of economic life, therefore, are only discoverable through the scientific study of capitalism. Accomplishing this task is why we need economic science in the first place (Westra 2018). Hence, it is only through unfolding of all the categories of capital, in their logical immanence, that the theory of a purely capitalist society demonstrates how capital wields a human society for its own self-aggrandizing purpose of value augmentation yet simultaneously meets general norms of economic life to reproduce the material existence of an actual historical society.[4]

Scientific precision required by the foregoing is precisely why, at the abstract level of theory, Uno explores the contradiction between value and use value in terms of "ideal" use values amenable to the capitalist chrematistic of value augmentation. Even, ideal use values, of course, pose resistance to capital. This is what makes capitalism an "alien" mode of economy for human beings. But, in theory, in following the way capital surmounts use value oppositions to consummation of its logic in a purely capitalist society, enough rope is given to capital to hang itself by revealing the innermost secrets of its one-dimensional plan for human society.

Applying the theory of a purely capitalist society to questions of really existing historical capitalism, however, brings to bear the necessity of problematizing "real" use value life for capital. However, in bridging the theoretical distance between the abstract theory of capital's logic and actual history with its rich, virtually infinite diversity of use value life, Uno again follows Marx's cue. Because the ultimate purpose of Marxian political economy is to produce complete knowledge of capitalism as a society where human material life is wielded for the purpose of value augmentation, Marx, in his specific treatment in *Capital* of the paradigmatic form value augmentation assumes in the mid-nineteenth century, examines the way capital strives to neutralize use value opposition in the key capitalist industry of the period, cotton production in factory manufacturing. To recapitulate, from Marx's historical vantage point and perspective on capital's actual historical tendency toward self-purification, there appeared little difficulty in conflating the inner logic of capital with laissez-faire capitalism of his day as typified by the cotton industry. As a key capitalist use value, "light" industry of cotton production is as close to an "ideal" use value for capital as imaginable.

However, for Uno, it is precisely at this juncture where the connector is established between the theory of a purely capitalist society as the abstract level of the theory and the mid-range, stage theory of capitalist development. Stage theory, as the mid-range level of analysis, according to Uno, involves the concretization of the contradiction between value and use value. In the theory of a purely capitalist society, use value recalcitrance to value is assumed to be neutralized. But in stage theory, theory construction commences around the ways paradigmatic use values, characteristic of world historic stages of capitalism, resist capital, refracting its logic of value augmentation into a specific type of capital accumulation. Moreover, because at the level of stage theory it is recognized that in capitalist history a modicum of material life always remains non-commodified and social relations non-reified, theory must analyze the range of superstructural supports capital receives in the stage. In this sense, the theory of a purely capitalist society is an economic theory par excellence. However, stage theory is necessarily interdisciplinary. As Uno explains (Uno 2016: 26):

> Apart from the general theory of capitalism, economics involves a wide range of specialised fields. It is my view that these fields must be studied… with reference to the word-historic stage of capitalist development…The question, therefore, boils down to how such determinations…are obtained. Clearly, the theory of any particular developmental stage of capitalism will have to consist of…a concrete-synthetic theory of the (bourgeois) state… with the assistance of political and juridical studies that relate to the specific developmental stage in question…The study of economic policies must, however, constitute the core of these studies, inasmuch as, and to the extent that, they directly bear upon the specific developmental stage of the evolution of capitalism.

But stage theorization always begins by identifying the paradigmatic use value of the capitalist period given that it resides in the degree of resistance posed by it to value augmentation that compels the particular accommodations by the logic of capital manifested in the structural transformations capitalism undergoes in a stage. Uno, himself, believed capitalism is marked by three world historic stages of development. He distinguishes them in terms of their representative policies. They are mercantilism, liberalism, and imperialism (Uno 2016: 27). Respectively, the paradigmatic use values of the three stages of capitalism are wool, cotton, and steel. Production of the stage-specific use values impels capital to assume a stage-specific form: merchant capital for mercantilism; industrial capital in the stage of liberalism; and, following Hilferding's cue, finance capital constitutes the form capital assumes in the imperialist stage. According to Uno, in each stage of capitalism, there exists a particular state or states where capital accumulation takes on its most typical, advanced shape. For both mercantilism and liberalism, it is Britain which arises as the dominant capital accumulator. In the world historic stage of imperialism, Uno maintains the stage-typical advanced accumulators are Britain, Germany, and the US, confirming the multifaceted nature of imperialism.

It is, therefore, precisely because stage theory is grounded in the theory of a purely capitalist society and its elaboration upon the fundamental contradiction of capital to expose what capital really is in its basic incarnation that it is not simply a stylizing of facts or ideal type. Rather, stages are "objectively unique" *material types* of capitalism. Sekine puts it thus: "A stage, in other words, should not be an arbitrary expedient by which to recount economic history in a systematic and orderly fashion; it should be a meaningful intermediary between deterministic theory and empirical facts" (Sekine 1975: 854).

It is from the cases of the advanced accumulators in a stage that Uno synthesizes the specific form and role of the state. In his book on stage theory and economic policies of capital, published initially in 1936, though only recently translated into English (Uno 2016), Uno fleshes out issues treated, at best, in passing in his only previous English-translated writing. He argues that up to the stage of liberalism, capitalism tended asymptotically to approach its ideal image captured in the theory of a purely capitalist society. However, drawing on work of theorists of imperialism, and engaging his own empirics, Uno theorizes the stage of imperialism with an eye to the way capital accumulation gravitates asymptotically away from its ideal image.

At the root of this gravitation are the exigencies of capitalistically managing the production of steel and its related complex of heavy industrial chemicals. As covered more fully in Chap. 2, the sheer magnitude of up-front costs and structural requirements of steel production morphed the very nature of the capitalist firm from its entrepreneurial type in the period of industrial capital to the monopoly/oligopoly form. Meeting the exorbitant costs and time scale of steel and heavy chemical production technologies of the second industrial revolution brought to bear new modalities of raising capital. Finance capital, as the new form of capital, drew in both direct bank involvement in industrial planning and equity markets in channeling investment to the limited liability joint-stock company. Imperialist state policy supported finance capital by promulgating a raft of protectionist measures for home markets and in coveting economic territories abroad. Uno zeros in on the specific way both the monopoly form of business and state policy impact upon the fundamental logic of capital in terms of its equalization in rates of profit, movement of business cycles, and absorption of the industrial reserve army. He declares (Uno 2016: 148):

> As heavy industries centred around the iron-and-steel industry become important, even the gradual working of the mechanism, which might otherwise correct the uneven growth of the economy—the mechanism which was available to industrial capital in the liberal era—can no longer be counted on. As the form of the Joint-stock company becomes more and more adopted in manufacturing industries, the tendency for this mechanism to be undermined is bound to be reinforced. The law of average profit, one of the most fundamental laws of capitalism, thus suffers a serious distortion.

What springs from Uno's levels of analysis approach and stage theoretic determinations is the compelling explanation for the ultimate limit to capitalism in history. That is, the limit to capitalism derives not from the general contradiction between the productive forces and relations of production hypothetically proffered by Marx in his pithy approach to human history in toto. Rather it derives from the historically specific contradiction of the capitalist commodity economy. This is the contradiction between value and use value. What it confirms is that capital reaches its limitations as use value life becomes increasingly difficult to manage according to the fundamental logic of capital. And, as capital seeks to maintain its "alien" grip on human material existence by relying on an expanding matrix of extra-economic, extra-capitalist policy supports, it only generates new, perverse forms of crisis that increasingly prove its exhaustion as a means of reproducing human economic life.

In a memorandum affixed to the 1970 reissue of his 1936 book on levels of analysis and stage theory (which appears in the current English translation), Uno asserts that he initially found himself nonplussed over whether WWII and the economic changes in the post-WWII period heralded the consolidation of a new stage of capitalism. Uno's early prognosis had been that imperialism was the final stage of capitalism as 1917 constituted the advent of socialism in the world. As put by Screpanti and Zamagni (2005: 449), "only Uno had the courage to make explicit...the history of capitalism ended in 1917; then began the history of the transition to socialism". Hence, in revisiting the question subsequently for the reissue of his book, Uno declares (2016: 237–41):

> What was clear to me, however, was that the development of capitalist nations, then, as remarkable as it was, did not demonstrate sufficient vigor in blocking the expansion of the socialist sphere...I have come to believe that the world economy after the end of the First World War must be studied not as capitalism in its highest, imperialist stage of development, but rather directly as a phase in the economic history of capitalism, which is free from such stages-theoretic determinations (that is to say, as capitalism moribund) in the sense of already presupposing the emergence of socialism...

Uno's statement here is at the root of a rift among major scholars working in the Uno–Sekine tradition of Marxian political economy who publish in English. The divide is largely between Sekine and Bell who follow Uno and Albritton and Westra who follow Uno and Sekine but see the post-WWII golden age period as amenable to stage theoretic analysis. What is emphatically *not* in question is whether the post-WWII stage or phase of capitalist history continues the asymptotic movement of capital away from its ideal image. The question is one of the extent of that movement and whether the logic of capital has been so distorted as to nullify the utility of the concept of capitalism in its specific sense for that period. Bell and Sekine (2001) may be referred to on the "yes" answer to the above question and Westra (2014: 48–52) for a succinct recapitulation of the issues and friendly rebuttal of the Sekine and Bell argument.

The Capitalist Stage of Consumerism as the Final Stage of Capitalism

While the debate will not be revisited in its entirety, here it is nevertheless necessary to develop two of its points that carry important ramifications for what follows in this book. One is that in his argument for imperialism as the final stage of capitalism, Uno does not focus upon the contradiction between value and use value, and another one is the issue of whether the use value space of the post-WWII period is amenable to capitalist management even with the panoply of non-economic, non-capitalist supports it receives. Instead, Uno highlights the advent and development of socialism which, from his historical vantage point, appeared destined to enlarge in scope. Sekine, accompanied by Bell, deviates from Uno's analysis on this point to lay emphasis upon the use value space of the post-WWII economy.

Sekine marshals two signal arguments, though both hinge upon the capacity of the law of value, elaborated as the "regulator" of capital in the theory of a purely capitalist society, to play its part in managing use value life under the post-WWII production regime of consumer durables, typified by automobile production. First, Sekine notes that in contrast to the oscillation of capitalist business cycles around prosperity and depression phases as captured in the theory of a purely capitalist society, where capital recovers by raising its organic composition, the Great Depression of the 1930s constitutes a watershed for capital in that no "automatic" recovery was forthcoming. Ergo, the operation of the law of value, is so severely blunted and non-capitalist supports given to economic recovery so extensive as to call into question the usefulness of referring to the post-WWII economy as capitalist in a determinate sense (Sekine 2013: 252–5). Second, Sekine maintains that the exigencies of consumer durable production and architecture of non-economic braces for capital in the post-WWII period pervert the working of the reconstituted economic oscillations to prevent clear determination of the value of labor power upon which its commodification and existence of capitalism hinge. This problem arises from the activities of oligopolistic transnational corporations (TNCs) in innovating selectively throughout business cycles without capital having been depreciated, along with the anathema of TNCs to price competition, as touched on by Mandel in Chap. 3, and the impact of this upon the law of population, which operates as the macroeconomic basis for the expansion and contraction of the industrial reserve army.

However, on the first count, Uno recognizes in his stage theoretic analysis of imperialism that the transmutations of capital occurring in the stage do not reprise the pattern of crises alternations captured in abstract theory, or approximated in the liberal stage of capitalism under the auspices of industrial capital. Uno claims, "these features did not follow straightforwardly from routine capitalist development which the pure theory of capitalism would lead one to surmise, since they even repudiate, to some extent, the free competition that capitalism, as a system, must presuppose in principle" (Uno 2016: 141). Further, there is hardly a seamless transition between the liberal stage of capitalism and the imperialist stage. After all, the historical record is clear: From the mid-1870s, a "great crash" wracked the global economy unraveling central pillars of the liberal order such as its trading system and financial arrangements (including staid financial institutions) with no recovery until the mid-1890s. And the recovery was hardly a fait accompli but was greatly assisted by historically contingent factors such as the discovery of new supplies of gold (Westra 2016: 122–3). This is why questions of transitions between capitalist stages with the contingent events they are punctuated by are treated at the level of empirical-historical analysis, not stage theory.

As well, what the theorizing of imperialism is all about is the seismic structural changes forced upon capital to meet the challenges of managing production of heavy or "bulky" steel and industrial chemicals as the new use value complex. Indeed, it is a hallmark of Uno's work that enjoins it in a family resemblance with RS and SSA, as opposed to theorists of imperialism along with Baran and Sweezy and Mandel, that periodizing of capitalism does not entail the "chain linking" of stages to a prime mover, but rather theorizes stages as discontinuous. Thus, on count two, as cited above, Uno already recognized the extent to which cyclical oscillations, even in the theorizing of imperialism, no longer revolve around the logic of capital and law of value in their pure incarnation. In fact, it is at the heart of the very scientific procedure animating Uno's levels of analysis approach to the political economic study of capitalism that scientific laws hold in "closed" systems and that is where their validity is incorrigibly established. In the "open" system existing across the sweep of capitalist history, scientific laws, in this case the law of value, never get things all their own way (Westra 2018).[5]

The second main point on the debate builds upon the original contribution to Uno's theory by Robert Albritton. Albritton's work takes as its basic presupposition the contradiction between value and use value to interrogate whether capital is able to structurally reconfigure itself to manage the forms of use value production, that are central to post-WWII economies, in a coherent enough fashion (Albritton 1991: 225). Albritton, on this, draws upon Sekine's reconstruction of Marx's *Capital* and Uno's two-volume *Principles of Political Economy* in Sekine's effort to refine the theory of a purely capitalist society. This provides Albritton with the touchstone for what capital is. Albritton further engages in his own empirical-historical analysis of capitalism, particularly as it impinges on Uno's construction of stage theories of mercantilism, liberalism, and imperialism. Albritton reveals the great distance between the theory of a purely capitalist society and the stage structure of mercantilism, for example, where commodification of economic life is tenuous at best. Yet, for him, mercantilism nevertheless deserves to be studied as a stage of capitalism rather than in terms of a historical analysis of an era given the strong gestating propensities of capital to shape society in its own image that the stage theory of mercantilism captures. Moreover, Albritton is informed by important empirical work produced by RS and SSA (Albritton 1991: 8–9). Uno had never been exposed to these theories. RS and SSA direct attention to the important ways a coherent period of accumulation derives from a complex institutional matrix designed to support capital's chrematistic workings toward wielding a human society for its abstract purpose.

Albritton, as well, enriches stage theory itself. Uno had confined it to theorizing the predominant form of capital and its economic policy for an era of capital, along with the politico-legal infrastructure of that policy. While Albritton keeps to Uno's naming of stages based on the paradigmatic state economic policy, he significantly expands Uno's stage distinctions to include stage-specific forms of ideology, class struggle, capitalist crises, and international dimension of capital for each stage commencing with mercantilism and ending with the post-WWII stage dubbed *consumerism* by him (see Fig. 6.1). In fact, Albritton's theorizing of the stage-specific ideology of the capitalist stage of *consumerism* fills an important gap left by RS and SSA on the "regulating" of capitalism. There are two

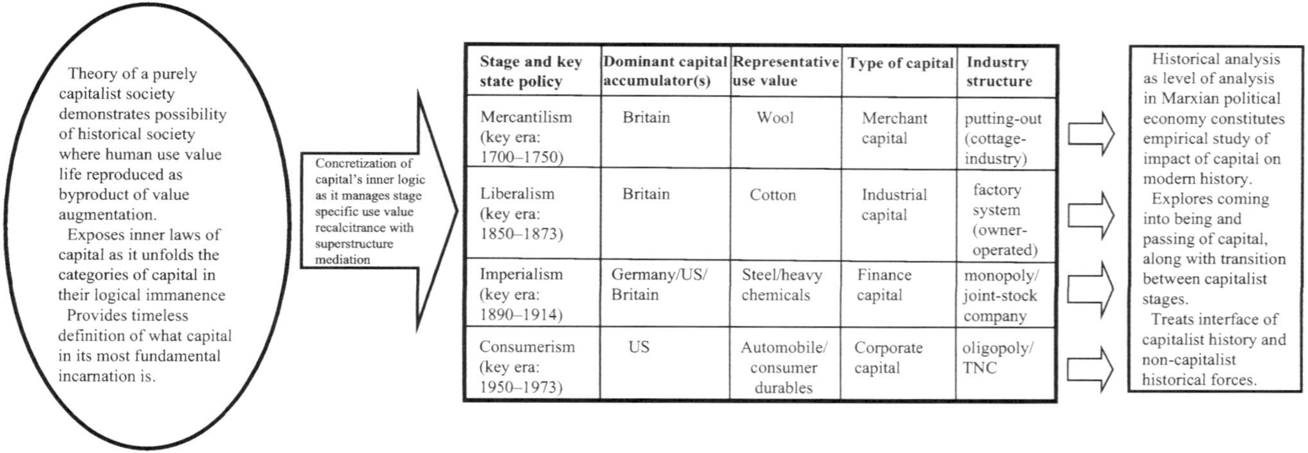

Stage and key state policy	Dominant capital accumulator(s)	Representative use value	Type of capital	Industry structure
Mercantilism (key era: 1700–1750)	Britain	Wool	Merchant capital	putting-out (cottage-industry)
Liberalism (key era: 1850–1873)	Britain	Cotton	Industrial capital	factory system (owner-operated)
Imperialism (key era: 1890–1914)	Germany/US/Britain	Steel/heavy chemicals	Finance capital	monopoly/joint-stock company
Consumerism (key era: 1950–1973)	US	Automobile/consumer durables	Corporate capital	oligopoly/TNC

Fig. 6.1 Stage theory in levels of analysis approach to Marxian political economy (Source: Author)

dimensions to the stage-specific ideology of *consumerism*. *Consumerism* is supported, on the one hand, by an ideology of "hyper-individualism". This fosters a peculiar subjectivity that turns mass consumption of an ever-expanding array of diverse gadget-like commodities into a secular religion. Both subject identities and the legitimacy of the state are predicated upon consumerist ideology. In fact, the "fragmented" narratives and identities Lash and Urry advert to (see Chap. 4), far from revealing a so-called postmodern condition, find material roots in the ideology of *consumerism*. On the other hand, a point we touched on in Chap. 4, ideology of unique individual difference in mass consumption is paralleled by an ideology of vehement anti-communism that serves to sublimate the extent to which capital accumulation and material reproduction generally in the post-WWII period is dependent upon vast collectivities such as the welfare state and giant corporations (Albritton 1991: 246–55).

My own earlier work picks up on Albritton's broader characterization of stage structures and concurs with his theorizing of the post-WWII era as the stage theory of *consumerism* (Westra 2009: Chapter 3, 2012: Chapter 1). Where my emphasis shifts in defending the theorizing of *consumerism* resides in the way I recall what is historically distinct about capitalism as confirmed by the theory of a purely capitalist society. That is, capitalism comes into being at a stage of development of human want satisfaction for standardized factory-produced material goods and as the technologies for producing these become available. After all, the production of material goods and market calculus of their direct costs in material accouterment and commodified labor power is the foundation for value augmentation and surplus value expansion and extraction. Capitalism, in other words, constitutes a production-centered society. Standardized mass production of consumer durables, the automobile being the representative type of use value production for the stage of *consumerism*, deeply entrenches standardized material goods production within the economic reproduction process of society. In no period of capitalist history does the sectoral component of the total labor force devoted to manufacturing and standardized material goods production, in advanced economies, approach 50 percent as it does in the post-WWII period. And in no period of capitalist history do production-centered economies materialize such full-scale wholly integrated industrial manufacturing systems as advanced economies in the post-WWII period do. To not analyze the period following WWII to the 1980s as a stage of capitalism—the stage of *consumerism* as dubbed by Albritton—on this ground alone contributes to confusion over what changes euphemized as globalization and financialization really entail for human material reproduction, and the future of humanity, as we shall see in the following chapters.

Adding to this, I accept Sekine's point of the constraint the operation of corporate capital places upon a market determination of the value of labor power as per the workings of the law of value. Though it may be interjected here that both Hilferding and Lenin had already recognized the possibility of this for the age of finance capital and imperialist policy supporting an "aristocracy" of labor (Westra 2015: 8). Of course, business cycles, under the umbrella of both corporate capital governing of the market and state macroeconomic policymaking, do contort further from their already-distorted form in the stage of imperialism. But the golden age economy never dispenses with the market principle as did the Soviet Union. State macroeconomic policymaking responded ex post to movements toward recession in the production-centered economy. With the form of business cycle in the stage of *consumerism* revolving around oscillations of full capacity utilization followed by output contractions and the maintenance of overcapacity with minimal price fluctuations of key commodities, a means of ensuring labor power remained, at least, partially commodified was embedded in the system. That is, slowing production and resultant overcapacity in industry set in at points where wages could no longer rise in the prosperity phase of the business cycle. Countercyclical policymaking and social wages to support ongoing effective demand ensured the real wage did not fall deleteriously during recessions. In this way, the modus vivendi or class accord (to use SSA's felicitous concept) between capital and labor in the stage of *consumerism* partially decommodified labor power to, paradoxically, maintain it as a commodity (Westra 2016: 141–2). In the end, as recounted in Chap. 5, with the increasing organic composition of capital across the consumer durable economy and concomitant absorption of the industrial reserve army, the foregoing cyclical tendency reached its "upper bound", leading to a sustained fall in profit rates, which sounded the death knell for the golden age of the stage of *consumerism*.

The demise of the golden age segment, or key era, of the stage of *consumerism* does not mean, however, that the stage of *consumerism* itself immediately ceased to exist. In fact, it is not from stage theory that the ultimate passing of a stage can be explained. Stage theory is synchronic and captures the predominant structures of capital accumulation as these crystallize in stage-specific forms around the capitalist management of production and value augmentation of the stage-specific use value. As pointed out above, stage theory constitutes a material type of capital by following what the theory of a purely capitalist society reveals about capital in its most fundamental incarnation to then abstract from capitalist history a specific type of capital accumulation. In stage theory, what is exposed is how under conditions of the concretization of the basic contradiction of capital, that between value and use value, it is nevertheless possible for capital to manage the production of a stage-specific use value selected for its representation of capitalism in its most advanced and idiosyncratic form for a stage.

Empirical-historical analysis as a level of analysis in Marxian political economy differs from empirical analysis in general. As a level of analysis, empirical-historical analysis revolves around capitalist history and is oriented toward studying capitalism in its manifold use value diversity, its coming into being, transformations, and transmutability, and the passing of capitalism from history. It is also concerned with human agency in all its potentialities, whether in the way human agency lends support to the current order or acts to oppose it. And empirical-historical analysis connects study of capitalist history with study of other "histories" or social forces such as patriarchy, race, and so forth, as well as that of natural forces like climate change. Thus, to explore not only the unfolding economic crisis of the golden age of *consumerism*, beyond examining it as a particular type of crises specific to *consumerist* capital accumulation, but its aftermath and the changes it wrought, falls to empirical-historical analysis, not mid-range theory.

What Albritton's theorizing of the stage of *consumerism* confirms is the almost overbearing fashion by which capital accumulation in the production-centered economy of consumer durables, with the automobile as the representative use value, is dependent upon a matrix of superstructural support. RS and SSA empirical work contributes to this understanding of post-WWII production-centered capital as Chap. 5 elaborated. It is this that lends credence to the Sekine and Bell argument that capitalism sensu stricto is never reconstituted in the post-WWII period. When we take account of all the ingredients of this matrix—social democratic welfare state provisioning and macroeconomic countercyclical policymaking; TNC capital itself eschewing market operations to develop "internal" transactional practices for its internationalized production and investment; the cocooning of "economic nationalist" production-centered edifices by an international order, led by the US, including the Bretton Woods international monetary system, a congeries of supranational political and economic institutions also instated under US auspices; and the role of the US in engendering this international order by supporting reconstruction of WWII adversaries and ultimately "policing" this order to "protect" its benefits for "free world" participants—it is evident that if there was ever any hope of resurrecting golden age–like prosperity, it hinged upon strengthening social democracy in a shift that would clearly purge advanced economies of much of what remained of their capitalist substance.

If we look at what is at stake conceptually and ultimately in terms of practice through the lens of Marx–Polanyi's notion of principles of economy, set out in Chap. 2, the question that confronts us is this. To paraphrase Marx: "What specific kind of production or principle predominates and whose relations thus assign rank and influence to the others"? Where I concur with Albritton is that across the near three decades following WWII, though the principle of "redistribution" or state-superstructure management or "regulating" of the economy was extensive, it was deployed to support what remains of the logic of capital or market principle of capitalism. It did this in numerous ways: among them, the perpetuation of capitalist class relations of production, the commodification of labor power the partial decommodification of which made a mass proletarian labor force available to capital, private ownership of the commanding heights means of production, macroeconomic programming that responded to oscillations in the private economy, and so forth. Hence, it was the market principle of capital, though truncated, which "assigned rank and influence" to other economic principles. And it was the fact that the principle of redistribution-superstructure regulation never completely superseded market forces that the golden age of the stage of *consumerism* plunged into a crisis of overaccumulation of capital in relation to the size of the industrial reserve army.

My argument, as elaborated more extensively in other writings (Westra 2009: Chapter 4, 2012: Chapter 3), is the following: Given the sheer scope and scale of the superstructural supportive architecture for capital accumulation under the stage-specific production-centered use value conditions of consumerism, to dismantle this architecture, as effectuated by the policy dictates of neoliberalism, while expecting to revive the dynamism of integrated systems of consumer durable production terminated by the crisis, is a fool's errand. As stated above, the only road to maintain elements of golden age-like economies at the juncture of the late 1970s was to strengthen social democracy to tip the market or superstructure management balance in the direction of social democratic redistribution and socialism. Yet precisely the opposite course was settled upon by US capital and its political class with European Union capital and Japanese capital (somewhat belatedly) and their respective political classes in tow. But the logic of capital in its final, belabored expression of managing the use value space of consumer durables in the capitalist stage of consumerism had already demonstrated its exhaustion and inability to contribute to managing human material affairs notwithstanding herculean superstructure reinforcement. This is what makes neoliberal policy claims about reloading the market such an insidious ideology. Indeed, it is instructive that if any significant vestige of the superstructure matrix of consumerism remains, it is its twin ideologies of hyper-individualism and anti-communism.

Where Sekine, Bell, Albritton, and Westra, among prominent Uno–Sekine approach theorists publishing in English, again meet up in their political economic analysis, hence, is over the view that the period following what I maintain is the capitalist stage of *consumerism* constitutes a transition away from capitalism. Bell and Sekine, of course, had included the post-1980s in their notion of an "ex-capitalist transition" commencing prior to WWII, though where no telos is inferred, such that the outcome might be socialism or potentially a kind of barbarism and destruction of human society and humanity.

While the following chapter will again move back to debates outside of the Uno approach over the question of what follows *fordism* or the post-WWII SSA, as well as revisit the other writings we have surveyed in Chaps. 3 and 4 with their prognosis for the future, the analysis will be guided by what has been elaborated in this chapter. That is, it is informed by the Uno–Sekine approach to the theory of a purely capitalist society as well as the stage theory of *consumerism*. It proceeds at the level of empirical-historical analysis as a level of the Marxian political economic study of capitalism. Among the theoretical threads that will be followed are points from Chap. 5 on the golden age crisis and its initial aftereffects on capital: the condition of "capital becoming surplus" (as Webber and Rigby put it) and the desperate search by capital to raise rates of exploitation.

Notes

1. For example, in 1975, Thomas Sekine published a major article in the US *Journal of Economic Literature* (Sekine 1975). Therein he outlined clearly the many ways Uno's approach to Marxism diverged from what he referred to as "conventional" Marxism. Also developed in the early going of the article is Uno's understanding of "stage theory" as the necessary mediating level of analysis in Marxian political economy.
2. It is upon the foundation of the economic "base" or substructure, Marx had argued in the famous *Preface*, that there arises a political and ideological superstructure.
3. What follows draws upon Westra (2018): For readers interested in pursuing the extended philosophical arguments over ontology and epistemology in science, scientific discovery and scientific theory building beyond the brief remarks here, there is where they will find satisfaction.
4. The general norms of economic life are as follows: (1) no human society can survive for long if the direct producers do not at minimum receive the product of their necessary labor (though any substantive social reproduction demands productive labor produce *more* than is required to reproduce his/her labor power); (2) no human society can survive for long if social demand for basic goods is not met with a minimum misallocation of social resources, primarily human labor power (this necessitating producing means of production and means of consumption in appropriate proportions); and (3) if the productive technology of a society remains

constant, the reproduction process of society cannot expand faster than the natural rate of growth of the working population (this ultimately is the root of conflicts between the forces and relations of production discovered in Marxian economic theory exploration of capitalist business cycle oscillations).

5. Sekine in his formative introduction to Uno's ideas refers to the question in science of open and closed systems in terms of the biological concept of "progressive mechanization" applied to organisms. As Sekine rephrases this, "organisms at some stage of their growth manifest a tendency almost to 'become machines' (progressively mechanize themselves), although they never quite make it". The method of Marx's *Capital*, refined and reconstructed by Uno, is to "copy" the factual tendency for capital to "mechanize" in a self-repeating logical system of value augmentation, and extrapolate this to conclusion in a closed system as a scientific experiment of sorts (Sekine 1975: 857).

References

Aglietta, M. 1987. *A Theory of Capitalist Regulation*. London: Verso.

Albritton, R. 1991. *A Japanese Approach to Stages of Capitalist Development*. Basingstoke: Macmillan.

———. 2007. *Economics Transformed: Discovering the Brilliance of Marx*. London: Pluto.

Barshay, A. 2004. *The Social Sciences in Modern Japan: The Marxian and Modernist Traditions*. Berkeley: University of California Press.

Bell, J. 2009. *Capitalism and the Dialectic: The Uno-Sekine Approach to Marxian Political Economy*. London: Pluto.

Bell, J., and T. Sekine. 2001. The Disintegration of Capitalism: A Phase of Ex-Capitalist Transition. In *Phases of Capitalist Development: Booms, Crises and Globalizations*, ed. R. Albritton, M. Itoh, R. Westra, and A. Zuege. Basingstoke: Palgrave Macmillan.

Hilferding, R. 1981. *Finance Capital*. London: Routledge & Kegan Paul.

Itoh, M. 1988. *The Basic Theory of Capitalism: The Forms and Substance of the Capitalist Economy*. Basingstoke: Macmillan.

Lenin, V.I. 1913. *The Three Sources and Three Component Parts of Marxism*. https://www.marxists.org/archive/lenin/works/1913/mar/x01.htm. Accessed 11 Dec 2018.

Marx, K. 1904. *A Contribution to the Critique of Political Economy*. Chicago: Charles H. Kerr & Co.
———. 1973. *Grundrisse*. London: Penguin.
———. 1977. *Capital Volume I*. New York: Vintage Books.
Marx, K., and F. Engels. 2018. Manifesto of the Communist Party. https://www.marxists.org/archive/marx/works/download/pdf/Manifesto.pdf.
Polanyi, K. 1957. *The Great Transformation*. Boston: Beacon Press.
Screpanti, E., and S. Zamagni. 2005. *An Outline of the History of Economic Thought*. Oxford: Oxford University Press.
Sekine, T. 1975. Uno-Riron: A Japanese Contribution to Marxian Political Economy. *Journal of Economic Literature* 13 (3): 847–877.
———. 1986. *The Dialectic of Capital*. 2 vols. Tokyo: Toshindo.
———. 1997. *An Outline of the Dialectic of Capital*. 2 vols. Basingstoke: Macmillan.
———. 2013. Towards a Critique of Bourgeois Economics. In *Towards a Critique of Bourgeois Economics: Essays of Thomas Sekine*, ed. J. Bell. Berlin: Owl of Minerva Press.
———. forthcoming. *The Dialectic of Capital: A Study of the Inner Logic of Capitalism*. Leiden: Brill.
Uno, K. 1980. *Principles of Political Economy*. Sussex: Harvester Press.
———. 2016. *The Types of Economic Policies Under Capitalism*. Leiden: Brill.
Westra, R. 2009. *Political Economy and Globalization*. London: Routledge.
———. 2012. *The Evil Axis of Finance: The US-Japan-China Stranglehold on the Global Future*. Atlanta, GA: Clarity Press.
———. 2012/2013. *Capital* as Dialectical Economic Theory. *Journal of Australian Political Economy*, Special Issue on *Capital* Against Capitalism: New Research in Marxist Political Economy, 70.
———. 2014. *Exit from Globalization*. London: Routledge.
———. 2015. From Imperialism to Varieties of Capitalism. In *The Future of Capitalism After the Financial Crisis: The Varieties of Capitalism Debate in the Age of Austerity*, ed. R. Westra, D. Badeen, and R. Albritton. London: Routledge.
———. 2016. *Unleashing Usury: How Finance Opened the Door to Capitalism Then Swallowed It Whole*. Atlanta, GA: Clarity Press.
———. 2018. Roy Bhaskar's Critical Realism and the Social Science of Marxian Economics. *Review of Radical Political Economics*, Online first September 21, 2018. https://doi.org/10.1177/0486613418787405.

7

Problematizing Capitalism in the Era of Globalization and Financialization

As submitted in the introductory chapter to this book, outside of work in the Uno–Sekine tradition of Marxian political economy, little concern has been displayed across the research field of periodizing capitalism in robustly defining what capitalism as a historical mode of production is in its most fundamental incarnation. This lacuna holds notwithstanding whether the research strategy proceeded by systematizing history in stylized facts or on the basis of a constant of capitalism which purportedly determines its historical trajectory. Non-Marxist perspectives which proceed by the first strategy, though animated by ostensibly Marxist concerns over technological change and modes of business organization, tacitly cling to mainstream economics perception of capitalism as always and forever. Marxist perspectives, with the exception of Regulation School (RS) and Social Structures of Accumulation (SSA), defend a constant or essence of capitalism, however draw it not from Marx's project in *Capital* as a whole but from Marx's pithy theory of historical materialism foretelling a socialist historical outcome (though they do back up their claims for a constant as such with supportive radical quotations from *Capital*). Between RS and SSA, RS in Aglietta's formative volume does veer conceptually in the direction of providing a basic theorizing of

R. Westra, *Periodizing Capitalism and Capitalist Extinction*, Palgrave Insights into Apocalypse Economics, https://doi.org/10.1007/978-3-030-14390-9_7

capital in what RS refers to as its abstract theory, yet Aglietta leaves it opaque and never makes connections between the levels or ranges of theory he maintains the RS research program is founded on.

A central theme of this book on periodizing capitalism is that during times of epochal economic change as engulfed Britain and Western Europe from the seventeenth century, when history thereby becomes "gray", both defining and explaining in the most substantive fashion what the precise constituents of a mode of production are represent the most pressing of tasks. Marx, of course, for good reason, only provided a complex "synthetic" definition of capital which unfolded all its deep structural categories. He was able to do this precisely because of the unique ontology of capital that tends toward reifying human material life, rendering it "transparent" for the first time in history. It is capitalist reification, in turn, which constitutes the foundation for the systematic scientific study of capital and, as argued elsewhere, the very possibility of economic theory per se (Westra 2018). The definition of capital that springs from the foregoing endeavor, first elaborated by Marx, and later refined by Uno and Sekine, serves our capacity to make judgments in gray empirical milieus on whether capitalism as a mode of production exists. Such theory informed judgment is vital in sorting out debates over the rise of capitalism in history as it is to us today in navigating the helter-skelter neoliberal world to discern what economic principles humanity has left to rely on to sustain its economic existence.

From Chap. 3 onward, in this book, we have explored a wide and diverse range of Marxist and non-Marxist theories on periodizing capitalism of the post-WWII period. Each seeks to explain through the prism of their own conceptualization the economic transmutations of the post–World War II (WWII) era of capitalism which mark it as a distinct type of capitalist economy. Those in Chap. 4, in particular, move to the next step in treating what follows in the wake of the breakdown of the post-WWII golden age period. In Chaps. 5 and 6, we added to the foregoing, periodization of the post-WWII era as stages of *fordism*, the post-WWII SSA, and *consumerism*. But we did not yet follow up in any sustained manner on how RS, SSA, and the Uno approach deal with the aftermath of the disintegrating of the post-WWII stage as they had theorized it. Signal issues raised by all the periodizations we have covered will now be brought back into the discussion. This will be done against the backdrop of our exploration of those seismic shifts in major economies and the world economy euphemized as globalization and financialization. But, as per the discussion in Chap. 6, critical attention is devoted to highlighting trends which demonstrate why the blithe assumption of major theories that the neoliberal era constitutes a form of capitalism which continues to manifest capitalist ability to meet the general norms of economic life to guarantee the longevity of human material existence, immiserated as that may be, is misguided.

Post, Neo, Flexible, and Other Late Twentieth-Century Tropes

It is felicitous to begin the discussion in this section with RS and its explanation for the crisis of *fordism*. As we may recall, RS held that the golden age crisis spilled out from the rigidity of mass production systems which reached their limits in raising productivity crucial to maintaining the high profit high wage economy, soon bringing the whole edifice of "regulation" from its state support system to its international infrastructure crashing down. One of the critiques of RS in its initial exposition, and SSA, for that matter as alluded to in Chap. 5, had been the ambivalence on the relationship between the RS purported intermediate range theory of *fordism* and its historical level of theory. This was exhibited in the inability of RS to account for the way elements of *fordism* mark different capitalist economies such that notwithstanding their empirical differences (e.g. between the US and Japan's economy), it is still possible to classify them as representatives of the *fordist* stage. This ambivalence carried over into debates over what follows *fordism*, what potentially had to occur to swing capital accumulation into prosperity, and how the constituents of this might be theorized in terms of a new era or stage of capitalism. Bracketing, for the moment, the fact that it was not a productivity crisis which sparked the fall of the golden age, the search for a solution to the apparent crisis catalyzing rigidity of *fordism* as RS had it concatenates with interests of a raft of other perspectives on periodizing capitalism.

Lash and Urry, we may recall from Chap. 4, while not directly weighing in on the causal dimension of *fordist* crisis, offer a description of change from large-scale organized capitalism to a disorganized capitalism marked by transformations in both scale and geospatial scope of capital. Piore and Sabel did weigh in on the crisis of what they set out as the mass production paradigm. They are in sync with RS in viewing mass production as a rigid technological system that is destined to reach limits in accelerating productivity. For Piore and Sabel, the only resolution to the crisis of mass production is the wholesale world economic shift to a full-fledged flexible production paradigm. Thus, their perspective goes against work we will treat below which suggests that there exist "varieties" of capitalist roads to the future (Webber and Rigby 1996: 84). Perez's argument also fastens on to the productivity slowdown root of crisis of what she names the mass-production techno-economic paradigm. Given her claim of technology as "the fuel" of capitalism, extrication from its crisis demands capital usher in a new techno-economic paradigm. Capital ultimately does this, on her account, commencing in the early 1970s, through the gestation and spread of the "microelectronic" paradigm. And, for Perez, the keyword of this paradigm and its productivity-enhancing kernel is precisely its "flexibility". Arrighi, as we recount, has no capital-specific causal argument on the crisis of the golden age (remember, he derides what he explains as Marx's focus on "domestic" accumulation cases around which Marxian crises debates swirl). Rather, his focus is upon a fuzzy world system crisis of global "growth" which leads to transitions among competing world system hegemons, one which then rides the wave of financial expansion to gain ultimate hegemony and thereby install a new era of material expansion in their image. Arrighi, in this regard, dwells on notions of disorganization and flexibility of capital as contributing to the growth travails of the US systemic cycle of accumulation. At the time of his writing, Arrighi detected the growing role of Japan as global creditor paralleled by Japan's economic retooling around microelectronics and related flexible production methods. He hints at the potential for Japan to assume the mantle of hegemon to kick-start a new systemic cycle of accumulation.

Initially attracting interest of RS in Japan as a potential forerunner of a new neo- or post-*fordist* stage of capitalism was the fact that its profit rate trends bucked those of other major economies the profit rates of which all began to fall by the early 1970s. Japan's, however, only displayed a marked downward trend from 1979 (Webber and Rigby 1996: 303, 324). As well, in response to the oil shocks and, under conditions of its particular variant of a post-WWII class accord, or wage relation in RS parlance—this including enterprise or "companyist" unionism and tenured long-term employment for core workers—wide application of the new information and computer technologies (ICTs) and robotics was facilitated. This in turn, it is argued, supported what are pegged as increasingly flexible business structure and work practices including the following: vertical disintegration of enterprises and cultivation of enduring ties with lower cost suppliers, such underpinning just-in-time (JIT) production strategies through which large firms are disburdened of bulky inventories; a shift from concern with quantity to quality with "quality control circles" for smaller batch production; a reconfiguring of the labor process toward "learning by doing" by work teams embodying increased skill polyvalence (see Table 7.1). Such elements of post-*fordism* are supported institutionally by state policy geared to infrastructure upgrading to support targeted economic sectors, and "main" bank financing for a "convoy" system of industrial groups bound by enterprise cross-shareholding (Westra 1996, 2003).

Part of the difficulty with claims that the so-called post-*fordism* represents a new techno-economic paradigm is that beyond the more rapid assimilation of available ICTs Japan's alleged post-*fordism* represents at

Table 7.1 *Fordism* vs. post-*fordism*

Fordism	Post-*fordism*
– Semi-automatic production	– Increased automation
– Long continuous flow runs	– Shorter runs with more variety
– Task fragmentation	
– Functional specialization	– Flexible specialization through work teams
– Separation of engineering and execution	– Learning by doing
– Just-in-case (JIC) inventories	– Just-in-time (JIT) or *kanban system*
– Hierarchical management	– Flattened management
– Vertically integrated companies	– Horizontal integration

Source: Author

best a neo-*fordism* of sorts in that it reconfigured mass production rather than replacing it (Wood 2001). In other words, the idea of an inherent rigidity of mass production systems proffered by Aglietta and RS is overstated. JIT, for example, was a response to state support of rationalization in the auto parts supply chain and commenced as a process innovation rather than a futuristic development of a new stage of capitalism. Work teams and skill polyvalence are schemes to intensify labor on the shop floor and fit well within Japan's form of the post-WWII class accord based upon lifetime employment and enterprise unionism. It is true that Japanese transnational corporations (TNCs) in automobiles exhibited a greater degree of vertical disintegration than the highly vertically integrated US auto companies, but horizontal relationships that were established between suppliers and core firms served the same technical purpose as vertical integration in *fordism*. It is also questionable whether robotics has rendered automobile production more flexible. Yes, early utilization of robotics in automobile body building and spray painting certainly injected a significant degree of flexibility into these components of auto production through the way robots can be reprogrammed to perform a wide variety of related tasks. But, as Williams et al. argue (2001: 235–7), this never transforms in any major fashion the scale of automobile production opening the door to small flexibly specialized firms as Piore and Sabel have it: Ditto for flexible manufacturing systems which come with exorbitant costs favoring large firms.

Lipietz (2001), for example, reads the strength of Japan's economy, along with that of Germany for that matter, as but one route out of the crisis of *fordism*. According to him, the same generalization of ICT has been remaking the frontiers of work across major economies including the US, the European Union (EU), and East Asia. Where the differences arise with the "models" of this transformation crystallized in Japan and Germany is that these economies have relied on institutional devices such as negotiated settlements with labor to win the battle of global competitiveness. Of course, such renewed settlements with labor do not necessarily translate into enhanced benefits for the working class. Under Japan's model, while ICTs raised productivity in manufacturing by 9.2 percent annually in the 1975–1980 period, real wages remained stagnant (Itoh 2000: 11).

It is the model adopted by the US and Britain to which Lipietz applies the notion of "flexibilization". In his usage, however, flexibilization is less about an industrial divide or new technological paradigm but more pointedly about an alternate reconfiguring of the wage relation or class accord in SSA's parlance. This reconfiguring entails, in particular, a more complete unraveling of the welfare state social support infrastructure than occurs in Japan and Germany along with the weaning of labor off "rigid ties to the firms" (Lipietz 2001: 24–5). In effect, what the latter notion captures is hurling of the lower middle and working classes into conditions of precariousness, either permanently excluded from employment through job redundancies or rendered subject to short-term contractual employment at the mercy of cyclical vagaries. What theorists of post-industrial society and flexible specialization tout as futuristic promise of new technologies only serves to reduce demand for labor where, in the absence of social protections, a permanent underclass is engendered. Lipietz declares: "The machine of exclusion more closely resembles a centrifuge, whose velocity expels those no longer useful to post-industrial society" (2001: 28–9). Lipietz's view thus vitiates the Piore and Sabel expectation that, as their new industrial divide of flexible specialization permeates the globe, all will benefit. The reality instead is that in a world economy increasingly opened to trade and international flows of investment in marketable productive capacity, a zero-sum game is perpetuated where states with more optimal institutional conditions covet shares of this at the expense of others (Williams et al. 2001: 241).

Mandel, we may recall from Chap. 3 and our discussion of the golden age crisis in Chap. 5, had correctly maintained that it was not a productivity slowdown that sparked the golden age demise but a falling rate of profit in the face of an increasing organic composition of capital and absorption of the industrial reserve army which then prevented capital from raising rates of exploitation. Japan did face the predicament of absorption of the industrial reserve army by 1973 yet, its rapid incorporation of ICTs and exacting of labor discipline through the settlement achieved with labor, as touched on by Lipietz, combined with a ratcheting up of exports to the US, in particular, reinvigorated profit rates to 1979 as noted above (Itoh 2000: 11–2). Mandel's point, however, is that the travails of late capitalism (what he dubs the period RS name *fordism*) demand attrition by capital against labor. This potentially occurs by reducing the value of labor power, increasing the intensity of work, or transforming conditions of production by diminution in turnover time of capital, costs of constant capital, or the organic composition of capital across key sectors or regions of the global economy. In short, the discourse of flexibility or flexible specialization actually captures the strategy of capital as it responds to its profitization discontents. The so-called flexibilization is not, in itself, the cause of changes underway to a new future (Webber and Rigby 1996: 85–6).

Varieties of What?

Problematizing capitalism with regard to what herculean exertions capital must undertake to meet the above profitability exigencies and, further, on the question of whether capital could continue to satisfy general norms of material life to reproduce a historical society as a byproduct of value augmentation was tacitly removed from much of the critical scholarly agenda in the 1990s and early 2000s. Part of this had to do with the unceremonious unraveling of the Soviet Union and Fall of the Wall. Scholars from within the Marxist fold, including those who had played significant roles in formulating RS and SSA, largely abandoned Marx. After all, if socialism "failed", does this not vitiate Marx's theories, particularly the conventional apprehension of Marxism as a master theory of historical directionality?

Another component of abdication from Marxism was deficiencies in the theoretical armature of *fordism* which, along with SSA, was presented as a resolution to abiding travails of the Marxist research program of periodizing capitalism and contextualizing capitalist change. We have addressed this issue in several places above yet it deserves restating. RS and SSA levels framework promised to mediate abstract theorizing of capitalism as a process of "homogenizing" value augmentation with a mid-range level of theory that periodized capitalism; then connect these with a third level of theory that studied capitalist history in all its heterogeneous diversity. However, in practice, the levels of theory were largely collapsed into intermediate theory to reproduce much of the alleged totalizing hubris of initial "single-level" Marxism that theorized capitalism as a subtheory of a master theory of historical directionality. What actually concerned critics of RS and SSA, however, were not directionality issues of the laws or logic of capital as treated by theorists of imperialism, monopoly capital, or late capitalism, but a question that was of little interest to the latter. This was the empirical variations among major economies which had been slotted into one or another stage (imperialism, *fordism*) typology. Finally, there is the issue of research strategy. Though SSA is not explicit here, RS certainly is in claiming to deploy the ideal type, stylized facts approach to systematizing empirical history in their periodization of capitalism. With the abstract level of theory as in Marx's *Capital* essentially disconnected from this stylizing of facts, it set the research field up for a perverse conceptual slippage away from any substantive foundation in the theorizing of capital from which periodizing of capitalism is logically nested.

It is into this perfect storm of historical conjuncture and theoretical misfiring that the "varieties of capitalism" (VOC) approach burst. To be sure, the roots of VOC stretch back quite deep into economic and historical sociological traditions such as work of Max Weber, the German Historical School and early mainstream analysis of "institutions" in modern economies (Coates 2015: 17). In fact, RS and SSA contributed to the rapid respectability VOC gained in Left and critical political economic circles through their emphasis upon the institutional dimension of the social and regulationist structures that supported long-term stability of capitalist economies. Unwittingly, VOC also imbibed what had always been a key tenet of Marxism as a theory of historical directionality. That is, in Marx's teleological scheme of historical materialism, modes of production follow each other successively such that if there is no socialism then, ergo, there must be capitalism. What purpose, hence, VOC blithely queries, is there for interrogations of what capital is in its fundamental incarnation as per the unconsummated promises of levels of theory? And, to the extent VOC does reference economic theory it does this through the prism of the way the yoga of rational choice apotheosized in neoclassical economics is treated in the so-called institutional economics as the "agency" their "structures" provide the context for (Hodgson 1998; Boyer 2005).

VOC, as Coates explains (2015: 12–3), spread rapidly within broad fields linked to comparative politics, political economy, and institutional economics to draw in a wide cross-section of researchers in paradigmatic fashion. Part of its attraction, as I have argued, is that due to the supposed failure of socialism, leaving capitalism as the only game in town, a mind-set is perpetuated around the view that if we all have to now live with capitalism as the "end of history", attention should be devoted among progressives on how it might be optimally honed for that purpose. This fed into what emerged as a key VOC discourse, the realization of a so-called progressive-competitive model of capitalism: competitive because lack of such purportedly contributed to disintegration of really existing socialism; and progressive to maintain as much of the *fordist* welfare state as possible while remaining competitive.

Commencing with Weberian and Polanyian notions of capitalism as an institutionalized order in which "the market" constitutes but one institution emplaced in a particular ordering, VOC turned to issues of how the potential orderings function to impart a modicum of coherence or balance to an economy. These orderings, or what VOC elaborates as institutional "complementarities", are shaped by their emergence in discrete national, social, and historical conditions to reflect a strong "path-dependence". VOC thus initiates its research program from the beginning to explore a wide range of cases in comparative perspective. However, at the outset, it evinced little concern with institutional complementarities as stabilizing or regulating factors for capitalist crises tendencies to secure capital accumulation over the relatively long period. Rather, it sought to establish credentials for policy relevance by dwelling on three policy questions: What institutional complementarities optimally promote economic growth and global competitiveness? Is there a particular complementary relationship among institutions which advances competitiveness while yielding a progressive "variety" of capitalism? Are tendencies afoot toward convergence of economies in a particular variety that proves its combined progressive-competitive mettle (Westra 2009: 64–6)?

At the core of VOC policy debates, then, were three taxonomies of institutional complementarities. One is a "liberal" or market variety of capitalism associated with the US and the UK. Second is a "coordinated" or "negotiated" variety which is associated with Germany and possibly Japan. Lipietz above alludes to this in his discussion of roads from the crisis of *fordism*. Three is a "state-led" variety which potentially includes Japan as well as South Korea. Though, to be sure, more variant taxonomies or so-called varieties of capitalism abound across the literature. Where a variety fits in VOC taxonomies follows upon things like the modalities of labor organization vis-à-vis the state and business, the extent and role of the state in the economy, and the relationship between the financial sector and production-centered business.

Why VOC persisted as long as it did, according to Coates, derives from its research trajectory spanning a period that US mainstream economists dub the Great Moderation where the cyclical tumults, inflation, unemployment, and so forth, which marked the demise of the golden age and early 1980s, appeared to be banished. Major economists could be heard loudly proclaiming from prestigious rostrums that problems of business cycle oscillations through periodic depression or recessions had been solved (Coates 2015: 18). Neoliberal triumphalism stemmed from several factors. There is the growth rate posted by the US of 3.6 percent between 1992 and 2000 even though this was well below the golden age average between 1959 and 1973 of 4.4 percent. Real hourly wages rose 0.6 percent in the 1990s, however paling in comparison with the 3.5 and 3.7 percent real wages rose in the 1950s and 1960s, respectively. Productivity also grew by 1.81 percent in the 1990s: again, well below the halcyon years of the golden age. Nevertheless, because these apparent feats were driven by only a marginal expansion of government spending, much of that on militarization, neoliberals argued for the superiority of the US "market" VOC, calling for its replication around the advanced economy world (Westra 2012: 120–2).

Those working either in or at the critical edges of VOC maintain the global meltdown of 2008–2009 constitutes a watershed moment for VOC erasing what eminence it held in comparative political economy. Coates declares: "What had been ignored...underlying capitalist contradictions...and...cross-national linkages...suddenly in 2008 moved centre-stage again, and a conceptual universe preoccupied with minute institutional variation could suffice no more" (2015: 23). The literature, McDonough explains (2015: 119), was "so enamored with its discovery of the trees that it…started to ignore the wood to its cost". Yet, as debates over the demise of the golden age clearly demonstrate, the economic "contradictions" and "the wood" were always there in plain sight. With a paucity of theoretical underpinning over what VOC in fact was all about—capitalism—the whole VOC enterprise was largely based on assertion. And, its near two decades run diverted much scholarly attention from forces unraveling the world built over the previous century. Let us look at these.

Transition from the Stage of Consumerism

We left off discussion in Chap. 5 with two economic problematics saddling moribund capital in the waning years of the golden age: the desperate search by TNCs of major economies for means by which to raise rates of exploitation, and the tendency for what Webber and Rigby refer to as "capital becoming surplus". Conducing the former, as touched on above in this chapter, potentially rests upon increasing the rate of surplus value production by reducing the value of labor power, accelerating the intensity of work, or by transforming conditions of production such as shrinking turnover time of capital or the organic composition of capital in major sectors or regions of the global economy. Costs of maintaining value augmentation as a social goal, as such, it is argued over the remaining chapters of this book, demand capital abdicate its responsibility for meeting general norms of economic life to form a historical society that viably reproduces human existence. Even more intractable, it is explained, is the problematic of "capital becoming surplus" or what in this book is defined as the problem of idle money. The latter is routinely generated in capitalist economies in the withdrawal of funds from the capitalist production centered, value augmenting circuit during business cycles. It becomes hazardous to humanity when pools of idle funds bloat into oceans with no possibility of ever being converted into real capital to be "activated" in production-centered circuits.

Remember, the capitalist stage of consumerism structurally congeals around the capitalist management of the use value complex of consumer durables, the automobile being the representative type. Its form of capital, corporate capital as represented in history by the TNC, coordinates production of a welter of standardized components in integrated, multidivisional business systems which eschewed market pricing by internalizing transactions domestically while reconfiguring global trade around intra-industry, intra-firm flows of goods. It also self-financed, as noted in earlier chapters, which imparted to management a significant degree of flexibility to advance TNC production centered, value augmenting interests. The profit model of corporate capital with its gargantuan fixed costs in automobile production revolved around high throughput and low unit costs where output is absorbed by ever-expanding mass consumption. Such mass consumption, in turn, is fortified by a matrix of extra-economic institutional supports and class accord, both of which contributed to partial decommodification of labor power to, paradoxically, maintain labor power as a commodity. Sustaining mass commodified labor forces in this paradoxical fashion hinged on cultivating their "alter egos as consumers" (Fleetwood 2008). This was required under the golden age's economic exigencies of relatively closed advanced economies where ever-expanding mass consumption largely depended on wages paid to workers as noted in Chap. 5. The edifice of "economic nationalist" *consumerist* accumulators is then cocooned by an international architecture of supranational institutions centered upon the Bretton Woods international monetary system (Westra 2009: 89–90).

Certainly, historical variances in the extra-economic institutional matrices existed during the golden age, but their "similarities far outweigh their differences" (Frieden 2006: 238–47). In fact, the stage-specific structures of *consumerism* launched first, historically, in the US such that even the "coordinated" or "negotiated" variant of these harked back to the New Deal response to the Great Depression and were exported to Western Europe vis-à-vis the Marshall Plan following WWII (Van der Pijl 2015: 41). Ditto for financial systems which, notwithstanding US "liberal" propensities, were governed by state policy or state-sanctioned banking organizations that set interest rates and maintained a stable banking population to preclude any significant bank failure among major advanced economies from the end of WWII to 1974 (Grossman 2010:

255–9). Though stable banking systems in consumer durable producing economies played an important part in "activating" funds for production-centered activities. Tendencies in the golden age toward the increased pooling of idle funds had to be managed. As briefly discussed in Chap. 3, the "roundaboutness" of consumer durable production with the complex layering of interconnected business temporally separating production of inputs from final consumption draws banks into financing short-term TNC debt as it prompts TNCs to take on "money manager" duties (Westra 2016: 147–8). Further, notwithstanding ever-expanding mass consumption of consumer durables, social and individual savings, in the case of US capitalism, significantly outstripped domestic investment needs. These idle funds were subsequently mopped up in the US by the welfare-warfare state along with US individuals and businesses coveting for foreign assets (Eichengreen 2010: 12–4).

Empirical-historical analysis of the late 1970s and 1980s following the crisis of the golden age thus shows how, against the backdrop of the above constituents of *consumerism*, the twin problems of raising rates of exploitation and bloating of idle money pools interpenetrated as they played out in the global economy. As *consumerism* began to decompose following the profitization crisis of the golden age rates of accumulation slowed and capital from major economies set off on a trek across the globe seeking investment outlets. However, the causal argument found in literatures on a "new international division of labor" drawn upon by Lash and Urry and Piore and Sabel, that it was capital flight to newly industrializing economies (NIEs) in search of low wages from which diminution in rates of accumulation of the golden age derived, is wrong. Private financial flows to NIEs only ratchet up from 1974 well after profit rates in major golden age economies plummeted. As well, foreign direct investment (FDI) in East Asian NIEs of South Korea and Taiwan, for example, was negligible contradicting the initial story of NIE export platforms leaching investment and jobs from golden age economies (Webber and Rigby 1996: 444–7). And the financial flows of surplus or idle funds trekking across the globe to escape diminishing investment opportunities in advanced golden age economies were parlayed by "strong" NIE states into indigenous "economic nationalist", full-scale industrial development models (Webber and Rigby 1996: 463). Arguably, even as structures of the capitalist stage of *consumerism* crumbled in the US, and other advanced economies, these were given as last gasp in South Korea's and, to a lesser extent, Taiwan's development (Westra 2006).

However, the absorption of the initial volley of idle funds from moribund golden age economies to produce NIE development of full-scale industrial competitors contributed little to the long-term problem of pooling idle money. Nor to the needs of capital to raise rates of exploitation in key sectors or regions of the global economy. Rather as NIEs rapidly approached the technological frontiers of erstwhile golden age economies, the result was simply the enlargement of the field of "mature" consumer durable producing economies that became subject to the same constraints that tumbled *consumerist* capital in the US, the EU, and Japan. To summarize: "As capital sought to unbind itself from constraints of labour and demand in industrial capitalist economies so it has brought additional economies into the bounds of those constraints" (Webber and Rigby 2001: 261).

Much the same may be said of other sources of nascent footloose funds. It is true as per circulating lore that the City of London attracted "surplus" or idle, largely dollar deposits from myriad sources to its newly constituted "offshore" Eurodollar market during the 1960s. These were then bolstered exponentially by idle dollars flooding out from the Organization of the Petroleum Exporting Countries in the 1970s. But recycling of these funds, as unregulated as the Eurodollar market was, only supported global redistribution through projects of "economic nationalist" catch-up development from the third world to the Soviet bloc as per the golden age institutional inertia (Van der Pijl 2015: 47). Further, the spiraling inflation the flooding of US dollars into world markets contributed to imparted a half-decade lease on life to the Keynesian welfare state in the US itself with federal, state, and local governments borrowing at well below the rate of inflation to fund programs between 1973 and 1981 (Frieden 2006: 368–9).

In 1980 the mess hit the fan when Paul Volcker, then US Federal Reserve Bank (FED) chair, struck with his "coup" (Dumenil and Levy 2004: 69). It has to be understood that while at the level of stage theory which studies capital synchronically by abstracting a material type of capital from its most advanced form and geospatial site, the US for the stage of *consumerism*, from the perspective of empirical-historical analysis, the US economy in the post-WWII period played an unrivaled part in maintaining post-WWII global stability in that the dollar was enshrined by Bretton Wood as world money. Advanced economies benefited from this "contract" given the way the US dollar furnished the necessary global liquidity for post-WWII reconstruction and reinvigorated international trade. And the US was to be kept honest by the Bretton Woods mandate that US gold be exchanged for dollars should this or that state end up holding an excess. Already in 1971 with the US economy in crisis, the Bretton Woods contract was unilaterally broken. This allowed the increasingly inflation hit dollars to flood global markets and unleash a dollar borrowing orgy. As the Volcker coup hit with its stratospheric interest rate hike, global debt became unsustainable overnight. Yet while Volcker's coup virtually bankrupted the US welfare state and nearly toppled the US banking system, in the end it proved a bonanza for the US capitalist class.

Globalization and Financialization Rising

Idle, largely unwanted dollars from across the globe flooded into US markets and US dollar denominated savings instruments. Inflation was quashed and the value of the dollar appreciated against other major currencies. For the production-centered economy, already thrashed by fallen rates of profit and diminution of investment, Volcker's interest rate hike created a perverse situation where real interest rates spiked not only well above rates of profit from TNC manufacturing but also over double the rate of growth of the advanced economy's national product. Funds now gushed out from production-centered activities toward burgeoning financial markets headquartered on Wall Street and the short-term arbitrage opportunities that were being hatched there (Westra 2016: 161–2). What through the 1970s had been attrition against the golden age class accord turned, in the 1980s, into a blitzkrieg with estimates of losses in manufacturing employment in the US reaching almost four million jobs equivalent to 25 percent of industrial employment in manufacturing (Westra 2012: 79). For those who remained in manufacturing jobs, capital pounced to radically increase rates of exploitation by intensifying labor. This period witnessed the introduction of performance measuring programs such as Six Sigma that "filled the pores" in working days. It is estimated that total break time in industry plummeted from 13 percent of the working day in the 1980s to 8 percent by the 2000s, thus effectively expanding the working day by 30 minutes at no further cost in wages or taxes on capital (Moody 2017: 15–6).

Rapid appreciation of the US dollar against other major currencies which created the financial bonanza for the US economy effectively priced US goods out of global markets. This exacerbated festering golden age crisis tendencies toward disintegrating of consumer durable mass production systems. From the 1980s, TNCs deverticalized and, then, disinternalized their integrated production systems, slicing, dicing, and disarticulating them across the globe. It is from this juncture, not the 1970s period of the NIE rise, where internationalized production by US and other advanced economy TNCs contributes to the wholesale disintegration of *consumerist* consumer durable production-centered capital accumulation. Ultimately, by the 1990s, US commanding heights TNCs essentially morphed into "not-at-all-manufacturing" brands that do not actually make anything. This great disintegration and disarticulation would reconfigure the US labor force such that by 1994 the "temp" agency Manpower ascended as the largest single employer only to be eclipsed in that role by the retail monster Wal-Mart by 2003 (Westra 2012: 84–5).

But, with investment potentialities in the production-centered economy vanishing, the problem of pooling idle money hypertrophies. And it is not a question of simply investing of monies withdrawn from the production-centered, profit-making circuit of capital held idle. Various categories of social savings including pension and insurance funds, later added to by money market mutual funds (MMMFs), compounded in the closing years of the golden age. Investment of these monies, whether by banks in blue chip companies or funds themselves in secure government debt, was tightly regulated by New Deal legislation. In 1980, pension and mutual funds combined totaled close to $1 trillion in the US. By the early 1990s, this amount was $6.4 trillion. In 1995, pension, insurance, mutual, and other "institutional" funds amounted to

$11.2 trillion or 140.8 percent of US gross domestic product (GDP) (Westra 2012: 111–2). Instructively, ever so prescient business guru, Peter Drucker, had noted by the early 1990s that the sheer magnitude of those monies composed of deferred wages and social savings eclipsed that of real *capital* tied to production-centered activities. And, in fact, their very bloated quantitative existence defied definability within the parameters of mainstream economics (Drucker 1994). Yet, the challenge such monies faced were sources of yield given the disintegrated production-centered economy and limitation of available government debt instruments. And, if scant investment opportunities for pension and sundry funds resided in the real production-centered economy, what about idle funds held by TNCs and banks?

After all, in slicing, dicing, and disarticulating production-centered activities across the globe, TNCs radically restructured the international production system emplacing manufacturing activities in largely low wage, weak regulatory regimes in the third world. Operating in this environment of pliant workers and, more often than not, authoritarian governments was a new breed of contract suppliers or "non-equity modes" (NEM) of TNC control. TNCs maintained suzerainty over this edifice through ICTs which reconnected the whole "value chain" from conception and high value-added activities in the hands of brands through the carrying out of varied tasks by myriad NEM suppliers around the world. Soon, traversing these global value chains (GVCs) were "intermediate goods" or subproducts touching down hither and thither in assembly mills to ensure the full gamut of consumer durables which had powered prosperity in erstwhile integrated, "economic nationalist" projects, now became the prerogative of no one country.

Where the TNC three-piece dream suit of divestiture miscarries, however, is over the fact that in abdicating its mass commodified labor force and non-economic support systems helping to sustain it, shifting manufacturing operations off TNC books and transferring work to pliant, low-wage workers, while raising rates of exploitation to restore profitability, the outlets for investing the profits are simultaneously reduced. Though TNCs had initially self-financed in the stage of consumerism, the drop in funding TNCs did require from banks only further exacerbated bank travails which were already mounting under the weight of the non-performing loans banks found themselves saddled with in the aftermath of Volcker's interest rate hike coup.

It would be precisely this triumvirate of institutional funds, TNCs and major banks, all holding oceans of idle money with zero chance of ever being converted into real capital invested in surplus value creating production-centered activity that were the loudest cheerleaders for the neoliberal policy package of deregulation and liberalization. As neoliberal ideology has it, if only this idle money, "capital" in mainstream parlance, is "freed" from golden age state regulatory shackles, entrepreneurial "animal spirits" of bygone years can again be unleashed to swing economies into golden age–like prosperity. Of course, this is ideological gibberish.

In the first instance, the very existence of oceans of idle funds inconvertible to real capital signals the decay of capitalism as a historical society as it exposes the inability of capital to allocate resources in socially redeeming, income generating, and profit-making ways. Second, what neoliberals ultimately "freed" is not capital. It is idle money. And "freeing" it, as per the neoliberal mantra, to potentially act on its own account, resurrects pathologies of antediluvian "loan capital" or usury that accumulates only by expropriation of wealth. This is precisely what Arrighi, in Chap. 4, never grasps. It may be the "dream" of capital to "set itself free" (to quote him) from the production-centered circuit but, once it does, it is no longer capital.

Deregulation "freed" idle funds held in TNC coffers from 1982 by legalizing practices which had previously been considered stock market manipulation. What neoliberal ideology concocted as "agency theory" essentially claimed that TNC profitization languishing in the doldrums from the demise of the golden age meant that Galbraith's "technostructure" management was shirking its responsibility to shareholders and that another metric was needed for business success. This is "shareholder value" reflected in the equity market capitalization of the business. Without factories and production in which TNCs had invested both borrowed and earned monies, then TNCs turned to gambits selling and buying back their own stock: this activity exploding from the 1990s with US businesses spending $7 trillion on buybacks, equal to half their profits, since 2004. As put by Rana Foroohar (2016: 124–31):

> Over the last thirty years, buybacks have come to represent the main form of corporate "strategy"…corporations haven't been issuing stock to raise money for their own investments for years. Rather, they've been buying back equities in order to push up the value of their own stock prices.

It has to be understood here as well that it is idle funds sloshing around financial markets that flow in to publicly traded companies. Such flows represent 80 percent of business investment in the US. Monies composing these flows are raised largely from pension and other social savings funds, now rechristened as "institutional investors", and channeled via a new breed of "asset management" or "private equity" firms into the stock market. Institutional investors with obligations to pensioners and other savers are more than happy to park their holdings with asset management companies which then feed them into the stock market in search of yield with little concern over the fact that stock prices bear little relation to what remains of a real production-centered economy (Foroohar 2016: 132–3, 218–9). Between 1990 and 2013, the value of public companies globally increased by 524 percent to $51 trillion. However, global GDP grew only 228 percent during that period (Westra 2016: 215). Financialization, as such, according to Satyajit Das, creates "an artificial economy with manipulated and unsustainable values". Equity markets which, from the stage of imperialism, were developed by capital to draw idle funds from across society into production-centered endeavors as business investment needs expanded "have increasingly decoupled from the real economy…threaten[ing] the market's viability" (Das 2016: 43–4). In fact, net issuance of stocks for public companies today (new equities minus buybacks) constitutes a staggering *minus* $3 trillion, something that helps explain why with increased global demand for equity investments stocks are priced at 25 times corporate earnings (*Washington Post* 2018).

Where financialization and globalization initially interpenetrate is in the way financialization constitutes a surreptitious industrial policy. Its compulsion for businesses to increase shareholder value by downsizing to their "core competencies" such as research and development, finance, and design, while ensuring exorbitant payouts to shareholders, metastasizes a "downsize and distribute" dynamic over the global economy. This in turn further drives TNCs to shed the last vestiges of their production-centered manufacturing accouterment and transfer it to NEM contractors setup in global low wage locales. Figures demonstrate that TNCs most vigorously outsourcing and carving up production in GVCs populated by ruthless, wage-cutting NEM suppliers are the same TNCs devoting the greatest share of profits to equity buybacks and dividend payments to shareholders (Milberg and Winkler 2013: 210–34).

Explored from another angle, the financing of TNC downsize and distribute gambits by asset management companies channeling institutional funds, or by sundry funds themselves, means that savings by ordinary working people are supporting the very businesses that are slashing jobs and draining the laboring capacities of human beings across third-world segments of GVCs. And, to add insult to injury, the gains from stock market gamesmanship flood into the hands, in the US, of the top 10 percent of wealthy individuals who own 91 percent of all equities (Foroohar 2016: 123). Finally, captivated by the downsize and distribute dynamic, with its short-term, finance gambit horizons, for the US real economy in the 2000s "underlying investment…was less a percentage of GDP than in any decade since World War II" (Foroohar 2016: 55).

Interpenetration of globalization and financialization is impelled by two further factors related to seismic transformations in global production from the decomposing capitalist stage of *consumerism*. One factor, as discussed above by Lipietz, is the competitiveness battle among advanced economies which saw Japan and Germany retain vestiges of their production-centered accouterment through "negotiated" settlements with workers. The second factor follows the disarticulation of the bulk of production-centered activity from advanced economies into GVCs. Statistics tracking this latter process showed manufacturing activity exploding across the third world (Westra 2012: 92). Yet, on close inspection of the figures, it was actually the case that the most pronounced spike in manufacturing value added and manufactures as a proportion of total exports of third-world economies, along with FDI stimulating it, occurred within the East and Southeast Asian region, though China in particular. Why Asia emerged as the central locus of manufacturing GVCs owed much to the initial strategies of Japanese capital in the aftermath of the golden age crisis shifting low value-added production to regional suppliers under original equipment manufacturing and original design manufacturing arrangements. China's integration into the regional economy occurred after its 1978 reform opening. Its attraction stemmed from the literacy, skill, and health endowments of its labor force given the low level of its per capita GDP and the fact that its post-1978 government offered foreign capital attractive terms and infrastructure support to set up export operations in newly opened special economic zones (SEZs). Manufacturing in Asia GVCs, however, epitomized much of what so-called globalization is all about. High and medium value-added intermediate goods streamed from Japan, the US, the EU, South Korea, and Taiwan through Southeast Asia and into China's SEZs for final assembly and export around the world. Export dependency ratios of Southeast Asian middle-income countries jumped as did those of newly industrialized economies NIEs South Korea and Taiwan. China ultimately opened a yawning trade surplus with the US and much of the world even as it ran a trade deficit with Southeast Asia (Hart-Landsberg 2013: 31–9).

If the neoliberal policy support roster for "freeing" bloated pools of idle money from advanced economy production-centered institutional anchors to operate on its own account included institutional funds, TNCs, and big banks (the role of the latter to be visited momentarily), among major states it is the US which has the greatest stake in compelling deregulation and liberalization within the world economy as a whole. After all, the Bretton Woods international monetary system, integral to remaking the post-WWII "free world" order on an "economic nationalist" foundation, instated the dollar as global hub currency in a setting of capital controls. It is true that the hub currency role of the dollar granted an "exorbitant privilege" to the US. However, the Bretton Woods "contractual" pledge by the US to convert excess global dollars into gold kept it on a relatively tight leash as but one economy (though a transcontinental, productivity leading, economy to be sure) within a "free world" trading order superintended by supranational institutions. In unilaterally abrogating Bretton Woods to render the global dollar moored only to US T-Bill IOUs (I owe you), then instigating an interest rate hike coup which ravaged advanced state production-centered economies and dashed "economic nationalist" aspirations across the third world, the US and its capitalist elite stumbled upon a new orientation to the world.

The US as the Singular Global Economy

With the T-Bill IOU based US dollar as world money, participation of states in the global economic order mandated they either export for dollars more goods than they buy or borrow dollars to buy. When the US was "workshop of the world" in the post-WWII golden age, Bretton Woods fostered a virtuous circle which injected liquidity in the global economy to support construction of full-scale industrial "economic nationalist" competitors. Under conditions of its abdicating much of its production-centered economy, yet where the T-Bill IOU based dollar is global hub currency, the US is absolved of the aforementioned constraints on participating in the world trading order. Advanced states such as Japan, Germany, South Korea, and Taiwan that retained vestiges of their *consumerist* integrated production accouterment as well as third-world economies like China within which manufacturing GVCs concentrate, as noted earlier, accumulated mammoth US dollar surpluses. These are then invested in US dollar denominated savings instruments in the deep and versatile Wall Street-centered US financial market. "By 2007 the US was absorbing up to 85 percent of total global capital flows (US$500 billion each year). Asia and Europe were the world's largest net suppliers of capital" (Das 2016: 40). Today, foreign holdings of US public debt alone amount to $6.21 trillion (see Fig. 7.1).

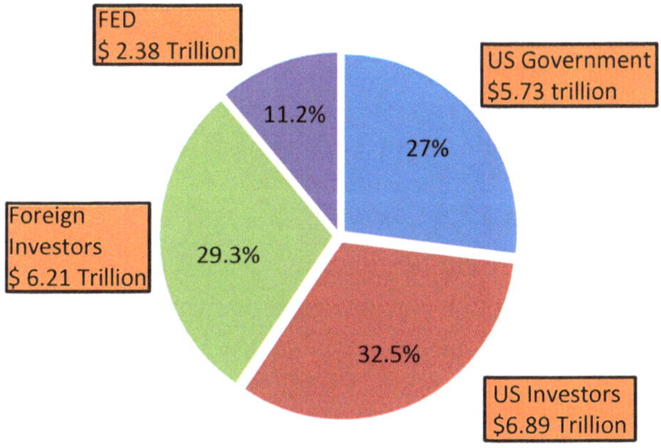

Fig. 7.1 Foreign holdings of US debt in August 2018 (Source: https://www.marketwatch.com)

It is precisely on the foundation of the effectively unanchored US dollar as world money that the US economy gains an automatic borrowing mechanism giving it global policy autonomy denied all other states in the world. Hence, though the US runs widening trade, budget, capital account, and domestic savings deficits, it remains as firmly in the global driver seat as it was at the outset of the golden age when it was workshop of the world. From the demise of the golden age, US consumers first devoured their savings then resorted to an orgy of borrowing in attempting to maintain consumption of consumer goods viewed as tantamount to their "freedom". However, the consumer goods largely emanate from disarticulated manufacturing GVCs with production and assembly based in economies holding US debt. Thus, borrowing to finance consumption in the US exercises little pressure on interest rates which the FED easily manipulates to zero. With its current account deficit financed by savings of the world, US government spending on global military domination and other budget priorities can expand without "crowding out" private sector borrowing. In the end, the US spends well in excess of its domestic savings plus government tax revenues without engendering the sort of price inflation which caused the "stagflation" debacle of the 1970s.

As Tony Smith (Smith 2015: 81) succinctly declares,

> [I]t makes little sense to speak of a US "variety" of capitalism that other regions could emulate. Only a region with the "exorbitant privilege" of a national currency functioning as world money could expand credit money on such a vast scale for such an extended period, while simultaneously enjoying an unprecedented flow of capital inflows receiving relatively low rates of return. It follows that no region could expand debt-fueled speculative bubbles and domestic consumption on the same scale.

Indeed, as I have maintained, given the role of the dollar as world money and the US financial system headquartered on Wall Street constituting a vortex through which global savings and investments engendered by the post-1980s reconfiguring of the world economy pass, globalization is, at bottom, a sexed-up term for the US transubstantiation into a *global economy* (Westra 2012: 81). Wall Street, and the broad spectrum of financial institutions and practices the reference to it here euphemizes, emerges

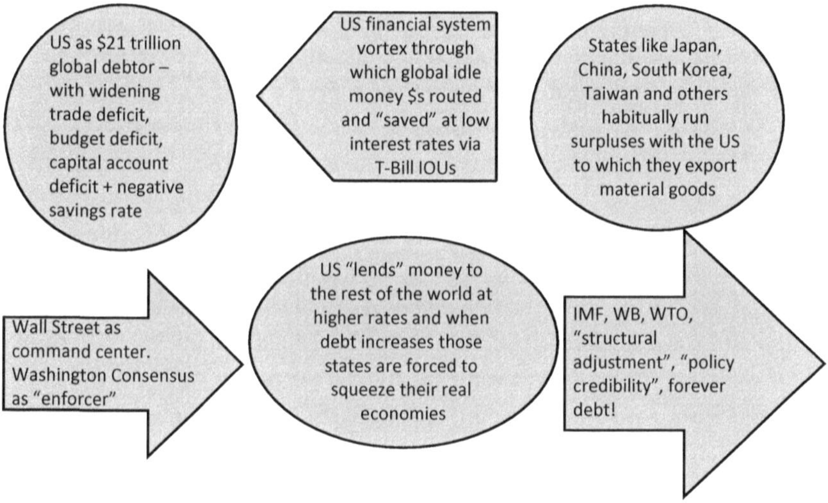

Fig. 7.2 US as a "global" economy (Source: Author)

in the US transubstantiation as the command center for remote control management of the world economy (see Fig. 7.2). Their lending and credit actions are backstopped by the FED and Treasury "serving as de facto central banker of the world, with an unparalleled ability to determine where the horrors of financial crisis would fall with full force and where they would be alleviated" (Smith 2015: 81).

Before we further specify the financial transformations the notion of financialization refers to, beyond the definition above of pooling idle money in capitalist economies with no possibility of ever being converted into real capital—then set "free" to operate on its own account, let us clear up one final matter from the VOC debate. While neoliberal wizards marveled at the paucity of business cycle activity in advanced economies during what is dubbed the Great Moderation, the period was anything but "moderate". Rather it is marked by a series of rotating meltdowns: "the 1987 stock market crash, the 1990 collapse of the junk bond market, the 1994 great bond market massacre, the 1994 Tequila economic crisis in Mexico, the 1997 Asian financial crisis, the 1998 collapse of the hedge fund Long-Term Capital Management, the 1998 default of Russia, and the 2000 dot-com crash". Even Japan, eulogized in the flexible specialization and post-*fordism* literature, fell into a decades-long slump in 1989 which is what supported the claim of superiority of the US liberal market model (Das 2016: 26). In fact, it has been calculated by the International Monetary Fund that between 1970 and 2011 the world economy was wracked by 147 banking crises (Tett 2018).

What ultimately misled analysis of the so-called Great Moderation is the fact that it was precisely during its duration that the production-centered economy, from which cyclical oscillations spring, is disintegrated and disarticulated in GVCs. Capitalist business cycle oscillations, then, which revolve around innovation and economy-wide replacement of fixed capital, as touched upon at several points in earlier chapters, did tend to lose their force. The problem is that they were replaced by a perverse new form of cyclical oscillation of financial bubbles and bursts (Westra 2016: 195–6). As one analyst of the 1997 Asian financial crisis put it in his critical response to various explanations of the debacle, "we should recognise that the financial system is now driving itself, independent of conditions in the real economy, so the chain of causation is: financial system → east Asia" (Webber 2001: 10).

Merchant of Venice Banking and Global Securitization

As treated in Chap. 2 discussion of Hilferding's contribution to theorizing imperialism, and to some extent in our Chap. 4 critique of Arrighi, Marx's theorizing of capital demonstrates how capitalism subsumes and transforms the antediluvian activity of money lending or "loan capital" to generate modern banking in the service of industrial capital. Modern commercial or "relationship" banking plays a vital capitalist social role in capitalist economies. Its role in socializing idle funds withdrawn from the efficient capitalist production-centered circuit has been explained. Because commercial banks exist "outside" anarchic operations of private units of production-centered capital, they are able to agglomerate idle monies from various units and lend it at rates of interest to varied other units, irrespective of their sphere of commodity production, and to commercial capital, all in the service of hastening the conversion of idle money into profit making capital. The notion of "relationship" is also an important part of the capitalist commercial banking equation as banks engage with businesses to discount bills of exchange and extend commercial credit and, therefore, function to assess creditworthiness. Banks' profits are derived from financial intermediation and are received in the form of the interest rate spread between what banks pay to depositors and what they charge borrowers. Interest rates themselves are set in the money market according to supply and demand for funds. Quite simply, the capitalist production-centered commodity economy could not exist without relationship banking in some form.

Investment banks, on the other hand, enter the banking population in capitalist economies with the rise and spread of the joint-stock corporate form. They are the denizens of equity markets and function as broker-dealers in the buying and selling of securities. Between 1946 and 1980, the value of total financial assets of all investment banking securities traders in the US never expanded above two percent of US GDP. Yet, investment banks profited handsomely from their stock market trading monopoly. Further, the Great Depression era 1933 Glass–Steagall Act established a firewall separating investment banking which engages in proprietary trading and commercial banking responsible for lending depositors' money (Westra 2012: 99). Nevertheless, neither interest rate caps nor reserve-to-lending requirements, or even strict separation of investment from commercial banking under golden age financial regulations left either investment banks or commercial banks hard put.

But, in the waning years of the golden age with the US economy struck by simultaneous economic stagnation and inflation or stagflation and with banks increasing loss of TNC customers, the US government began to look the other way as a new coterie of private financial intermediaries (PFIs) bearing new kinds of savings instruments made their debut. First, negotiable certificates of deposit (CDs), then MMMFs, offered higher yielding savings and investment vehicles to be traded in secondary markets at just the time when the virtuous connect between business profitization and safe, "boring" banking imploded (Foroohar 2016: 46–8).

These are the forerunners of what is today referred to as the *shadow banking* system. A spate of legislation soon followed removing restrictions on interest rate arbitrage, categories of assets banks could invest (other peoples' money) in, and even on concentration and centralization of banking to create a world of megabank behemoths. This effectively operated as a countertrend to the fact that between 1978 and 1993 financial sector assets in the hands of institutional investors expanded from 32 percent to 52 percent at the expense of commercial banks in the US; though a similar tendency marked the financial sector in Britain, France, and Germany (Westra 2016: 182). Finally, the Financial Services Modernization Act of 1999 in the US sounded the death knell for Glass-Steagall regulations by eliminating the firewall separating commercial, investment banking, and insurance provision. In the end, neoliberal deregulation engendered a seamless financial web ensnaring erstwhile commercial banks, investment banks, and shadow banking, globally headquartered on Wall Street.

What needs to be factored into the foregoing financial institutional transformation is the fact that during its unfolding debt multiplies exponentially. And it exploded, as Michael Roberts illustrates, in formation of financial bubbles which precede each major bubble burst globally including Japan's credit bubble in the late 1980s, the dot com bubble, the meltdown of 2007 and sovereign debt bubble of 2008–2009. "In the United States between 1950 and 1980, the ratio of nonfinancial debt…was quite stable at 130 percent of GDP. After 1980, it nearly doubled to more than 250 percent; for advanced economies, the average weighted mean ratio has risen 80 percent" (Roberts 2016: 98). Satyajit Das notes, a "2015 study covering twenty-two developed economies and twenty-five developing economies found that between 2000 and 2007 total global debt grew from US$87 trillion to US$142 trillion, an increase of 7.3 percent per annum, double the growth in economic activity" (Das 2016: 33). To accommodate such gargantuan borrowing appetites, Das continues, total global financial assets including equities and securities exploded from $51 trillion in 1990 to $294 trillion by 2014; an aggregate increase of 3.8 times that of global GDP and an annual growth rate of 8 percent also significantly outpacing "real" economic growth (2016: 34).

It is now time to more deeply explore how financialization plays out beyond its specification as bloating oceans of idle money with no possibility of being invested in real economic activity then "freeing" itself to engage in casino games on its own account. Borrowing and the vast agglomerating of debt must be financed. When capitalist economies are not in recession or depression, this occurs through production-centered activity which generates profit rates above costs of borrowing, along with real incomes that pay off loans, are saved, or spent. But, we have already emphasized how bloating of idle money pools was only exacerbated by disintegration of production-centered economies and the disarticulation of production across GVCs. And notwithstanding the accumulation of idle funds in corporate coffers which they increasingly ply in shareholder value gambits, US TNCs incurred $5.3 trillion debt in outstanding bond issues (*Washington Post* 2018). As TNCs zapped their high wage and benefit, mass commodified labor force, workers ratcheted up credit card and mortgage debt to maintain semblances of their golden age lifestyles. Thus, of the debt explosion adverted to above, "80-85 percent financed existing corporate assets, real estate, or unsecured personal finance" (Das 2016: 36). Hence, among advanced economies in 2014, non-financial TNC debt reached 113 percent of GDP with household debt at 90 percent of GDP (Roberts 2016: 99).

Thus, if swelling debt is not being repaid through productive, profit-making investment and the real incomes such generates the only other means of dealing with it is further borrowing or reductions in current consumption. Reductions in current consumption, today politely dubbed austerity, forms part of the discussion in the following chapter. Here, the question of more debt to settle preceding debt takes us back to the commercial banking system which operates on a fractional reserve basis (mandating banks hold cash reserves equal to a fraction of their deposit liabilities): And, to ensure bank solvency, with a given capital adequacy ratio equal to a percent of bank "risk-weighted" assets.

However, in the face of the foregoing constraints on banks credit expansion, and given that production-centered business cycles have been superseded by rotating bubbles and meltdowns that only compound past liabilities, rendering global debt virtually non-repayable, the financial system responded with *securitization*. Securitization in the simplest sense allows banks and PFIs to take illiquid assets off their balance sheets by packaging them off to an investment "vehicle". In this fashion, securitization reduces the amount of capital the financial system as a whole must hold against lending as it enables it to circumvent capital reserve requirements imposed on commercial banks. Among the off-balance sheet items conjured up by securitization are the arcane forms of derivatives, a contractual obligation deriving its value from the performance of some underlying instrument, asset or rate. Following the 1982 Volcker coup induced third-world debt crisis which perpetuated a neoliberal holocaust on so many of the worlds impoverished economies (Bond 2008), as major US banks were bailed out by big government from their non-performing "relationship" loans, third-world debt was rapidly securitized through swaps. Swaps are a form of derivative held off-balance sheet which allowed banks to trade obligations, usually fixed for variable or floating obligations, on interest rates or currencies, all the while enjoying lucrative fees yet without putting new loans on their books that compromised capital adequacy ratios.

In the US economy a smorgasbord of new-fangled securitization instruments that read like an alphabet soup were conjured up to expand lending over credit cards, mortgages and even securitization to "insure" derivative bets. First, asset backed securities (ABS) packaged off credit card debt. Then mortgage backed securities (MBS) helped supersize mortgage lending. ABS, MBS, and other loan obligations were repackaged into collateralized debt obligations (CDOs) that allowed banks and PFIs to "bundle" debts of varying sources and quality into a single derivative vehicle. The icing on the cake was the credit default swap (CDS) which purported to "insure" ABS, MBS, CDOs, and so on (as the later were also "squared", "cubed" and repackaged if such is imaginable). While the story of what sparked the meltdown of 2007–2008, and how the vortex for global finance constituted by Wall Street transmitted meltdown impacts across the world's major financial systems, has been told and retold (Westra 2016: 190–2). What concerns us here, on the one hand, is that no lessons were really learned. On top of bond issuances, for example, TNCs are now ramping up borrowing from megabanks which are securitizing this debt in collateralized loan obligations (CLOs) as fast as they can get it. Banks are then selling CLOs to yield-hungry institutional investors such as pension and insurance funds from Japan (*Washington Post* 2018). Even student loans are being securitized in student loan asset backed securities (SLABS). At end 2017, SLABS packaging the $1.3 trillion US student debt represented the second largest source of consumer debt in the US after home mortgages (*Business Insider* 2017).

On the other hand, and most importantly, are the broader implications of securitization for the financial system as a whole and capitalism as a mode of economy. Remember, the fundamental purpose of securitization is to reduce the amount of capital the financial system needs to hold against lending by effectively removing loans from bank balance sheets by packaging them off into securities. This, however, transforms the very nature of capitalist lending based upon commercial or relationship banking. Under relationship banking, because it is banks to which loan plus interest is paid, banks assume a capitalist social responsibility in lending to evaluate creditworthiness of borrowers and to avail themselves in that regard as to what socially redeeming, income generating activity loaned funds are to be put toward. As advanced economies' financial systems are enveloped by securitization, the role of banks in financial intermediation is replaced by financial disintermediation by banks and assorted PFIs. Here banks simply "originate" loans which are then "distributed" to end buyers of securities. In this "originate to distribute" banking model loan plus interest is not paid to banks but to end buyers of securities. Banks thus disclaim any accountability for creditworthiness of borrowers or to what ends loans are put.

This, of course, raises a crucial question. As maintained above relationship banking in some form is essential to the existence of the capitalist commodity economy. Yet, major TNCs in the process of morphing into "not-at-all-manufacturing" brands and shareholder value buyback arbitragers no longer have much need for relationship services of banks. Banks turn toward household lending in advanced economies largely for mortgage purposes, and channeling of household savings into financial markets, has proved problem fraught (Lapavitsas 2013: 238–41). Therefore, as Costas Lapavitsas queries, if what remains for banks beyond their key relationship purpose in evaluating creditworthiness is simply creating money and operating payment systems, tasks potentially undertaken by institutions such as the post office, "what is their social and economic function" in current economies (Lapavitsas 2013: 321)?

Securitization and shadow banking with which commercial and investment banks are now entwined in fact already established a parallel mode of money creation from the networks of commercial banks operating under the umbrella of a central bank as marked capitalist economies from the mid-nineteenth century. Central to this new money creation is the "repurchase agreement" or repo. As Erik Gerding explains, repos are "one of the primary reasons financial institutions created the entire shadow banking system" (Gerding 2014: 409–10). Succinctly stated, a repo entails a borrower selling a security below its "market" price. An agreement is then made by the borrower to repurchase the security at a higher price in the future, often at an "overnight" rate. The magnitude of both leverage gained by one party and collateral held by the other is predicated on the price difference dubbed the "haircut". For the whole originate to distribute banking system, it is the repo which constitutes the principal form of funding. Shadow banking and repos thus render sundry forms of long- and medium-term "assets" magically money-like in the short term. However, as evidenced from the meltdown, securitization, and derivatives, trading in the shadow banking network is an opaque affair carried on unregulated, "over the counter" by counterparties. Further, the substantive basis of credit creation in capitalist economies is eradicated by repos. In relationship banking whether it is businesses borrowing directly from banks or the latter discounting bills in chains of commercial credit, the collateral is always, ultimately, real goods. But, in the originate to distribute casino economy it is the repo which produces cash funding that acts as collateral with the whole exercise undertaken for purely financial purposes (Mohun 2016).

Yet, when the 2007–2008 meltdown hit, central banks of major advanced economies, including the US FED, the ultimate job description of which is to act as lender of last resort for commercial relationship banks, were forced to respond as lender of last resort to the now interwoven web of shadow banks, commercial banks, investment banks, and insurance companies. This effectively transforms the FED into a "broker-dealer of last resort" (Garcia 2014). Unfortunately for humanity, with erstwhile commercial banks that had played a vital capitalist social role in society now roped into casino games through their intermeshing in the shadow banking system, and central banks now transitioned into broker-dealers of last resort to backstop the whole casino, what remains of the real, production-centered economy is progressively starved for funds leaving it on a perpetual deflationary footing.

And the shadow banking system, even by the more "narrow" definition, has only enlarged following the meltdown of 2007–2008 to mammoth dimensions today estimated at $45 trillion, over 30 percent of which is rooted in the US financial sector. Shadow banks via repos thus constitute "net providers of cash to the financial system…while banks remain net recipients of cash" (Financial Stability Board 2018: 2–3). Even more disconcerting is the predominating role US shadow banking plays, both through the dollar as hub currency and T-Bill IOUs as "collateral" for gambits, essentially enshrining the US economy and Wall Street as the engine of global financialization (Tokunaga 2018; Tokunaga and Epstein 2018). This only reconfirms the position of the US as a global economy adverted to above and Wall Street as the command center managing economies through their financial sectors by remote control.

We will look further at the dynamic irrationalities of this system in the following chapter. After all, lending of idle funds in capitalist commodity economies is governed according to market rational supply and demand setting of interest rates. Commercial banks' role is essential to the efficient circuit of capitalist value augmentation or profit making. And it is the same conditions by which value is augmented that capital is able to meet the general norms of economic life and reproduce capitalism as a historical society as profit makings byproduct. Originate to distribute banking is governed by no such commodity economic rational principle; thus, as in the *Merchant of Venice*, repayment conditions are set arbitrarily in ways potentially leading to ruination of the debtor or compelling debtors to strive for ruination of others.

References

Bond, P. 2008. Against Volcker. *Counterpunch*, November 12. https://www.counterpunch.org/2008/11/12/against-volcker/.

Boyer, R. 2005. How and Why Capitalisms Differ. *Economy and Society* 34 (4): 509–557.

Business Insider. 2017. GOLDMAN SACHS: There's an Attractive Way to Profit from the $1.3 trillion Student-loan Bubble. December 9. https://www.businessinsider.com/student-loan-bubble-investment-is-private-abs-goldman-2017-12.

Coates, D. 2015. Varieties of Capitalism and the 'Great Moderation'. In *New Directions in Comparative Capitalisms Research: Critical and Global Perspectives*, ed. M. Ebenau, I. Bruff, and C. May. Basingstoke: Palgrave Macmillan.

Das, S. 2016. *A Banquet of Consequences: The Reality of Our Unusually Uncertain Economic Future*. Harlow: Pearson Education.

Drucker, P. 1994. *Post-Capitalist Society*. New York: Harper Business.

Dumenil, G., and D. Levy. 2004. *Capital Resurgent: The Roots of the Neoliberal Revolution*. Cambridge, MA: Harvard University Press.

Eichengreen, B. 2010. *Global Imbalances and the Lessons of Bretton Woods*. Cambridge: MIT Press.

Financial Stability Board. 2018. *Global Shadow Banking Monitoring Report 2017*. http://www.fsb.org/wp-content/uploads/P050318-1.pdf#page=4.

Fleetwood, S. 2008. Workers and Their Alter Egos as Consumers. *Capital & Class* 32 (1): 31–47.

Foroohar, R. 2016. *Makers and Takers: The Rise of Finance and Fall of American Business*. New York: Crown Business.

Frieden, J. 2006. *Global Capitalism: Its Fall and Rise in the Twentieth Century*. New York: W.W. Norton.

Garcia, C. 2014. Cash Pools, Fed Rev-repos, and the Stagnationist, Future Part 1. *Financial Times*, July 3. http://ftalphaville.ft.com/2014/07/03/1890002/cash-pools-fed-rev-repos-and-the-stagnationist-future-part-1/.

Gerding, E. 2014. *Law, Bubbles and Financial Regulation*. London: Routledge.

Grossman, R. 2010. *Unsettled Account: The Evolution of Banking in the Industrialized World Since 1800*. Princeton: Princeton University Press.

Hart-Landsberg, M. 2013. *Capitalist Globalization: Consequences, Resistance, and Alternatives*. New York: Monthly Review Press.

Hodgson, G. 1998. The Approach of Institutional Economics. *Journal of Economic Literature* 36: 166–192.

Itoh, M. 2000. *The Japanese Economy Reconsidered*. Basingstoke: Palgrave Macmillan.

Lapavitsas, C. 2013. *Profiting Without Production: How Finance Exploits Us All*. London: Verso.

Lipietz, A. 2001. The Fortunes and Misfortunes of Post-Fordism. In *Phases of Capitalist Development: Booms, Crises and Globalizations*, ed. R. Albritton, M. Itoh, R. Westra, and A. Zuege. Basingstoke: Palgrave.

McDonough, T. 2015. Social Structures of Accumulation: A Marxist Comparison of Capitalisms? In *New Directions in Comparative Capitalisms Research: Critical and Global Perspectives*, ed. M. Ebenau, I. Bruff, and C. May. Basingstoke: Palgrave Macmillan.

Milberg, W., and D. Winkler. 2013. *Outsourcing Economics: Global Value Chains in Capitalist Development*. Cambridge: Cambridge University Press.

Mohun, S. 2016. Inequality, Money Markets and Crisis. In *The Great Financial Meltdown: Systemic, Conjunctural or Policy-Created?* ed. T. Subasat. Northampton: Edward Elgar.

Moody, K. 2017. *On New Terrain: How Capital Is Reshaping the Battleground of Class War*. Chicago: Haymarket.

Van der Pijl, K. 2015. Varieties of Capitalism or Dominant Fractions? In *The Future of Capitalism After the Financial Crisis: The Varieties of Capitalism Debate in the Age of Austerity*, ed. R. Westra, D. Badeen, and R. Albritton. London: Routledge.

Roberts, M. 2016. *The Long Depression: How It Happened*. In *Why It Happened and What Happens Next*. Chicago: Haymarket Books.

Smith, T. 2015. The End of One American Century…and the Beginning of Another? In *The Future of Capitalism After the Financial Crisis: The Varieties of Capitalism Debate in the Age of Austerity*, ed. R. Westra, D. Badeen, and R. Albritton. London: Routledge.

Tett, G. 2018. Have We Learnt the Lessons of the Financial Crisis? *Financial Times*. https://www.ft.com/content/a9b25e40-ac37-11e8-89a1-e5de165fa619.

Tokunaga, J. 2018. *US Dollar Based Financialization in the 2000s: A Marxian Approach*. Paper presented to 2018 International Symposium on K. Marx in the 21st Century – Bicentennial Anniversary of Karl Marx's Birth, Hosei University, Tokyo, Japan, December 23.

Tokunaga, J., and G. Epstein. 2018. The Endogenous Finance of Global-dollar Based Financial Fragility in the 2000s: A Minskyan Approach. *Review of Keynesian Economics* 6 (1): 62–82.

Washington Post. 2018. Beware the 'Mother of All Credit Bubbles'. June 8. https://www.washingtonpost.com/business/economy/beware-the-mother-of-all-credit-bubbles/2018/06/08/940f467c-69af-11e8-9e38-24e693b38637_story.html

Webber, M. 2001. Finance and the Real Economy: Theoretical Implications of the Financial Crisis in Asia. *Geoforum* 32: 1–13.

Webber, M., and D. Rigby. 1996. *The Golden Age Illusion: Rethinking Postwar Capitalism*. London: Guilford Press.

———. 2001. Growth and Change in the World Economy Since 1950. In *Phases of Capitalist Development: Booms, Crises and Globalizations*, ed. R. Albritton, M. Itoh, R. Westra, and A. Zuege. Basingstoke: Palgrave.

Westra, R. 1996. Periodizing Capitalism and the Political Economy of Post-War Japan. *Journal of Contemporary Asia* 26 (4): 431–451.

———. 2003. Social Theory, Economic Crisis, and the Japanese Political Economy: A Review Article. *Review of International Political Economy* 10 (2): 363–373.

———. 2006. The Capitalist Stage of Consumerism and South Korean Development. *Journal of Contemporary Asia* 36 (1): 3–25.

———. 2009. *Political Economy and Globalization*. London: Routledge.

———. 2012. *The Evil Axis of Finance: The US-Japan-China Stranglehold on the Global Future*. Atlanta, GA: Clarity Press.

———. 2016. *Unleashing Usury: How Finance Opened the Door to Capitalism Then Swallowed It Whole*. Atlanta, GA: Clarity Press.

———. 2018. Roy Bhaskar's Critical Realism and the Social Science of Marxian Economics. *Review of Radical Political Economics*. Online first September 21, 2018. https://doi.org/10.1177/0486613418787405.

Williams, K., T. Cutler, J. Williams, and C. Haslam. 2001. The End of Mass Production? In *Regulationist Perspectives on Fordism and Post-Fordism: Regulation Theory and the Crisis of Capitalism 3*, ed. B. Jessop. Northampton: Edward Elgar.

Wood, S. 2001. The Japanization of Fordism. In *Regulationist Perspectives on Fordism and Post-Fordism: Regulation Theory and the Crisis of Capitalism 3*, ed. B. Jessop. Northampton: Edward Elgar.

8

Landlordization of Capitalism and Extinction of an Economic Species

In his timely intervention into debate over financialization, Francois Chesnais hits on an important feature of the world economic transformations captured by the term in what he describes as the permeation of "capital as function" by "capital as property" (Chesnais 2016: 16). His allusion here is to the way the doctrine of shareholder value concocted by bourgeois economics through "agency theory" has shifted the relations of ownership and control of transnational corporations (TNCs), particularly by the insertion into the ownership equation of the aforementioned (in Chap. 7) private equity or asset management companies which hold vast institutional portfolios hunting for yield (Chesnais 2016: 104–5). However, the notion of capital as property or asset, hit on by Chesnais, carries deeper, far-reaching implications for current economic goings-on than Chesnais grasps (Westra 2019: 120–2).

To probe these, it is necessary to step back into Marx's analyses in *Capital*. Readers familiar with the work know well how, in Volume I, Marx makes the case for the commodification of labor power is the sine qua non of capitalism. By commodification of labor power Marx means the "freeing" of labor power in a "double sense": "freed" from access to the means of livelihood in land and means of production, and "free" to

R. Westra, *Periodizing Capitalism and Capitalist Extinction*, Palgrave Insights into Apocalypse Economics, https://doi.org/10.1007/978-3-030-14390-9_8

sell their remaining commodity (the ability to work) on the market for capital, which now owns the means of production, to purchase (Marx 1977: 272–3). Because the very existence of capitalism is predicated upon the availability for capital of the direct producers already separated from land and other means of production, Marx engages in a lengthy historical excursus at the end of the volume on the process of primitive accumulation by which in Britain, the first really existing capitalist economy in human history, the commodification of labor power is brought about (Marx 1977: 873–913).

Yet it is not until Volume III of *Capital* that Marx treats questions of ownership and "value" of land. The first reason for this is that in preceding volumes of *Capital* Marx is concerned with the fundamental capital–labor relation through which the labor and production process of society is subsumed by capital for the purpose of producing commodities as value objects. Land, per se, plays no part in this. However, while land in itself has no role in production of commodities as value objects, it is a necessary component of the production of commodities as *use values*. Thus, in Volume III of *Capital*, in further elaborating the categories and structure of capitalist social relations, Marx explains how capital relates to land and the products of agriculture as a key sphere of social production and component of the capitalist division of labor (Marx 1991: 773–4).

Second, capitalist value augmentation has no need for landlords. In theorizing capitalist agriculture Marx assumes that landlords neither invest in agriculture nor work themselves. He puts it thus: capitalism in agriculture "dissolves the connection between landownership and land so thoroughly that the landed proprietor can spend his entire life in Constantinople, while his landed property remains in Scotland". Marx continues, as investment in land by capitalist farmers raises its productive value, "[property owners] put away in their private purses the result of a social development achieved without their participation" (Marx 1991: 755, 757).

Third, we arrive here at the crux of what Marx's theorizing of capital as property exposes about our current economic malaise is the way Marx deals with the owner of land. Though the landowner plays no economic role in production or investment in Marx's theorization of capitalist agriculture, the category of *rent* constitutes the nexus by which land and its legal owner are brought in to the capitalist economy in a capitalistically rational fashion. But capital must tread carefully in this process given that private property and private ownership of means of production constitute its own presuppositions. On the one hand, Marx notes that landed property is an alien principle for capital because ownership titles of land are bound to murky historical inheritances. Such an ownership condition is diametrically opposed to the way titles to property in commodities circulate on the capitalist market. Commodities are bought and sold on the market based upon the fact that a capitalistically rational "original" price has been paid for them. For capital to deal with landed property then (without upending its own presupposition), Marx argues, it needs to create a *legal fiction*. This fiction is that land, bequeathed to humanity by nature, but at the dawn of the capitalist era is found monopolized in hands of a particular social class, is the legal prerogative of its current owners as is the case of all commodity owners in capitalist society.

On the other hand, with the legal fiction of landownership established, land is thus integrated into the circulation of commodities as an "asset" the ownership of which constitutes entitlement to the income stream of *rent*. Through rent accruing to property ownership capital essentially bends its principles by recognizing an entity "external" to it as a claimant on surplus value. Nevertheless, in bending its principles, it resides in the way levels of rental incomes are arrived at in the market, that capital establishes capitalist class predominance over the wielding of the productive forces of society for the purpose of value augmentation. That is, capital does not pursue a modus vivendi with landownership to buy and sell land as an "asset" or thrive on rental income from such activity. The latter was already viewed as anathema by David Ricardo who bemoaned circumstances where rent gobbled up profits from manufacturing asserting, famously (in his chapter "On Profits"), how such "will have arrested all accumulation" and be "an end of accumulation" (Ricardo 1817). Rather the price of land and its rental is arrived at by the "method of capitalization" which in the case of land is based upon its potential productivity through the application of productive labor (Albritton 1991: 20).

However, to fully explicate the method of capitalization, Marx's Volume III of *Capital* turns to elaborate the concept of interest. In establishing the principle of property ownership as entitlement to an income stream for an entity "external" to it, what Marx demonstrates is the way capital applies this principle "internally" to itself with the category of interest. That is, when idle or "dormant money reserves", as Marx initially dubs idle money (Marx 1991: 738), are withdrawn from the productive, profit-making circuit of capital, they cease to be capital. Instead, when they are socialized in the banking system, which superintends the money market where idle funds are placed, capital itself is converted into a commodity or "asset". And to the banks that own the funds as their custodian, it is an income stream of interest, rather than profit, which accrues to ownership of their asset. Again, under relationship or commercial banking, interest rates are set in the capitalist market according to the supply and demand for funds. This latter, in turn, depends upon investment conditions for the potential application of commodified labor power in production-centered, profit-making, and income-generating activities. Thus, antediluvian "loan capital" or money lending with its predatory feeding upon social wealth is neutralized as capital subsumes and transforms it in a commodity economic rational fashion, and turns it toward socially redeeming purposes in relationship or commercial banking. It is, therefore, through the prism, the method of capitalization substantiated by the case of capital itself traded as a commodity, that it is possible to grasp how land may be purchased as a commodity or held as an income-generating asset, the price for which is determined by the method of capitalization (Sekine 1997: 132–3). Only in this fashion is rent endowed with its capitalistically rational form.

Euthanasia of the Rentier

If Ricardo had agonized over the power of the landed class ratcheting up rent to devour profits, John Maynard Keynes lived the Depression-era nightmare of potential income accruing to financial assets drawing investment from production-centered activity in a way that also "arrested all accumulation" as Ricardo put it. Keynes, thus, famously advocated for the euthanizing of the rentier class at the time. But likely both Ricardo and Keynes would writhe in their graves if they witnessed the simultaneous leeching of profit-making, production-centered wealth to rent and interest as occurs in today's economic excrescence. We may recall from the previous chapter our point on business guru Peter Drucker decrying the fact that money held in the hands of a coterie of funds was of a greater magnitude than real capital and that neoclassical economics had no theory to capture the exigencies of this. Drucker further claimed how such a constellation coming to pass heralded the advent of a society of "capitalism without capitalists" or "post-capitalism" (Drucker 1994: 69–70, 77–8).

In Chap. 4 of this volume we commenced with a review of theories which sought to address changes among major economies occurring from the 1970s and proceeding through the 1980s and 1990s. Designations applied to these changes included post-industrial, disorganized, flexibly specialized, and so forth. Critically summarizing this work, I highlighted the lacuna they all shared in failing to problematize capitalism; a deficit which stems from the epistemological strategy the theorists employed of stylizing facts with no foundation in understanding what capitalism is in its fundamental incarnation. Descriptions of transformatory processes such as the diminution of the manufacturing working class and rapid expansion of the service sector, as well as the increased application of information and computer technologies (ICTs) such as robotics were marshaled by the authors to critique Marx's pithy theory of historical materialism. Marx's famous "Preface" had projected the historical course of modes of production in terms of developing forces of production gestating a new social order coming into contradiction with relations of production which constrained the emergence of the new. This, then, leads to a period of social revolution. In the case of socialism, it was believed tendencies toward enlargement of the working class, industrial agglomeration, restructuring of ownership of increasingly gigantic monopolistic, market eschewing firms managed by functionaries rather than entrepreneurs, all presaged the socialist future of society-wide rational planning. But, with these tendencies subverted by the actual course of history, so proponents of post-industrial society claimed, Marx is proven "wrong".

However, the schema of historical materialism, which remains the best meta-theoretical explanation of historical change on offer to this day, is not "wrong" in broad brush terms. Where it does mislead is in its lack of precision over the specific contradiction of capitalism and what analysis of that contradiction tells us about capitalist change and the historical delimitations of capitalism as a historical society.[1] Marx, of course, knew this, as following publication of his pithy theory of history he turned to the in-depth study of capital that consumed the remainder of his life. In *Capital*, which constitutes Marx's most systematic theorizing of the capitalist commodity economy, Marx specifies the fundamental contradiction of capital as that between value and use value. As elaborated above, in Chap. 6 of the present book, the very historical existence of a capitalist society is predicated upon the amenability of human use value life to management by capital for the abstract purpose of value augmentation. What stage theory as a level of analysis of Marxian political economy tells us in its periodizing of capitalism is that "light" use values such as cotton textiles are particularly suited to capitalist value augmentation. However, exigencies of capitalist management of heavier, more "roundabout" production involved in steel and industrial chemicals, as well as the mass production of consumer durables, compel capital to enlist an enlarging matrix of non-capitalist, extra-economic supports for value augmentation.

What much of the futuristic thinking about post-industrial society elides is the cardinal question of whether the use value dimensions of such an economy as these have been set forth by theorists lend themselves to management by capitalist commodity economic "market" principles (even with a matrix of extra-economic supports). There are several issues involved in answering this question. One relates to the big problem of "measuring" things that are "post" or not "industrial" or "material" as is the case with non-financial intangibles or "intangible assets" such as knowledge, "branding", design, research and development (R&D), and much of the incorporeal accouterment of ICTs as per Perez's "microelectronic paradigm" (Haskel and Westlake 2018: 22). This measurement problem involves both market pricing and assessing "indirect costs" of individual intangible assets as well as how these are dealt with at an economy-wide level. A second issue entails treatment of remaining components of the industrial economy under conditions where indirect costs supersede direct costs. The third issue is most paradoxical and cuts to the heart of the problematizing of capitalism. It swirls around the fact that intangible assets per se are *not* capital (though their incorporation into material wherewithal of production-centered activity sees them "act" with real capital). In themselves, however, intangibles constitute a form of property or "asset". And, while they may factor into production-centered, profit-making activity of real capital, their ownership is remunerated in the form of rent. Thus, what emerges here is a similar question to what Drucker posed concerning the pooling of idle funds exceeding magnitudes of real capital, which led him to dub the current economy as characterized by capitalism without capitalists. In this case, Jonathan Haskel and Stian Westlake pose the question in terms of "capitalism without capital" (Haskel and Westlake 2018).

In the US economy, 1985 was the pivotal year when financial services first contributed more to national income (according to conventional measurement, a vital point to be revisited) than manufacturing. Current estimates have financial services contributing over 40 percent of US gross domestic product (GDP). According to the World Intellectual Property Organization, knowledge- and technology-intensive industries which now account for over 30 percent of global output gain more rental income from intellectual property rights than through production of goods and services. The critical year for the ascendancy of intellectual property in branding, design, copyright, patents, and so on is 1995 (Standing 2017: 24, 50). For both the US and UK economies, evidence has it that intangible investment surpassed tangible investment in terms of value added in the mid-1990s. Averaging among major European Union (EU) economies, including Germany, Austria, Denmark, and the Netherlands which continue to maintain a significant element of tangible capital intensity, along with the US and UK and others which maintain less, shows the share of GDP contributed by intangible investment outstripping overall tangible investment around 2008 (Haskel and Westlake 2018: 24–7). Another estimate has intangible assets such as patents accounting "for between one third to half of the US corporate sector" today (Seabrooke and Wigan 2014: 259).

Patent filings globally, in fact, have increased dramatically in conjunction with the "downsize and distribute" processes of TNC globalization which disarticulate production into global value chains (GVCs). The two million patent filings in 2011 were more than double the number filed around the world in 1995. In 2013, 2.6 million patent applications were filed globally and in 2014 the figure rose to 2.7 million. Indeed, in 2014 it is estimated that 10.2 million patents were in force around the world.

Already in 2009 when 6.7 million patents were in force their estimated global value was $10 trillion. On the assumption that patent value globally increases with patent "stocks", the 2015 estimate of patent value globally would be $15 trillion or 20 percent of world GDP. In 2014 it is the US that held 25 percent of the 10.2 million patents in force globally with Japan coming in second at 19 percent (Standing 2017: 51–2, 59). Cross-border payments for use of intellectual property in 2014 amounted to approximately $300 billion, over three times the 2000 estimate and ten times the 1990 figure. It is the US which accounts for around 40 percent of cross-border payments. In 2013, of US $129 billion in intellectual property exports, $45 billion went to patents, $43 billion to software, and $17 billion from trademarks. The latter tripled from 1995 reaching 7.5 million in 2014. Thus, from 1987 to 2011, US investment in brands amounted to 22 percent of all investment in intangible assets, greater than that devoted to R&D or design. US business also led in the $466 billion globally invested in brands in 2011. Apple's brand, worth an estimated $145 billion in 2015, constitutes 20 percent of its market value with its stock of patents being even more valuable (Standing 2017: 62–6).

Dealing with the enigmatic third question posed above, of whether capitalism without capital can, in fact, be considered as a kind of capitalism, brings us back to the problem Mandel noted about late capitalism. That is, whether the ICT economy of "robotism" enabled a specifically capitalist economy to raise rates of surplus value sufficiently to offset the increasing organic composition of capital to rejuvenate accumulation. Mandel's skepticism is borne out by the fact that the full-scale industrial economies of late capitalism were never reconstituted in the attempt to raise rates of exploitation. Rather they are disintegrated, with commanding heights businesses disinternalizing their production-centered accouterment and disarticulating production into GVCs within which mostly subproducts traverse the globe.

Certainly, the disarticulating of production in GVCs concentrating the making of things in low wage locales such as China contributes to expanding the global pool of surplus value. This has been accomplished, in part, as I have argued, by remunerating labor power below the costs of its reproduction. China, in particular, offers fertile ground for such a pattern given the peculiar landholding arrangements that followed upon its post-1978 "reforms" and the Soviet era "internal passport" system, or *hukou*, which restricts the mobility of labor power in ways akin to the Poor Law or Speenhamland system studied by Polanyi (see Chap. 2). This pattern predisposes workers in China to part-time, contingent, and precarious employment forestalling the complete commodification of labor power as occurred in advanced capitalist economies. There, the working class was formed through wholesale absorption by urbanized industrialization and radical diminution of primary sector employment and rural population. In China, laborers "float" back and forth from manufacturing to subsistence agriculture leaving to the latter the reproduction costs of rearing their young and tending for the aged. If we take China's large primary sector employment level today and consider its "floating population" in statistics on urbanization, China evinces a profile close to what current advanced economies looked like in the early nineteenth century (Westra 2018b).

While the fact of the business of making things being outsourced to, at best, a semi-proletariat remunerated for work below the value of labor power, harking back to antediluvian forms of exploitation reminiscent of "putting out" systems at the dawn of the capitalist era, speaks volumes about the disintegration of capitalism, even more instructive in this regard are effects of the investment equation. As Duncan Foley explains, if we approach the question through the enchanted prism of bourgeois economics, it appears that the vast existing pool of surplus value extracted from productive labor globally, potentially equal to between one-half and two-thirds of global GDP, holds out "limitless" possibilities for businesses in the post-industrial, knowledge economy to accumulate wealth. Yet, what may benefit one country that is the strategic geospatial repository for intellectual property, or even one or two major businesses, does not hold for the economy as a whole. Human material reproduction in a capitalist society is still dependent upon the pool of surplus value generated by exploitation of productive labor power (Foley 2013: 264–5).

At the level of the global economy, while GVCs in consumer electronics and other consumer goods, for example, run through East and Southeast Asia into China for final assembly, the evidence shows how in 2016 the international intellectual property receipts directed to advanced, high-income economies were 100 times—$323 billion to $3 billion—more than accrued to low- and middle-income countries (Durand and Milberg 2018: 17). For the individual company, to continue with the Apple TNC exemplar, 60 percent of the retail price of its new iPhones wherever they are sold flow to it (as a US based company), giving Apple a 40 percent profit margin. This does not include its haul from rental income for its online sale of apps (Standing 2017: 69). Yet, according to a study by the Asian Development Bank of an early version of Apple's iPhone, while over 96 percent of its export value derives from re-exported components produced elsewhere, a paltry 3.6 percent of its cost is attributed to Chinese laborers (Smith 2016: 28).

Thus, to tally up here, our analysis presented above shows the surpassing of tangible investment in major economies by investment in intangibles. In the US, investment in equipment, new factories, and even the R&D category of intangibles plummeted in manufacturing businesses by 21 percent between 2000 and 2010 (Foroohar 2016: 68).[2] Across GVCs where manufacturing has been sliced and diced and disarticulated to low wage locales, the share of intangibles in the value of final products has been increasing from 2000. As well, evidence shows greater intangible intensity in the "lead segments" of GVCs (Durand and Milberg 2018: 5), something which explains the benefit flow of intellectual property receipts to advanced, high-income economies. Therefore, while the downsize and distribute model that sees TNCs maintain investment in core competencies which lead to expanding returns to intangible investment as the flipside to intensifying exploitation of labor (particularly in the third world, though not exclusively as touched on in the previous chapter) has produced wealth effects, it accomplishes this at the cost of increasingly unraveling remnants of the capitalist commodity economy.

Remember, the accrual of income to intangibles assets, which constitute an increasing proportion of advanced economy GDP, is as rent. It is not just a question here of the widening inequalities impelled in advanced economies by the combined intangible intensity embodied in technological change plus so-called globalization where the material production of the "new economy" technologies is outsourced to low wage workers in Asia, as Branko Milanovic argues (2016: 110). Rather, to paraphrase Ricardo, if rent siphons an increasing proportion of surplus value destined in a capitalist economy for conversion into profits to then be invested in the production centered, value augmenting circuit of capital, accumulation will be "arrested" and capitalism "end". This is the chimera of the view that advanced, purportedly capitalist economies "can accomplish the same trick…[as oil exporting economies coveting scarce resource rents] through specializing in finance and intellectual property rents" (Foley 2013: 266). Of course, the caveat here is that such Middle East states are rentier economies par excellence and never have been, nor will be, capitalist economies in any substantive sense. That such rentier economies are ruled by odious authoritarian monarchies does, however, beg political questions for the future of advanced societies pursuing the rentier tack. We will return to this in the final chapter.

However, advanced economies appear to be doubling down on just this chimerical belief. From 1995, as intangible assets and investment enlarged their footprint in the US economy, a spate of legislation issued forth extending durations of patents, copyrights, and so on. Through trade agreements and pressure, the US foisted its system of intellectual property protections upon the world (Baker 2016: 79–82). The so-called globalization era has thus witnessed the "proliferation of over 3200 bilateral or multilateral treaties on trade and investment, most of which have never been subject to any democratic mandate or accountability" (Standing 2017: 67–8). Though, as Standing continues, that these treaties are referred to as "trade" agreements is misleading to the highest degree. Their purpose, rather, is to weaken nation-state regulatory infrastructures while enforcing US-style intellectual property protection.

But the disintegration of capitalism is also impelled by issues of pricing and measurement of economic contributions made by intangible investment and the policy conclusions drawn from this. Enthusiasts of post-industrial, disorganized, and flexibly specialized capitalism had based a good part of their prognosis for the future on the massive employment shifts occurred following the demise of the post–World War II (WWII) golden age as service sector work exploded. Yet, excluding finance, insurance, and real estate (FIRE) service sector employment, of the 14.2 million new private sector service jobs created in the US economy between 1990 and 2010, that are likely performed by "working class" people, 57 percent have been in health care, social care, food services, and so on.

And, by 2010, 43 percent of these service jobs in the US were classified as "below low wage" (Moody 2017: 19–21), a designation which, in Marxian economic parlance, attests to employment remunerated below costs of reproducing labor power.

Services, of course, are found in virtually every society in human history. In capitalist economies, they are essential to efficient operations of even capitalist production-centered business. Unlike commodified labor power which is purchased on the capitalist market for its abstract general attribute that is applied by capital to production of *any* good according to shifting patterns of social demand and opportunities for value augmentation the market presents, services are traded in the capitalist market for their concrete specific attributes and do not directly produce surplus value. A "service economy" is, hence, an oxymoron in line with Kautsky's "petty commodity" economy in that no human society can allocate resources in a way that guarantees its economic viability on market principles with workers bound to specific tasks as is the case with services. It is true, as Moody maintains, that current economic practices increasingly regiment services (2017: 21–2), but even robotizing of housework personnel akin to depiction of such in the Hollywood film *Stepford Wives*, will not augment value.

Prices of services, unlike commodified labor power the price for which is set objectively in the capitalist market, are set according to subjective criteria. Without the anchor of commodified labor power, the requirement that resources are allocated in society to ensure the direct producers receive the product of their necessary labor is abrogated. This can only lead to increasingly arbitrary allocation of social resources in an economy attempting to salvage the market principle of capital in contradiction to the necessity for human material reproduction that the general norms of economic life are met as a byproduct of value augmentation. Such arbitrary allocation of resources following from swelling service sector employment is exacerbated by the impact of ICT and enlargement of the economic scope of intangible assets on market pricing. Specifically, capitalist market operations through which the law of value reproduces human use value life as a byproduct of value augmentation are attuned to direct costs of material inputs and commodified labor power. Periodizing capitalism as a level of analysis in Marxian political economy demonstrates how the exigencies of capitalistically producing heavier, roundabout stage specific use values bring to bear a growing panoply of extra-economic supports on both the investment side and consumption side of capitalism. But even heavy, expensive durable goods and their means of production in the stage of *consumerism* still embodied largely direct costs. Mainstream economics and accounting practices felt measuring indirect costs of an "asset", such as knowledge potentially embodied in a good could be safely ignored (Haskel and Westlake 2018: 8).

When mainstream economists began to take greater interest in predominating of intangible assets in production was when the "old" objects of the stage of *consumerism* were increasingly being "made intelligent". As buzzwords capturing this abounded, Paul Mason recounts, "the knowledge economy, the information society, cognitive capitalism...[the] assumption was that info-capitalism and the free-market model worked in tandem...To some the change looked big enough to conclude it was as important as the move from merchant capitalism to industrial capitalism...But just as economists got busy explaining how this 'third kind of capitalism' works, they ran into a problem: it doesn't" (Mason 2015: 110–2). One major difficulty besides dealing with indirect costs in production is the fact that many ICT products, such as software, have "zero marginal cost" as Jeremy Rifkin emphasizes. Of course, for capitalists, a condition "where the marginal cost of producing each additional unit is nearly zero" would be anathema. When "goods and services become nearly free, profits dry up, the exchange of property in markets shuts down, and the capitalist system dies" (Rifkin 2015: 85). Capitalists, with government in tow, responded by placing their intangible economic stocks in gargantuan monopolistic silos protected by the aforementioned phalanx of patent, trademark, and copyright legislation and global investment treaties (Rifkin 2015: 242ff).

Our final issue for assessing the capitalist substance of economies enveloped by exploding intangible intensity links up with one of the questions of the simultaneous impact of financialization, that of measurement. In the United Nations (UN) System of National Accounts investment is categorized as applying to production of material goods. On the other hand, a "producer" engaging in production is classified in terms of business, government, or a "third sector" which includes myriad services bought and sold on the market. In US National Income and Product Accounts (NIPA) created following the Great Depression to measure real production-centered categories of wages and profits in relation to real output, the third sector including FIRE was slotted into that calculus as producer of an "imputed" output (Foley 2013: 258). This system made some macroeconomic sense when intangible investment hardly registered on the radar and FIRE played a miniscule economic role. Given the blithe assumption, noted by Mason above, that financialized and info-capitalism "worked in tandem" with "the market", neoclassical economists, Foley continues, spun phantasmagorical models of endless growth from their output imputations.

With regard to technological change and growing intensity of intangibles in current advanced economies, the tendency for intangible investment to be mismeasured has been linked to propensities for equity investment and credit bubbles (Haskel and Westlake 2018: 114–5). Tony Smith suggests the leading role the US and US-based TNCs in technology sectors, bolstered by the automatic borrowing mechanism of the US dollar, carries the potential for one day valorizing the Himalayan debt mountain the US has compiled. Though he does recognize with Foley that while a TNC, such as Apple, has parlayed intellectual property into their own golden age, on an economy-wide scale much of the architecture of monopoly, patent, and other protections and conflicts mitigate this outcome (Smith 2015: 87–90).

If we add the antinomies of financialization and its measurement to the issue of the trend toward deflation driven by the rentier economy of intangible assets, the exhaustion of capitalism as a mode of organizing human material affairs appears even clearer. To treat the manifestations of financialization including explosion in financial assets—at the beginning of 2015 the US position here was worth $81.7 trillion, more than the combined total of Japan, the UK, and China (Foroohar 2016: 13)—the growth in financial assets of non-financial businesses; and the enlarging of financial profits within economies relative to profits from production-centered accumulation (Lapavitsas 2013: 217ff); how to "represent" this in NIPA accounts became a major concern. As Foley explains, however, in the case of financial sector incomes the imputing of output to the FIRE sector involves a double counting (Foley 2013: 263).

Much of what factors into this imputed output as salaries, or purchase of a financial service, derives from interest payments which are already a deduction from total surplus value. This is particularly acute with regard to exorbitant salaries and bonuses paid to financial executives and functionaries. Massive fees and commissions that myriad financial intermediaries receive for various services rendered are included here, such as what the financial sector garners in relation to equity buybacks or merger and acquisition (M&A) by non-financial businesses; foreign exchange trading, brokerage and wealth management for the über-rich, asset management for insurance and pension funds, and so on. NIPA captures all these as contributions of the financial sector to GDP growth. There is also the question of titanic movements in valuations on equity markets, including when new shares are issued through initial public offerings and M&A. Yet these wild speculative occurrences simply redistribute portions of surplus value, not create it (Chesnais 2016: 74–5).

As pointed out in the concluding paragraphs of Chap. 7, the policy decisions of advanced economy states and central banks which support this mishmash on the basis of its imputed contribution to GDP, only further leech wealth from the truncated real capitalist production-centered economy intensifying its deflationary tendencies already mounting through the predation of technological rentiers.

Capitalists without Capitalism and the Illusion of a New Stage

As suggested in the introductory chapter to this book, the longer capitalism persists or even argumentation to that effect made by the Left for its transfiguring in yet another form as per the schema of historical materialism, which suggests modes of production only "end" when they are supplanted by another, the greater disincentives for socialist change become. Why this is the case stems from the fact that while socialism entails a leap for humanity into the unknown (or, for many, the unpleasant "known" colored by the Soviet-style experience), capitalism's persistence gives some cold comfort that the world will not be turned completely upside down.

In Marxian political economy, work in the tradition of Regulation School (RS) and Social Structures of Accumulation (SSA), treated in Chap. 5, and follow-up writings of the varieties of capitalism (VOC) approach dealt with in Chap. 7, captivated a significant cross-section of critical scholarship with its foci upon the variegated "institutional" dimension of capitalist stability. RS and SSA, as explored in this volume, initially placed the study of "regulating" or institutional "structuring" of capital accumulation within frameworks that set out such studies in the context of one "level" of theory. Such intermediate or mid-range level of theory was ostensibly to be guided by an abstract, economic level of theory and serve its utility in informing complex historical divergences and transformations of capitalism. Yet, given the paucity of theoretical attention devoted by RS and SSA to cultivating the other levels of theory and specifying how they might work in concert to produce knowledge of capitalism, the intermediate range institutional concerns of these theories came to subsume the whole project. VOC essentially banished all semblances of abstract theorizing of capital, as per Marx's lifelong lucubration in *Capital*, to settle upon notions of "the market" as essentially one institution subsisting among others. Whether this "market" as ever more ingeniously modeled by the neoclassical apostolate is actually capitalist in any of its really existing historical incarnations of the twenty-first century never enters the analytical equation.

While SSA had initially left the question of a new stage of capitalism following the demise of the golden age swirling in debate (McDonough 2010: 34–8), important new work in the SSA tradition has endeavored to theorize the existence of a neoliberal stage of capitalism. Long-time adherent of SSA, David Kotz argues that the post-1980s economic shifts ultimately brought into being a "radically changed form of capitalism" (Kotz 2017: 8). Kotz, importantly, dubs the post-1980s period neoliberalism to highlight the particular policies supporting this purported new form of capital accumulation. For him, while multiplex tendencies investigated in literatures on globalization or financialization emerge as significant elements of the post-1980s world, what the rubric neoliberalism captures is the "internal coherence" the specific new set of policies reinforce among key economic, political, and ideological institutions and practices. This relates to the SSA position developed more fully in

Chap. 5, shared by RS, that social structures of accumulation arise to mitigate conflicts inhering in capitalism so as to promote and stabilize accumulation in the medium to long term (Kotz 2017: 3–4). It is in the US that neoliberalism germinates, according to Kotz, though the period may be designated a neoliberal era or stage because of the imbibing by other states of neoliberal economic restructuring dictates; particularly as these have been wielded through international institutions like the International Monetary Fund (IMF), World Bank, and World Trade Organization (Kotz 2017: 32).

In putting forward the characteristics of neoliberalism as a stage of capitalism, Kotz contrasts them with what he refers to as the "regulated" capitalism of the golden age. First, neoliberalism stands for rolling back state regulatory and supportive armature with regard to non-financial and financial business activities, social protections, social welfare programs, public functions and goods, progressive taxation, anti-trust (monopolization), and US commitment to international monetary stability, much of which is treated in earlier chapters. Second, neoliberalism promotes flexibilization of labor markets as discussed by Lipietz in Chap. 7. As one SSA theorist puts it, "the most dominant institutional feature of the neoliberal SSA is the power of capital over labor" (Lippit 2010: 68). Third, neoliberalism transforms the commanding heights corporate sector, accelerating intra-firm competition which prompts business to downsize, replaces the "company man" of Galbraith's technostructure with the extravagantly remunerated "outsider" CEO, and fosters the independence of the financial sector from the non-financial sector. As Kotz summarizes, if there exists one "unifying principle [it] is the greatly expanded role of market forces in regulation of economic activity, with a reduced role for regulation by other types of relations such as states, corporate bureaucracies, trade unions, and professional associations" (2015: 41).

SSA theorist William Tabb further emphasizes with Kotz that neoliberal capitalism is "globally coherent" (Tabb 2010: 147). Globalization, he argues, reinforces neoliberal renunciation of the welfare state by internationalization of the power of capital over labor through the disarticulation of production into GVCs. Financialization then adds to neoliberalism and globalization the increasing dominance of the financial sector over the economy at large. Tabb declares (2010: 149):

> It means that stock prices, currency values, and interest rates shape the economic prospects of working people and these in turn are at the mercy of speculators who increasingly constrain and shape corporate strategies and the choices of politicians. It is the predominance of financial activities over production of goods and services that powerfully characterizes the new SSA.

However, while there is nothing inherently objectionable in the SSA empirics on the world economic transformations of neoliberalism it is not clear from what is elaborated in their work why this period is considered a stage of capitalism, nor from where alleged neoliberal "coherence" springs. After all, as Kotz readily recognizes the impacts of signal economic changes he claims are compelled by neoliberalism were never foreseen (2017: 103). Neoliberalism as an ideology, a point we will return to later, has a history reaching back into the same period when the thought and practice of the golden age class accord and welfare state gained acceptance. Because, as Kotz also notes, the technologies of post- or neo-*fordism* began to reshape economies largely in tandem with the ascendance of neoliberalism (2017: 48–9), its early policy dictates were directed at reviving the dynamism of "economic nationalist", fully integrated systems of consumer durable production of the stage of *consumerism* and golden age prosperity that flowed from these which the crisis, that hit the US economy first in the late 1960s, terminated. And, notwithstanding increasingly shrill neoliberal chanting across the 1970s, US policymakers and capitalist class believed they could have their cake and eat it too by maintaining the global role of the dollar while reinvigorating US industry. But the logic of capital in its final, belabored expression of managing the use value space of consumer durables in the capitalist stage of *consumerism* had already demonstrated its exhaustion and inability to contribute to reproducing human material life notwithstanding herculean superstructure reinforcement. Thus, the only path to maintain elements of golden age–like economies at the juncture of the late 1970s was to strengthen social democracy in ways that tipped the superstructure superintendence balance much further in the direction of social democratic redistribution and socialism. While somewhere at a deep subconscious level it may have been this specter which animated neoliberal ideology, even the Volcker coup which heralded the dawn of the neoliberal era set off a chain of consequences that were unintended.

Remember the initial two neoliberal policy prescriptions—monetarism and "supply-side" economics? Really, the one thing neoliberals got right was part of the former which asserted that throwing an ice bucket on the supply of money and credit to the economy by manipulating interest rates to stratospheric heights will slay the inflation dragon. But, the rest of the story that in an economy structured around a use value complex of consumer durables, rather than a neoclassical textbook economy modeled vaguely on nineteenth-century liberalism, this would subsequently reload capitalism was nonsense. As we have seen, the opposite occurred with the production-centered, profit-making economy and its mass commodified labor forces largely abdicated by capital. And the "power of capital over labor", at least in advanced economies like the US, was that commodified labor remunerated at its costs of reproduction was no longer needed in that capital is able to resurrect antediluvian modes of exploitation akin to putting out systems of merchant capital across the globe.

Neoliberal supply-side mythology, quite simply that supply creates its own demand, which catalyzed the rollback of state regulatory and supportive armature covered by Kotz, to purportedly put money back into the hands of capitalists that will invest it, drove the deregulation and liberalization agenda. But deregulation and liberalization did not "free" capital, but idle money, from golden age tethers. In fact, the paucity of attention devoted to the vital role relationship banking and holding of idle funds in the financial system plays for maintaining capitalist commodity economies is a major lacuna in much Marxian analysis of the post-1980s era. Pools of idle money with no possibility of ever being converted into real capital and "activated" in production-centered, profit-making activity had already begun to agglomerate by the 1970s. Neoliberal policies only exacerbated the impacts of this, as we have shown, in further unraveling what remained of capitalist production-centered economies. And, with specifically capitalist profit making supplanted by predatory rentier activities of financial casino games and monopolistic rents to holders of "property" in intangible assets and the like increasing deductions from available surplus value, economies manifested deflationary propensities which can only be countered in decayed capitalism by compounding debt.

For example, from 1952 to 1968, in the US economy, credit expanded approximately five percent annually. GDP growth, on the other hand, increased on average, almost four percent annually, leaving a one percent gap. Arguably, that gap was engendered by exigencies of complex, layered financing of TNCs in *consumerist* stage specific consumer durable mass production industries. This increased roundaboutness of production brought to bear gargantuan up front, fixed costs with extended real depreciation periods, and massive continuing finance requirements. The fact that competition induced technological change, as adverted to by Mandel, compelled capital to innovate at various points throughout the business irrespective of depreciation time of fixed capital, only added to financing demands. As touched on earlier, it is precisely to meet this condition in consumer durable production that Minsky's "big bank" springs into credit infusing action which then saddles golden age economies with mild inflationary tendencies.

However, in the neoliberal era from end of 1982 to end of 1987, credit explodes at an average annual pace of 10.1 percent adjusted for inflation. At this point the gap between expanding credit and GDP growth spikes to 5.6 percent annually on average. From the end of 2000 to end of 2007 expansion of credit averages 6.4 percent annually compared to GDP growth of only 2.4 percent per year (Duncan 2012: 87–8). Such a quantum leap in expansion of credit in relation to economic growth persisting to this day, notwithstanding a modicum of household deleveraging following the meltdown, shows that it is debt that drives what growth there is to be had in the US economy rather than vice versa (see Figs. 8.1 and 8.2). This "kind" of economy is much more appropriately dubbed *creditism* than capitalism (Duncan 2012: 133–4).

Theorists of monopoly capitalism visited in Chap. 3 have conjured the approach back to life with claims of monopoly capitalism itself reaching a new stage. Keeping in mind their continued adherence to the wrongheaded notion of economic surplus and its purported tendency to rise due to underconsumption, which we have already satisfactorily critiqued, monopoly capitalism is repurposed, in their view, to deal with shifts in the global economy grasped in terms of globalization

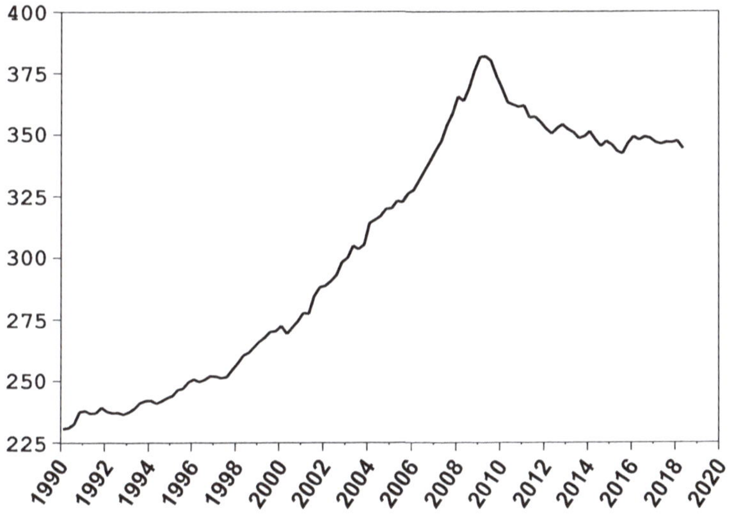

Fig. 8.1 US total credit market debt as a percent of GDP (Source: economagic.com)

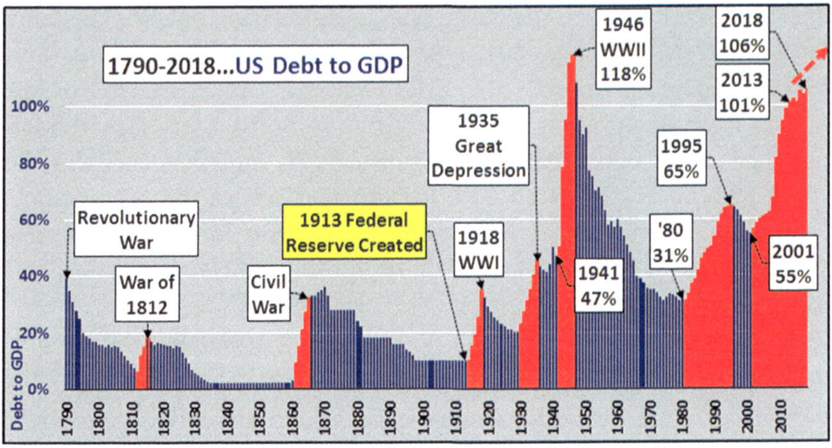

Fig. 8.2 US public debt as a percent of GDP from the Revolutionary War to today (Source: Chris Hamilton https://econimica.blogspot.com)

and financialization as SSA has attempted. In the words of Bellamy Foster and McChesney (2012: 15),

> [T]he "intricately related" aspects of monopolization, stagnation, financialization, and globalization have produced a new historical phase, which we refer to as "monopoly-finance capital". In this period the Triad economies are locked in a stagnation-financialization trap, while linked to the growth in the emerging economies via the global labor Arbitrage—whereby multinational corporations exploit the differences in wage levels in the world in order to extract surplus profits. The result is the worsening of the overall problem of surplus capital absorption and financial instability in the center of the world economy.

This new phase, ensnaring capital in a "stagnation-financialization trap", has become a "fix" for the system, yet is unable to overcome its "structural weaknesses" which rest on its outlets for surplus absorption. Overlaying overaccumulation in the real economy is the attempt by capital "to promote growth in production as a secondary effect of the promotion of speculative financial assets". But the difficulty of promoting this growth remains the rising rate of exploitation of labor (Bellamy Foster and McChesney 2012: 45). Correctly, Bellamy Foster and McChesney grasp the role of central banks as "broker-dealers" of last resort, as we described it in Chap. 7, but go on to assert that, though financialization boosts capital accumulation, it somehow corrodes the entire system by extracting wealth from the "rest of the population". Neoliberalism, thus, constitutes the political and ideological "expression" of the stagnation-financialization "fix" (Bellamy Foster and McChesney 2012: 63–4).

Again, everyone in the academic business of specifying the twenty-first-century economic transmutations draws from the same international databases. Where the problems lurk is in the conceptual frameworks and theoretical huffing and puffing to make the case for the capitalist substance of current advanced economies. Bellamy Foster and McChesney use the term "finance capital", however finance capital in its determinate meaning captures the early period of monopolization in the stage of imperialism with regard to the investment requirements of the then new heavy steel industries. Finance capital refers to the role big banks play in seeking to tap idle funds scattered in various hands across societies beyond idle money made available in the money market. This, in effect, draws rentier incomes into production-centered endeavors. The lure for attracting these idle funds is the joint-stock corporate form of enterprise which uses the capital market to sell equity shares in its ongoing production-centered business. Marx's, and later Hilferding's, use of the term fictitious capital in relation to finance capital, as explained in Chap. 2, applies to the fact of the efficient profit-making circuit of production-centered capital proceeding irrespective of the buying and selling of shares in the capital market. These shares are only "property" titles to income and reflect the commodification of capital *in* an ongoing business. The values at which the shares are traded are "fictitious" precisely because the changes in their ownership occur independently of the motion of real capital operating in its production-centered circuit. They will only become real capital if a business closes and its material parts physically sold off. Major shareholders may then be able to grab some of its capital goods.

But it cannot be stressed more that the bloating oceans of funds which slosh around the world today constitute not capital in any form but idle money with virtually no chance of ever being invested in real production-centered activity. The dearth of capitalist growth and disintegrating of capitalism springs from the fact that with the demise of the golden age, except for ICT infrastructural emplacement during the 1970s and a brief episode in the 1990s, capital has not attempted "to promote growth in production" in advanced economies as Bellamy Foster and McChesney claim. Indeed, even in the case of the 1990s productivity rise captured in statistics, evidence suggests that this was stimulated not by direct investment in production-centered accouterment, but by massive intangible investment initiated by Wal-Mart in its retail chain computer database which stimulated a spate of spending by rival retailers on computer networks to meet the Wal-Mart challenge (Westra 2012: 121–2). Thus, given the redirection of the pool of available surplus value from investment in profit making, production-centered activity toward the financial sector along with technological and other property or "asset" rent, the steep descent in growth of net capital stock among advanced economies is paralleled by a marked deflationary trend as clearly shown by Roberts (2016: 239–42).

Drucker dubbed the current constellation capitalism without capitalists given his belief that that the societal management of the pooling social savings would obviate the task of the specifically capitalist investor and the real capital they wielded. Haskel and Westlake see it as capitalism without capital because of the hypertrophic role of intangible assets, not only in terms of intellectual property income accruing within advanced economies as a whole, but due to the fact that the indirect costs of intangibles overwhelm direct costs of capital in its material incarnation as production-centered accouterment to subvert market operations. Duncan claims the sheer expansion of credit to animate economies in the neoliberal era disqualifies it as a capitalist, hence dubs the period *creditism.* We commenced this section with the heading capitalists without capitalism. If major TNCs have abdicated their production-centered activities, as they morphed into brands, and divested themselves of pesky mass commodified labor forces in advanced economies, is there still a way for them to extract wealth from "the rest of the population" as Bellamy Foster and McChesney obliquely put it?

To answer this question confronts us with the bedeviling issue of financial profits. One answer that takes account of the fact addressed above in relation to financialization of non-financial TNCs which devote increasing proportions of their revenues to equity buybacks and M&A is that, as Chesnais notes, the income flows deriving from financial gambits involved here along with the shifts in valuations of companies, constitute deductions from, and redistributions of, surplus value. Not its creation. Thus, the flipside to financialization as such is embodied in the disarticulation of production through GVCs to labor forces in the third world that are remunerated at extreme low wage levels, often below costs of the reproduction of labor power. This, however, does not amount to a new, "third form" of surplus value extraction, as maintained by John Smith (2016: 236–40). Rather it involves a retreat by capital from the commodification of labor power to antediluvian forms of exploitation redolent of the putting out system of merchant capital in the eighteenth century. What links this excrescence to TNC brand profitization given that such production is outsourced to non-equity mode (NEM) contract suppliers, according to Durand (2017: 128ff), is the particular power imbalance between branded

TNCs and retailers like Wal-Mart *and* contract suppliers. The latter are compelled not just to engage in a race to the bottom in terms of labor costs, but to pay up-front costs for their participation in a branded TNC GVC, a benefit that appears to generate wealth for TNCs through their financial gambits which occupy them in their advanced economy heartlands.

Another side to the question of financial profits treats potential forms of financial expropriation from wages of various categories of worker in advanced economies. Much of the arcane structure of financialization with its opaque securitized instruments is built upon exploding debts of average working people over home mortgages, credit cards, student loans, and so forth. Chesnais argues, however, that profits which accrue to financial institutions from their role in this process do not derive from "secondary exploitation" independent from surplus value realized from surplus labor performed by productive labor in the capitalist circuit and its distributions among sectors of capital (Chesnais 2016: 75–7). He asserts that workers must receive the product of their necessary labor to reproduce their livelihood. If confusion over this arises, it does so due to the fact that a growing proportion of the panoply of goods equivalent to the product of the workers' necessary labor is purchased on credit such that any expropriation amounts to deductions from profits of production-centered capital.

Yet, in my view, Chesnais overlooks the perverse economic goings-on in a world where capital lurches toward extinction. In Volume I of *Capital* Marx emphasizes that assessments for what factors into the product of the workers' necessary labor depend "on the level of civilization attained" and "contains a historical and moral element" (Marx 1977: 275). In the post-WWII golden age of capitalism, the historical and moral element included the family home, automobile, consumer appliances, and the trappings of "middle class" life. It is true as covered in earlier chapters that state social wage and welfare policies contributed to this, but such partial decommodification of labor power paradoxically ensured the maintenance of labor power as a commodity under exigencies of *consumerist* capital accumulation. In advanced economies, during the period of financialization and globalization, the basket of goods required to reproduce workers livelihoods, at "the level of civilization attained", has not changed. But incomes have plummeted with dwindling work opportunities rendering worker debts hypertrophic and virtually unrepayable. This is precisely the incoherent thrust of the neoliberal, supply-side policy of austerity in advanced economies. It seeks to force worker incomes downward below the existing "historical and moral" threshold (Westra 2019: 124). As well, worker mortgage, credit card, and student loan debts metastasize into securitized claims of lenders on worker wage incomes, not surplus value. Whether or not these will ever be actually validated at some future juncture is beside the point. As Lapavitsas explains (2013: 167–8), financial intermediaries therefore tap into worker income streams to expropriate financial profits by trading the sundry securitized credit instruments. This all proceeds with *Merchant of Venice*–like abandon with scant concern over whether borrowers will ultimately be destroyed.

Neoliberalism as the Ideological Last Stand

In a book written just after the 2007–2008 financial meltdown, an analyst queried about the "strange non-death of neoliberalism" given the overwhelming evidence of its policy package exacerbating those economic tendencies euphemized as globalization and financialization that are leading humanity to ruin (Crouch 2011). As we have seen, while neoliberal policies were embraced by capitalist ruling classes, or forced into their adoption through US international dollarization as the US morphed into a global economy dependent upon such, their real economic ramifications unraveled what remained of the stage structures of *consumerism* hence visiting upon the world tendencies that are destroying humanity. Though I disagree with the SSA claim of "coherence" in any capitalistically rational sense for neoliberalism, Kotz's argument for the staying power of neoliberal ideology is instructive. Keynesianism and social democracy, he avers, never commanded the sort of deep-seated societal allegiance as neoliberalism because of its fence-sitting over what economic principles should govern society. Neoliberalism, on the other hand, expresses the original zeitgeist of the rising bourgeois class when it presented itself as the beacon of individual liberty, meritocratic society, and bulwark against tyranny and arbitrary authority in its challenge to the decaying feudal order (Kotz 2017: 121–2).

Of course, as John McMurtry cautions, this does not mean that neoliberalism and neoclassical economics upon which it rests have not marshaled an inquisition-like structure across intellectual spaces to help galvanize neoliberal ideology as a global common sense world view (McMurtry 1999: 23ff). Kotz had suggested that a crisis of sufficient dimensions potentially acts to dislodge such a common sense. However, nothing of the sort happened following the meltdown of 2007–2008. Estimates have it that to cover bailout and support costs of major financial and non-financial businesses advanced economies will need overall spending of approximately three percent of GDP going forward. It knocked standards of living across major economies down ten percent below where they were in pre-crisis years and there standards will likely stay in "perpetuity". And public debt in advanced economies enlarged from 2007 to 2014 by 34 percent (Turner 2016: 3).

Unperturbed, global ruling classes and their ideological and political mouthpieces only doubled down on the pre-meltdown course. Through a device known as "quantitative easing" (QE) where myriad modes of debt issuance are deployed by states to expand the monetary base of economies, the US Federal Reserve Bank (FED), European Central Bank (ECB), Bank of England, and Bank of Japan (BOJ) pumped $6 trillion into flailing economies from mid-2008 to early 2014. By early 2016, central bank assets of the foregoing plus Switzerland, Denmark, and Sweden amounted to 35 percent of global GDP. Much to the chagrin of neoliberals, who believed a simple reversal of their policy for slaying the inflation dragon will rejuvenate economies, nothing of the sort occurred. When so-called zero interest policy failed to revive economies, governments turned to negative interest rate policy (NIRP), such that in 2016 the share of global GDP at NIRP leaped to 25 percent (Westra 2016: 225). Yet, the money continues to pool aimlessly as idle balances with little incentive, even at NIRP, for banks to lend to businesses in a dead economy.[3]

In its analysis of global economic risk, the IMF warns that global debt has reached "historic highs" resting by the end of 2016 at a "record peak" of $164 trillion equal to 225 percent of global GDP. The depth of this debt is now 12 percent greater than its previous peak in 2009 immediately following the meltdown (IMF 2018). Yardeni Research shows asset holdings of the FED, ECB, and BOJ as of November 2018 at $14.3 trillion. In terms of local currency, at nominal GDP, the BOJ has performed the extraordinary feat of compiling an asset base in the third quarter of 2018 of 100.3 percent of Japan's GDP. The figures here for the ECB and FED, respectively, are 39.7 percent and 20.4 percent of GDP. When we add the $5.2 trillion of assets held by the Peoples Bank of China (PBOC) in November 2018 into this unholy mix the total debt in major central bank hands leaps to $19.4 trillion (Yardeni Research 2019).

As disturbing as the specter of such debt revealed by these current figures is, in themselves they do not explain what is happening in the world. Argument above was presented to the effect that the sort of real economic business cycles which impelled oscillations of prosperity and depression have, since the late 1980s, been supplanted by rotating asset bubbles and subsequent bubble bursts. The QE injections into major economy central bank balance sheets feed the same tendencies toward financial games with existing corporate assets, real estate, and so on which characterized debt-fueled spending and leverage prior to the meltdown. It has been suggested that we are now in the middle of an "everything bubble" which is starting to deflate (Das 2018).

If cyclical oscillations of the golden age, notwithstanding state macroeconomic policymaking, could still be explored by applying Marxian crisis analysis of falling profit rates and overaccumulation of capital in relation to the size of the industrial reserve army, this dynamic no longer carries much economic force today (though to the extent Marxian economists continue to detect oscillations based upon profit fluctuations, these are driven by bubble and burst dynamics; the tail wagging residues of the commodity production dog, so to speak). This, of course, begs an important question. At several points in this book, we have referred to Marx's statement that in every mode of production in history "one specific kind of production" or economic principle is determinant in ensuring the material reproduction of society. Uno drew upon what Marx demonstrated in his study of the capitalist commodity economy to further specify the determinate role of the "specific kind of production" in satisfying the general norms of economic life. These norms—that the direct producers must receive the product of their necessary labor; basic goods required by society must be supplied according to changing patterns of social demand with minimal misallocation of social resources, primarily human labor power; and a balance must be achieved between technology and the reproduction process of society—are met by capital, so *Capital* shows, under constraints of capitalist social relations of production as a byproduct of value augmentation. Marx, of course, was well aware that in actual economic history no mode of production operates in a pure fashion. Other principles always exist in every mode of production though operate subsidiary to the "specific kind of production" of that mode. This is what enables us to talk about feudalism as a mode of production, for example, being different from capitalism.

During the capitalist stage of *consumerism*, the state performed herculean tasks attempting to program advanced economies. Yet this involved a balancing act which tilted in the direction of maintaining capitalist social relations of production and a modicum of market force. Neoliberal ideology proclaims a reloading of the capitalist market. However, while neoliberals and neoclassical economics may have some "market" in mind when they make their assertion, a *capitalist* market demands a capitalist production-centered economy which neoliberal policies contribute to eviscerating. Thus, if the capitalist market principle no longer predominates along with its enabling substructure of production-centered profit making and relationship banking, what principles guarantee that the general norms of economic life are met?

The short answer to this question is that as occurred during past epochs of transition between modes of production the predominating "kind" of production or principle, in this case the operation of the capitalist market in reproducing human material life as a byproduct of value augmentation, no longer performs its central role. This is one reason why inequality, particularly *global* inequality, emerges as a new topic of widespread interest in the capitalist era only in its late twentieth-century period of disintegration (Milanovic 2016: 123). Indeed, it goes without saying the every class society, including capitalism, will be an unequal society. But, under the current trajectory of the looming extinction of capitalism, capitalists without capitalism perched atop Himalayan piles of financial, intangible, and real estate assets drive wealth divisions to unimaginable extremes. For example, the Credit Suisse 2018 Global Wealth Report reveals that the bottom half of adults the world over collectively owns less than one percent of total global wealth. Yet, the richest top 10 percent own 85 percent of all global wealth (Credit Suisse 2018: 9). What the World Inequality Report adds is that in China, Europe, and the US, the top 10 percent owns over 70 percent of total wealth, while the bottom 50 of the population owns less than 2 percent; and "the global wealth middle class", composing 40 percent of the population, owns less than 30 percent of global wealth. However, if recent tendencies persist, the top 0.1 percent of the global population is projected to own more wealth than the global middle class by 2050 (World Inequality Report 2018).

Again, it has to be recalled that the same capitalist logic or law that augments value reproduces material existence in capitalist societies as a by-product of this. Capitalist commodity economic "market" reproduction is attuned to measuring direct costs of commodified labor power and tangible capital inputs in production-centered economies. It thus provides an objective metric for ensuring labor power is remunerated with the product of its necessary labor. A similar metric exists for effecting an allocation of social resources, particularly human labor power, to ensure the viable reproduction of capitalist economies as historical societies. This is the regulation of average profit rates across capitalist sectors of the division of labor. But, in the current economy of capitalists without capitalism bent upon aggrandizing wealth, with the only metric being their subjective whims, there remain only two major principles standing in the way of social implosion. The first of these, which is a topic for another book, are the variations in cooperative and sharing forms of economy including the proliferation of cooperative, community forms business, local employment/exchange and trading systems, soup kitchens, charities, and so on.[4]

Then there is the contribution of the state. Neoliberal ideology shrilly condemns the state or "big government" assuming a market management role. Yet the economic footprint of the state is larger than ever. According to the Organisation for Economic Co-operation and Development (OECD) database, only two economies within the OECD have levels of general government spending below 30 percent of GDP in 2016. US government general spending reaches near 38 percent of GDP despite frenetic efforts of the neoliberal political class to reduce it. At the top of the list are EU economies Belgium and France with government spending in 2016 equal to 53 percent and 56.4 percent of GDP, respectively

(OECD 2019). Even in the arch neoliberal US, the "food stamp", or Supplemental Nutrition Assistance Program (SNAP) served around 45 million people in 2015 with an average benefit of $1500 per annum. For 2016 US government spending on SNAP was projected to be $75 billion or 1.9 percent of GDP (Baker 2016: 23). Despite being disinclined toward such spending, the costs to the neoliberal state for maintaining order and minimal social welfare are only slated to grow even as its tax base shrinks. This has pressurized neoliberal states to turn to regressive "value added" and "consumption" taxes that only further leech incomes away from real economic growth inducing spending. Further, even the edifice of financial casino games and asset markets only exist at the behest of states. As one analyst starkly puts it (Noland 2015),

> [T]he entire marketplace was constructed upon the explicit and implied guarantees from the Treasury and Federal Reserve. The resulting "moneyness" of this Credit apparatus ensured excesses neared catastrophic extremes...The reality is that governments globally have now overtly commandeered so-called "market-based finance." Securities markets are openly manipulated. Trillions of securities have been monetized. Prices and risk perceptions throughout global securities and derivatives markets have been perverted like never before. The upshot has been a globalized Bubble of unprecedented scope.

In short, without the programming role of the neoliberal state in bailing out and supporting virtually insolvent commanding heights institutions, as well as managing a modicum of social welfare, current advanced societies will simply collapse. The neoliberal final solution is austerity to scrape the final pounds of flesh from the bones of humanity to pay for this morass.

Notes

1. Marx's precision analysis in *Capital* also offers a very different approach to thinking about socialism which, in fact, vitiates critiques of socialism and its potentiality implicit in the works of Bell, Lash and Urry, and Piore and Sabel reviewed in Chap. 4. That discussion, however, takes us too far outside the bounds of this book on periodizing capitalism. Interested readers are encouraged to look at Westra (2014, 2018a).

2. It is a telling fact that notwithstanding the proliferating of patents, R&D expenditure in the US held at 2.5 percent of GDP from the 1970s; and there is further, little evidence that patent proliferation has served to raise productivity growth which also has largely remained flat in the 2000s (Baker 2016: 85).
3. For the uninitiated, under the "gold standard" the state has *no* policy role in regulating the money supply. The gold reserve of each country, secured in respective central bank vaults, constitutes the foundation for both credit creation by commercial banks and the "legal tender" or banknotes issued by the central bank. Money issuance, whether for discounting bills of exchange or to meet cash payment needs, occurs "automatically" in response to ebbs and flows in buying and selling of goods. If defaults hit an economy, gold reserves are drained from central banks besetting economies with deflation and austerity until gold stocks were replenished. Under "fiat money" regimes marking economies from the 1950s, and the global economy with the 1971 demise of Bretton Woods, state debt security IOUs serve as monetary reserves. It is the holding of these government securities or bonds between the central bank and commercial banks connected to it that determines the level of the "monetary base" and extent of credit creation in the economy. Unlike the gold standard, the arrival at an "optimal" supply of money in fiat money regimes can *only* be achieved through state policy. Flexibility to set this policy was one of the reasons for the shift away from the gold standard in the post-WWII golden age. The faddish notion of central bank "independence" to day simply means the state has allocated to central bank officials the role of setting monetary policy.
4. See the sources in Note 1.

References

Albritton, R. 1991. *A Japanese Approach to Stages of Capitalist Development*. Basingstoke: Macmillan.

Baker, D. 2016. *Rigged: How Globalization and the Rules of the Modern Economy Were Structured to Make the Rich Richer*. Washington, DC: Center for Policy Research.

Bellamy-Foster, J., and R. McChesney. 2012. *The Endless Crisis: How Monopoly-Finance Capital Produces Stagnation and Upheaval from the USA to China*. New York: Monthly Review.

Chesnais, F. 2016. *Finance Capital Today: Corporations and Banks in the Lasting Global Slump*. Leiden: Brill.

Credit Suisse. 2018. *Global Wealth Report 2018*. https://www.credit-suisse.com/media/assets/corporate/docs/publications/research-institute/global-wealth-report-2018-en.pdf.

Crouch, C. 2011. *The Strange Non-Death of Neoliberalism*. Cambridge: Polity Press.

Das, S. 2018. The Bubble's Losing Air. Get Ready for a Crisis. *Bloomberg*, December 15. https://www.bloomberg.com/opinion/articles/2018-12-15/central-banks-have-few-options-to-deal-with-another-crisis.

Drucker, P. 1994. *Post-Capitalist Society*. New York: Harper Business.

Duncan, R. 2012. *The New Depression: The Breakdown of the Paper Money Economy*. Hoboken: Wiley.

Durand, C. 2017. *Fictitious Capital: How Finance Is Appropriating Our Future*. London: Verso.

Durand, C., and W. Milberg. 2018, July. *Intellectual Monopoly in Global Value Chains*. Working Paper 07/2018, Department of Economics, The New School for Social Research.

Foley, D. 2013. Rethinking Financial Capitalism and the 'Information' Economy. *Review of Radical Political Economics* 45 (3): 257–268.

Foroohar, R. 2016. *Makers and Takers: The Rise of Finance and Fall of American Business*. New York: Crown Business.

Haskel, J., and S. Westlake. 2018. *Capitalism Without Capital: The Rise of the Intangible Economy*. Princeton: Princeton University Press.

IMF. 2018, April. *Fiscal Monitor: Capitalizing on Good Times*. https://www.imf.org/en/Publications/FM/Issues/2018/04/06/fiscal-monitor-april-2018.

Kotz, D. 2015. *The Rise and Fall of Neoliberal Capitalism* 1st Edition Cambridge: Harvard University Press.

———. 2017. *The Rise and Fall of Neoliberal Capitalism* 2nd Edition Cambridge: Harvard University Press.

Lapavitsas, C. 2013. *Profiting Without Production: How Finance Exploits Us All*. London: Verso.

Lippit, V. 2010. Social Structure of Accumulation Theory. In *Contemporary Capitalism and Its Crises: Social Structure of Accumulation Theory for the 21st Century*, ed. T. McDonough, M. Reich, and D. Kotz. Cambridge: Cambridge University Press.

Marx, K. 1977. *Capital Volume I*. New York: Vintage Books.

———. 1991. *Capital Volume III*. London: Penguin Classics.

Mason, P. 2015. *PostCapitalism: A Guide to Our Future*. Milton Keynes: Penguin Books.
McDonough, T. 2010. The State of the Art of Social Structure of Accumulation Theory. In *Contemporary Capitalism and Its Crises Social Structure of Accumulation Theory for the 21st Century*, ed. T. McDonough, M. Reich, and D. Kotz. Cambridge: Cambridge University Press.
McMurtry, J. 1999. *The Cancer Stage of Capitalism*. London: Pluto Press.
Milanovic, B. 2016. *Global Inequality: A New Approach to the Age of Globalization*. Cambridge: Harvard University Press.
Moody, K. 2017. *On New Terrain: How Capital Is Shaping the Battleground of Class War*. Chicago: Haymarket.
Noland, D. 2015. *Out of Thin Air*. Credit Market Bulletin. http://creditbubblebulletin.blogspot.com/2015/05/my-weekly-commentary-out-of-thin-air.html.
OECD. 2019. *General Government Spending (Indicator)*. https://doi.org/10.1787/a31cbf4d-en. Accessed 2 Jan 2019.
Ricardo, D. 1817. *On The Principles of Political Economy and Taxation*. https://www.marxists.org/reference/subject/economics/ricardo/tax/. Accessed 5 Dec 2018.
Rifkin, J. 2015. *The Zero Marginal Cost Society: The Internet of Things, the Collaborative Commons, and the Eclipse of Capitalism*. New York: St Martin's Griffin.
Roberts, M. 2016. *The Long Depression: Marxism and the Global Crisis of Capitalism*. Chicago: Haymarket.
Seabrooke, L., and D. Wigan. 2014. Global Wealth Chains in the International Political Economy. *Review of International Political Economy* 21 (1): 257–263.
Sekine, T. 1997. *An Outline of the Dialectic of Capital*. Vol. 2. Basingstoke: Macmillan.
Smith, T. 2015. The End of One American Century…and the Beginning of Another? In *The Future of Capitalism After the Financial Crisis: The Varieties of Capitalism Debate in the Age of Austerity*, ed. R. Westra, D. Badeen, and R. Albritton. London: Routledge.
Smith, J. 2016. *Imperialism in the Twenty-First Century: Globalization, Super-Exploitation and Capitalism's Final Crisis*. New York: Monthly Review Press.
Standing, G. 2017. *The Corruption of Capitalism: Why Rentiers Thrive and Work Does Not Pay*. London: Biteback Publishing.
Tabb, W. 2010. Financialization in the Contemporary Social Structure of Accumulation. In *Contemporary Capitalism and Its Crises Social Structure of Accumulation Theory for the 21st Century*, ed. T. McDonough, M. Reich, and D. Kotz. Cambridge: Cambridge University Press.

Turner, A. 2016. *Between Debt and the Devil: Money, Credit and Fixing Global Finance*. Princeton: Princeton University Press.

Westra, R. 2012. *The Evil Axis of Finance: The US-Japan-China Stranglehold on the Global Future*. Atlanta, GA: Clarity Press.

———. 2014. *Exit from Globalization*. London: Routledge.

———. 2016. *Unleashing Usury: How Finance Opened the Door to Capitalism Then Swallowed It Whole*. Atlanta, GA: Clarity Press.

———. 2018a. *Socialism in the Twenty-First Century*. Hauppauge, NY: Nova Science Publishers.

———. 2018b. A Theoretical Note on Commodification of Labour Power in China and the Global Putting-Out System. *Journal of Contemporary Asia* 48 (1): 159–171.

———. 2019. Financialization and Marxism. *Science & Society* 83 (1): 117–126.

World Inequality Report. 2018. https://wir2018.wid.world/files/download/wir2018-summary-english.pdf.

Yardeni Research. 2019, January 4. *Global Economic Briefing: Central Bank Balance Sheets*. https://www.yardeni.com/pub/peacockfedecbassets.pdf.

9

Concluding Words

This short conclusion avoids the temptation of summarizing the complex and diverse material presented in an often-intense book. It rather offers concluding words on a literature, the periodizing of capitalism and theorizing of capitalist stages of development, which effectively begins its journey, as we have seen, in the mid-nineteenth century. As promised, let us turn to some of the apocalyptic intimations set out in the first pages of the introductory chapter.

In utilizing the metaphor of "cancer" to describe the current period of economic change, McMurtry alludes to the way disease infects the human body only to elicit an immune system response (McMurtry 1999: 100–2). Extrapolating this view to society as a whole today, the questions are whether, in fact, the cancer has spread, thus destroying its human host, and whether human immune system survival mechanisms are able to salvage humanity from the cusp of agonizing death. Polanyi (1957), in his work on the *Great Transformation* of the mid-twentieth century, evolved a like concept with the idea of a "double movement". The "market" economy, and its belief systems, he asseverates, disembed the economy from society and its myriad and enriching social practices. Polanyi believed, given his temporal emplacement, that the post–World War II

R. Westra, *Periodizing Capitalism and Capitalist Extinction*, Palgrave Insights into Apocalypse Economics, https://doi.org/10.1007/978-3-030-14390-9_9

economy of the golden age just then gestating, will re-embed "the market" into its proper social and institutional setting which history only confirms is necessary for human survival. Marx, for his part, well before Polanyi's time, had more precisely explained the phenomenon of capitalist market operations somehow seeming to levitate the economy from the social. For Marx, this constitutes a manifestation of a socially and ontologically unique tendency—that of capital reifying human material life in the capitalist era. Reification not only involves economic life in the capitalist commodity economy appearing as a separate sphere but also entails capital wielding human material life for its own self-aggrandizement, that is, the augmentation of value or profit making. This is what makes capitalism an "upside-down" or "alien" society par excellence, as it inverts the fundamental purpose of human material reproduction, relegating it to a byproduct of value augmentation. Capitalism, in this sense, may be considered an inversion of what a human society should be. Human society and its economic life should be devoted to human flourishing as its fundamental purpose.

At no time in actual history does capitalism ever completely consummate its abstract chrematistic. Other concrete "human" or non-capitalist, non-economic social practices always persist, even during the period of liberal, laissez-faire capitalism, when capital accumulated most true to its basic principles. Periodizing of capitalism and theorizing of stages of capitalist development, whether explicitly elaborated or held tacitly, capture shifts in the changing nature of capitalism and non-economic support armature it battens upon during its historical march. Marxian periodizations of capitalism tended to distinguish themselves from non-Marxian approaches by holding fast to the view that there is some constant or essence of capitalism that is reproduced notwithstanding transmutations of capital and its institutional buttresses. Where much of this literature misfires is over the specification of what that constant is.

Marx had unabashedly declared capitalism to be a historically delimited society. His claim is rooted in the position that capitalism comes into being at a historical point where human use value life—the transhistorical transformation of nature by human beings in a labor and production process which furnishes the goods necessary to reproduce human economic existence—lends itself to value augmentation. Possibility of capitalist management of this transhistorical human substructure is delimited, according to Marx, because of the circumscribed range of use values, essentially standardized production of material goods, that capital is able to ensure production of as a byproduct of profit making. This is the case even with potential enlargement of a non-capitalist support infrastructure. Where aspects of Marx's work misled followers, and we have to remember here that much of what Marx wrote had never been published or refined by him in his lifetime, is over the notion that particular industrial tendencies appearing at the historical conjuncture of his writing portended socialism. Again, Marx was not completely wrong here. Thus, what the periodizing of imperialism captures is the dampening of market forces necessary to ensure continuing value augmentation under use value conditions of heavy steel production by monopolistic combines. This is an exemplar of the delimitation of capitalism which inheres in the recalcitrance of use value life (heavy steel and industrial chemical production in the case of the imperialist stage) to capitalism's abstract principle of value augmentation. What ultimately misdirected Marx's followers was the idea he expresses at points in his writings: that capitalist change in the direction of socialism is teleological. And that capitalism's own historical movement toward monopolization and organizing of economies was building socialism rather than capitalism in an altered, "capitalist social" form.

However, as has been belabored across the pages of this book, as capitalism proceeds to augment value, it must nevertheless meet general norms of human economic life to constitute a historical society. It is precisely the nexus between the economic logic by which capital accomplishes this feat, and theorizing of its transmutability that, outside of the Japanese approach introduced in Chap. 6, is never clearly problematized by periodizations of capitalism. Again, particularly in Marxist approaches, because the focus was on identifying inherent tendencies of capitalism driving it toward socialism, Marx's deeper concern with explaining how such an "upside-down" society like capitalism actually works to viably reproduce a human society in the first place has been serially elided. This is ultimately what haunts Regulation School (RS) and Social Structures of Accumulation (SSA) works on regulation or social/institutional structuring of capital. The great theoretical effort of such approaches to escape from earlier teleological renderings of Marxian periodization by treating capitalist change at a structural or institutional level ended up losing touch with the object of such "structuring" of capital. For different reasons that same theoretical elision blunted what potential initial approaches to post-industrial, disorganized, or flexibly specialized society, covered in Chap. 4, held out for dealing with the economic implications of the swelling service sector and information and computer technology change on capitalist market operations. Each approach blithely assumes the visions they spin could be consummated in a capitalist economy. Nothing is further from the truth.

What I have argued is the final stage of capitalism, which exhausts the potential capitalism holds for managing human material life, is the stage of *consumerism* (late capitalism or *fordism* as other theories dub the period) where capitalist production congeals around a use value complex of standardized mass producible consumer durables. This constellation pushes capitalism to its historical limits with the matrix of non-capitalist, non-economic supports it calls forth, without which capital accumulation would have been impossible. The fatal conceit of neoliberalism is that globalization and financialization, projects with scant aforethought that neoliberal ideological affliction ultimately impels, would resurrect their beloved market society. However, as the final two chapters demonstrate this not only is hardly the case, as capitalism is increasingly dismantled in its substantive workings by globalization and financialization, but neoliberal ideological zeal is fomenting the ruination of society in a global movement toward a future of untold barbarism. Hence, there will be no recurrence of Polanyi's "double movement" in a capitalist economy. Polanyi's own antipathy toward Soviet socialism blinded him to the historical delimitation of capitalism residing in the contradictions use value life poses to value augmentation and "the market" irrespective of potential institutional embedding, which Marx so clearly grasped.

If McMurtry's conceptualizing of cancerous decay of society speaks to the extremely disconcerting possibility that human society will have been so irreparably damaged, and other major principles of human economic life that might be cultivated to bring about a future society of human flourishing irredeemably repressed, ideas of "gore" and "carceral" capitalism reflect on the horrors of what may be referred to as consequences of the "B-side" of globalization. Here, levels of violence wrought by globalization and financialization in the third world are far beyond the pale of what so many in the "A" world of advanced economies are able to fathom (Valencia 2018: 23–4). While we have stated at the outset that the foci of periodizing capitalism as a research program largely involves the advanced economies, briefly following up in the foregoing context on what was said in the previous two chapters is important. That is, it is not readily understood how conditions of wretchedness enveloping third-world peoples stem from the fact of third-world economies persisting in an economic twilight zone. What capitalist development they experienced had always been stunted thus limiting capitalist wealth effects and transformations of third-world social relations of production. The unraveling of advanced economy production-centered industrial edifices which disarticulate manufacturing in global value chains scattered across the third world, as per our discussion of globalization and financialization, serves to essentially freeze these economies in perpetuity in that twilight zone mold. Rather than industrialization promoting overall development and growth that, in turn, leads to urbanization, more sophisticated industrialization and rising incomes for working people. Today growth is decoupled from development as development is decoupled from the sequences of industrialization which marked capitalist development heretofore (Westra 2017: 28–9).

Of course, the "gore" of globalization is not limited to the third world as the neoliberal experiments in austerity which had been enforced upon third-world societies are now making a full circle return to the advanced economies within which the policies originated. This process, Valencia maintains, has engendered powerful transnational criminal classes plying their activities in both the third-world and advanced economies. Such classes share a predatory orientation with financialization and participate alongside it in the hyper-consumption of exorbitant incomes and wealth inequalities (Valencia 2018: 104). In turn, it is the dissemination by a transnational corporation–dominated mass media culture of fear of this B-side of globalization and its increasing importation into erstwhile advanced economies which, in turn, as Jackie Wang summarizes, conjures up tropes of social control and necessity of a "carceral" society. But this is not just one of building prisons; though these increasingly private monstrosities abound in places like the US and China (in the latter, however, the prisons remain "public" for now). Carcerality, Wang suggests, will increasingly "bleed in" to society through burgeoning total surveillance mechanisms and the like to render "the distinction between the inside and the outside of prison…blurrier" (Wang 2018: 39–40). This all follows from the fact that globalization and financialization, along with the neoliberal policies that promote them, "are ushered in by or generate a palpable share of violence that results in new security concerns for every region they touch" (Brown 2010: 95).

In Chap. 8, I evoked the specter of looming authoritarianism akin to its entrenchment in twentieth-century rentier societies (the Saudi Arabia's of this world) where coveting of rental income flows accrues to a narrow, quasi-feudal class cohort. In advanced economies, the increasingly predominating rentier dynamic of financialization, intangible asset patents, trademarks, sundry "property" rents, and so forth is central to what I dub the landlordization of capitalism. Peter Bloom argues that while neoliberalism, the ideological banner under which the foregoing transformation has played out, harks back to the liberationist proclamations of the nascent bourgeois class defense of "the market" as tantamount to human freedom, neoliberal political practice shifts decisively toward authoritarianism (Bloom 2016: 5–6). In later work, Bloom links the mass desensitization among publics toward this authoritarian shift to the portrayal by neoliberals of the existence of the capitalist market that they defend as the only bulwark against the very demise of civilization (Bloom 2018). Carcerality under neoliberalism then demands the imprisoning and surveillance not only of people but also of ideas which challenge neoliberalism as the ideology giving cover to the trajectory of globalization and financialization in capitalist and human extinctions. Only in this way can a social order predicated upon extraction of all manner of rents while consigning material reproduction of human life to happenstance be maintained.

What is at stake is something initially introduced in Chap. 2 and adverted to at several junctures across the pages of this book. When Marx asserts how in each mode of production "one specific kind of production predominates over the rest and assigns rank and influence to others" he is referring to ideas discussed decades later by Polanyi in terms of economic principles (see Chap. 2, Note 1). What Polanyi defines as reciprocity corresponds to social practices Marx had theorized as predominating in primitive communist modes of production that entail forms of interpersonal and collective cooperation. Small-m markets where face-to-face "exchange" of use values based upon the qualitative considerations, as can be found in various precapitalist economies, fall under this rubric as well. Polanyi's concept of redistribution corresponds to Marx's conceptualizing of slavery and feudalism as modes of production. In Polanyi's rendering, "the market" principle corresponds to Marx's theorizing of the systems of self-regulating markets characterizing the capitalist commodity economy. Redistribution as an economic principle which, in Polanyi's definition, entails movement of goods, tribute, tithes, taxes, and so forth from scattered producers to the center, these then being reallocated or redistributed from the center according to hierarchical status of social claimants, arguably further applies to Soviet-style socialism and the welfare state in the capitalist stage of *consumerism* (Westra 2014: 138–47). In slavery, feudalism, and the Soviet socialist model, such redistribution brings to bear interpersonal relations of domination and subordination and extra-economic coercions over the direct producing classes.

From the waning years of *consumerism*, I have argued, humanity in advanced economies finds itself in circumstances where the logic of the capitalist commodity economy which reproduced material life of societies as a byproduct of value augmentation has been rendered dysfunctional in a far deeper fashion than in the anarchic crises' oscillations capital exhibits from its inception. Of course, this does not mean that capitalist social practices and residues of commodity production no longer exist in advanced economies. It is simply that human use value life has outpaced the capacity of capitalist market operations to viably manage a human economy notwithstanding extensive superstructural support. Globalization and financialization, that appeared as initial panaceas for capitalist profit making travails, only exacerbate the disintegration of material goods producing commodity economies within which capital performed its feat of simultaneously meeting the general norms of economic life while wielding society for its abstract purpose of value augmentation. In this sense, the research enterprise of periodizing capitalism, broadly conceived, ultimately explores the contradictions and limits capital faces in its attempt to perform this "alien", "upside down" balancing act, so to speak.

What makes neoliberalism as an ideology so insidious, to follow up on elaborations of Kotz, from the previous chapter, and Bloom here, is its shrill claim that there is no economic alternative to "the market", and its bellicose policy compulsions that suppress the transformatory force of those principles or "specific kinds of production" which will be necessary to salvage human society from the detritus of capital. To the extent advanced economy states have deployed the planning principle of state redistribution, this has been directed toward extremely dysfunctional ends that support the financialization which predatorily expropriates wealth in a *Merchant of Venice*–like dynamic. Where shoots of cooperative forms spring forth neoliberal policies seek either to co-opt them or to crush their potential sources of nourishment.

No human society can survive for long, no matter how wealthy it was, without "one kind" of production or operating principle, or potentially two of them working in tandem, to ensure general norms are met to viably reproduce human economic life. Our examining of economic pathologies besetting advanced economies from the 1980s shows that the market mechanism, even with superstructural support, is unable to meet this test of economic reproducibility. Making this claim is not just an academic quibble to assert that the period referred to variously as neoliberalism, globalization, and financialization cannot be conceptualized as a stage of capitalism. It is to emphasize what in fact careful exploration of the literature on periodizing capitalism confirms that capitalism as a mode of organizing human material affairs is lurching from the endangered species list toward extinction. Humanity and civilization now hang in the balance of the decisions that we make.

References

Bloom, P. 2016. *Authoritarian Capitalism in the Age of Globalization*. Northampton: Edward Elgar.

———. 2018. *The Bad Faith in the Free Market: The Radical Promise of Existential Freedom*. Basingstoke: Palgrave Macmillan.

Brown, W. 2010. *Walled States, Waning Sovereignty*. New York: Zone Books.
McMurtry, J. 1999. *The Cancer Stage of Capitalism*. London: Pluto Press.
Polanyi, K. 1957. *The Great Transformation*. Boston: Beacon Press.
Valencia, S. 2018. *Gore Capitalism*. South Pasadena: Semiotext(e).
Wang, J. 2018. *Carceral Capitalism*. South Pasadena: Semiotext(e).
Westra, R. 2014. *Exit from Globalization*. London: Routledge.
———. 2017. From Development to BRICS: The Policy Magical Mystery Tour. In *The Political Economy of Emerging Markets: Varieties of BRICS in the Age of Global Crises and Austerity*, ed. R. Westra. London: Routledge.

Index[1]

[1] Note: Page numbers followed by 'n' refer to notes.

R. Westra, *Periodizing Capitalism and Capitalist Extinction*, Palgrave Insights into Apocalypse Economics, https://doi.org/10.1007/978-3-030-14390-9

R

S